S0-ATF-849

CHINA

TAIWAN

Hong Kong

Irrawaddy River

Ha Noi

Gulf of Tonkin

LAOS

MYANMAR

Mekong River

THAILAND

VIETNAM

South China Sea

Yangon (Rangoon)

Bangkok

CAMBODIA

Gulf of Thailand

Ho Chi Minh

Andaman Sea

BRUNEI

Strait of Malaca

MALAYSIA

SARAWAK

Singapore

BORNEO

SUMATRA

Java Sea

FREE THE CHILDREN

FREE THE CHILDREN

A Young Man's Personal Crusade Against Child Labor

Craig Kielburger

with Kevin Major

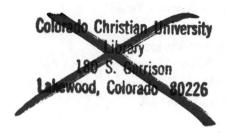

HarperCollins*Publishers*

FIRST EDITION

Library of Congress Cataloging-in-Publication Data

Kielburger, Craig, 1982–
    Free the children : a young man's personal crusade against child labor/
    Craig Kielburger.— 1st ed.
        p. cm
    ISBN 0-06-017597-4
    1. Kielburger, Craig.   2. Social reformers — Canada — Biography.
    3. Children — Employment.   4. Children's rights.   I. Title.
    HD6231.K53A3 1999
    331.3'1'092 — dc21   98-42653
    [B]

*To Munnilal, Nagashir, Mohan, Muniannal,
and all of the other children who shared their lives with me.
May your stories of courage inspire many to help free
the millions of labouring children.*

Contents

Acknowledgements

Ever since I can remember, I have had a poster in my room that says, "The journey of a thousand miles begins with a single step." The day I read about the murder of Iqbal Masih, when I was twelve years old, I never imagined that my first steps to the library to find out more about the issue of child labour would lead me to the many thousands of steps, both in miles and in knowledge, that I have travelled over the past three years.

Writing this book has been a challenging but enjoyable experience. While rereading my journal, which documented my thoughts at the end of each day, and listening to the more than fifty hours of video and audio tapes recorded during my travels, I was able once again to hear the voices and the stories of the children I had met.

This book, and the growth of Free the Children, would never have been possible without the love and understanding of my parents, Theresa and Fred, my mentor and older brother, Marc, and my Aunt Pat and Uncle Dave. They stood by me through the most challenging of times and gave me a helping hand and a hug when I needed it the most. In many ways I think that I am the luckiest kid in the entire world because of the unwavering support of my family. I could never pay them a great enough tribute.

Of course, I must thank Alam Rahman, who proved to be such a

ix

trustworthy companion and chaperone. My parents' decision to allow me to go to South Asia was based on their trust of Alam and the values he lived. Never did Alam put words into my mouth. Never did he seek recognition or the limelight, as adults sometimes do through children. Alam was a friend and he respected me as an equal.

I am rather fortunate when it comes to finding good mentors, because I hit the jackpot once again with Kevin Major. I soon discovered that writing a book was not as easy as it appears. The many weeks he and I spent at our computers were supplemented by long conversations on the phone. To quote my mother, "Kevin has the patience of Job." Working in collaboration with him was a marvellous learning experience. He proved to be invaluable in helping me to understand the structure of a book and the art of allowing room for readers to draw their own impressions and conclusions.

I would like to thank all my friends, whose loyalty has never wavered and who have always reminded me never to miss a good party. A special thanks to all of the thousands of children from the United States who have worked in support of labouring children. To each person who has ever written a letter in defence of children, organized a fundraiser, volunteered in the office, or attended one of our conferences: You are the true spirit of Free the Children. This story is as much yours as it is mine.

I am also grateful to the many adults who have given us both moral and financial support. They include the workers from human-rights organizations who were so very kind in sharing their time and knowledge with me during my visit to South Asia; the many people and organizations in the United States; the Christophers in New York; St. Mary's Church Community in Pompton Lake, New Jersey; the State of the World Forum in San Francisco; Fame in Los Angeles; The Association of Family and Conciliation Courts; the Roosevelt Foundation; Daryl Chamberlain, Rowene and Christine Nutter, Carol and Gregg Lacy, Theresa Bonner, Kate English, Roberto Bruni, Denise Clapham, Donna Carter, and other members of our U.S. board of directors; the many educators, church groups, human rights groups, and school groups throughout the American states, who have supported our cause; and the individuals who read the manuscript and offered their insights and advice, especially Kathleen Ruff and our editor, Alex Schultz.

Acknowledgements

Finally, and most importantly, I wish to thank the street children and working children whom I had the honour of meeting throughout my travels. They taught me more about respect, friendship, and myself than I might otherwise have learned in a lifetime. They allowed me into their world and shared their lives, their challenges, and their dreams with me. These children are the true heroes of this book, and I am indebted to them for all they have taught me.

Prologue

THE ROOM BROKE INTO THUN-derous applause as he climbed onto the stool behind the podium. He was a mere four-feet-two-inches tall, but his presence filled the room.

His name was Iqbal Masih, a freed child labourer, a champion fighter for the freedom of his peers, and he had come to the United States from Pakistan to receive the Reebok Youth in Action Award in recognition of his courage in exposing the horrors of child labour.

As Iqbal turned to the microphone, young children craned their necks to see him more clearly. His small frame made him look no older than some of them. For many in the audience it was hard to imagine him as a powerful activist for human rights.

The story Iqbal told was not unlike that of many children in South Asia, sold into bondage as a result of loans taken out by poor families. Iqbal's parents, to pay for the wedding of their eldest son, had bor-rowed six hundred rupees (about twelve U.S. dollars) from the owner of a carpet factory, a rich and influential man in the community. In exchange, Iqbal, said to be only four years old at the time, was forced to join several other child weavers squatting before looms in the owner's factory, tying tiny knots to make the carpets of elaborate design that sell for high prices in markets around the world. Until his family's loan, called a *peshgi*, was paid off, Iqbal would belong to the

I

factory owner. The man had not only the right to Iqbal's labour, but also, if he wished, the right to sell him to any other factory owner.

Iqbal's days were long. He worked from early morning until seven at night, twelve hours a day, six days a week.

He learned quickly not to bring on the wrath of the factory owner. If he made mistakes, fines were added to the sum owed by his parents. He worked with the threat of getting a beating, or having his legs tied together and being hung upside down in a back room. Many of the children had scars on their hands and feet where they had been whipped or struck with sticks or sharp metal tools for falling asleep at the loom. Often, too, they cut themselves accidentally with the carpet knives, especially when first learning the trade. The foremen would dip the wounds into hot oil to stop the bleeding, or fill the cuts with matchstick powder and set them alight so the skin and blood would bond together quickly. Then the children would be sent back to work.

When Iqbal was ten years old, he realized he would never be able to pay off his family's debt and, like many others in his village, would remain a slave forever. The debt had increased to thirteen thousand rupees, the fines for his mistakes and the charges for the bowl of rice he ate each day.

With the help of a human-rights organization, Iqbal was able to escape and go to school. Iqbal completed two grade levels that first year. He learned to read and write, and he became an uncompromising critic of child servitude, leading child workers in many marches to protest this exploitive practice. He developed into an eloquent and powerful speaker. He travelled to places very distant from his home.

In the spring of 1994, Iqbal spoke at a press conference in Stockholm, organized by the Swedish Industrial Union. "Now I am not scared of the factory owner," Iqbal told the reporters. "He is scared of me!"

Later that year he arrived in Boston to receive the Reebok Youth in Action Award.

Holding a pencil in one hand and a carpet tool in the other, Iqbal stood before the audience. And in his small but commanding voice he spoke of the horrors of child labour. The room was intensely silent.

(Richard Sobol/Reebok)

Iqbal Masih travelled to Boston to accept the Reebok Human Rights Award. He called upon everyone in the audience to celebrate his freedom by chanting with him, "We are free! We are free!"

3

"We have a slogan at school," Iqbal said. "When children get free, we all together say, 'We are free! We are free!'"

By this time the audience had risen to its feet.

"We are..." came his voice, filling the room.

"Free!" shouted the crowd.

"We are..." Iqbal called again.

"Free!" bellowed the well-dressed men and women, and their well-fed young children.

Iqbal's dream was to become a lawyer and help more children in his country gain their freedom. Inspired by his courage, Brandeis University in Waltham, Massachusetts, offered him a full scholarship for when he finished his schooling in Pakistan. A representative from Reebok set up an appointment with an American doctor to provide Iqbal with a year's supply of hormones to improve his stunted growth. His future looked bright. And millions of child labourers now had a spokesperson.

But on Easter Sunday, April 16, 1995, four months after Iqbal's trip to the United States, tragedy struck. Iqbal had taken the bus from Lahore to visit his family in Muridke. He spent most of the day with his mother, his half-brother, and his younger sister. He proudly showed them his report card from school. Then at seven o'clock that evening, he left by bus to return to Lahore. Two cousins of his boarded the bus at the same time to return to their own home a short distance from Muridke.

When the cousins got off the bus, Iqbal decided to go with them, to visit his uncle, whom he hadn't seen in some time. When the boys reached the uncle's home, they discovered he was working in the fields. They headed off by bicycle in search of him. All three rode on the same bicycle, one on the carrier in the back, another pedalling, Iqbal sitting on the front handlebars.

On the deserted stretch of land leading to the fields there was a rough, seldom-travelled road. From out of the dark came a blast from a twelve-bore, double-barrelled shotgun. One of his cousins was struck in the arm. Iqbal fell dead.

The next day Iqbal's body was placed on a funeral platform and carried through his village. A white headdress surrounded his face. A bright-red blanket covered his body. A large cross lay beside him, a symbol of his Christian faith. Death, in dreadful contrast to the jostling stream of people through the streets, had taken Iqbal. The voice of freedom from child labour was silenced.

One young girl, Shenaz, who had been forced into bonded labour in a brick kiln, looked on and declared, "The day Iqbal died, a thousand new Iqbals were born."

CHAPTER *1*

Thornhill

My mind goes back to April 19, 1995. I woke to sun streaming through my window, a welcome sign that summer was on its way. It was Wednesday, another school day, one I was looking forward to, in fact. Today were the tryouts for the cross-country running team.

As I stretched my way from under the blankets, I watched my dog go through her own waking-up ritual at the foot of my bed. I hauled on a pair of jeans and a sweatshirt.

"Hey, Muffin. Let's go, girl." I gave her a playful rub about her neck and off she went, racing ahead of me and down the stairs.

My mother, up for an hour or more already, was in the kitchen making lunches. The Kielburger household would soon be heading off to school. Both my parents are teachers. There were just the three of us; my older brother, Marc, had gone away to a junior college in January.

"Hi, Mom. The paper arrived yet?" I said, pouring cereal into a bowl.

"It's on the chair."

Every morning I read the comics before heading off to school. *Doonesbury. Calvin and Hobbes. Wizard of Id.* These are my favourites. If I find one particularly funny, sometimes I'll cut it out and post it on my bulletin board, or tape it to one of my school books. We all can use a good laugh every day.

6

I picked up the *Toronto Star* and put it on the table. But I didn't make it past the front page. Staring back at me was the headline "BATTLED CHILD LABOUR, BOY, 12, MURDERED." It was a jolt. Twelve, the same age as I was. My eyes fixed on the picture of a boy in a bright-red vest. He had a broad smile, his arm raised straight in the air, a fist clenched.

I read on. "Defied members of 'carpet mafia.'" Scenes from old movies came to my mind. But this wasn't any such mafia; the dateline was Pakistan. The boy was someone named Iqbal Masih.

I read quickly through the article, hardly believing the words before me.

ISLAMABAD, Pakistan (AP) – When Iqbal Masih was 4 years old, his parents sold him into slavery for less than $16.

For the next six years, he remained shackled to a carpet-weaving loom most of the time, tying tiny knots hour after hour.

By the age of 12, he was free and travelling the world in his crusade against the horrors of child labour.

On Sunday, Iqbal was shot dead while he and two friends were riding their bikes in their village of Muridke, 35 kilometres outside the eastern city of Lahore. Some believe his murder was carried out by angry members of the carpet industry who had made repeated threats to silence the young activist.

I turned to my mother. "Have you read this? What exactly is child labour? Do you think he was really killed for standing up to this 'carpet mafia,' whatever that is?"

She was as lost for answers as I was. "Try the library at school," she suggested. "Maybe you'll find some information there."

Riding the bus to school later that morning, I could think of nothing but the article I had read on the front page. What kind of parents would sell their child into slavery at four years of age? And who would ever chain a child to a carpet loom?

Throughout the day I was consumed by Iqbal's story. In my Grade Seven class we had studied the American Civil War, and Abraham Lincoln, and how some of the slaves in the United States had escaped into Canada. But that was history from centuries ago. Surely slavery had been abolished throughout the world by now. If it wasn't, why had I never heard about it?

The school library was no help. After a thorough search I still hadn't found a scrap of information. After school, I decided to make the trek to the public library.

The librarian knew me from my previous visits. Luckily, she had read the same article that morning and was just as intrigued. Together, we searched out more information on child labour. We found a few newspaper and magazine articles, and made copies.

By the time I returned home, images of child labour had imbedded themselves in my mind: children younger than me forced to make carpets for endless hours in dimly lit rooms; others toiling in underground pits, struggling to get coal to the surface; others maimed or killed by explosions raging through fireworks factories. I was angry at the world for letting these things happen to children. Why was nothing being done to stop such cruelty?

As I walked through my middle-class neighbourhood, my thoughts were on the other side of the world. And my own world seemed a shade darker.

That evening I had great difficulty concentrating on my homework. I pulled out the articles I had brought from the library and read them over, again and again. I had often seen the faces of poverty and malnutrition on television. At school we had discussed the famines whole nations have been forced to endure. But this was different. For some reason these descriptions of child labour had moved me like no other story of injustice.

Perhaps it was because the stories were of people my own age, and many even younger. Perhaps it was because these few words had shattered my ideas of what childhood was all about – school, friends, time to play. I had work to do around my house – carrying out the garbage, cleaning up the backyard – but it all seemed so trivial compared to what these children had to do.

I thought of how I would react if I found myself in their place. I felt sure I would rebel, gather everyone together and stand up to the cruelty. But I *wasn't* in their place; I could only *imagine* what I would do.

I opened our world atlas on the kitchen table and searched the index until it led me to a map of Pakistan. I discovered it wedged between Iran, Afghanistan, and India, with the Arabian Sea along its southern edge. My eyes ran over a maze of names I had never heard before, and some I could barely pronounce. I searched for the places mentioned in the story on Iqbal. I couldn't locate Muridke; it was too small to be on the map. I did find Lahore, and repeated the word several times out loud. It seemed so far away, a world I didn't know at all.

I had to find out more.

"I have a friend who worked overseas, in Africa," my mother told me. "Why don't you give her a call? If she can't answer your questions, I'm sure she'll know of someone who can."

That first telephone conversation led to calls to several human-rights organizations. Little did I think, in the months to come, it would lead to hundreds of other calls and faxes around the world, all in a quest to get to the heart of the issue of child labour.

Two things struck me right away. First of all, none of the organizations I talked to seemed to know much about child labour. But equally amazing – every person who tried to answer my questions was an adult. Without a single exception. Even though the issue was all about children, there were no young people involved in these organizations. I could hardly believe it. Shouldn't other children be speaking out in defence of children?

I'm always fascinated by coincidences, how one random event can come on the heels of another and together alter the whole direction of a person's life. Early the following week, in the Life section of the *Toronto Star*, there was a full-page article in celebration of Youth Week. As part of the activities, an organization called Youth Action Network was sponsoring an event at a downtown convention centre that coming Friday. Youth organizations were invited to set up displays and distribute information.

I'm not sure why, in the end, I decided to call the number in the article. I guess it was because I was tired of being able to speak only to organizations run by adults.

By a stroke of good fortune, my call was directed to Alam Rahman. Alam, whose parents were from Bangladesh, was a recent university graduate. I had no way of knowing it at the time, but Alam would become a very central figure in my life. I spoke to him for more than an hour about Iqbal and child labour. I tested the idea of getting some friends together and starting a children's group to fight such cruelty.

Alam didn't hesitate. "It's a great idea, Craig. You should try it!"

That was all I needed. The following day I asked my Grade Seven teacher, Mr. Fedrigoni, if I could have a few minutes to speak to the students before class began. I'm sure he must have thought it was about some social function or a football game I was organizing during lunch break.

As usual, we stood by our desks while the morning announcements came over the public-address system, followed faithfully by the national anthem. Then we sat down and quietly listened to Mr. Fedrigoni say how there had been a few problems with discipline the day before, but that he hoped this would be a better day. When he had finished, he simply said, "Craig has a few comments he would like to make to you." He looked at me and nodded.

I walked to the front and turned to face the thirty students in my class. The room was silent except for a couple of boys whispering in a back row. When I began they, too, were quiet. But I was still nervous; I always found speaking in front of my peers a tough thing to do, and I still had no idea how they would react to what I would say.

"I was wondering if anyone saw this article on the front page of last Wednesday's *Toronto Star*," I began.

I had made photocopies of it, which I passed around the classroom. As I did so, I started to tell Iqbal's story. I described his struggles and his dream, and how that dream had been cut short by an assassin's bullet. I presented the alarming statistics on child labour. As I spoke, I could see that many of my classmates were just as shocked as I was by the story. Anger, sympathy, disbelief filled the room.

"So this is the issue," I said. "I don't know a lot about it, but I want to learn more. Maybe some of us could start a group to look at it together." And then came the fateful question, "Who wants to join?"

About eighteen hands shot up, and I very quickly jotted down their names. I thanked Mr. Fedrigoni and the class for the half-hour of their time I had taken.

And through that simple action, it began.

At lunchtime that day, some of us got together and talked about what we could do. I was amazed at how enthusiastic they all were. I told them about the youth fair on Friday.

"Do you think we could put together a display?" I asked. "We haven't got much time."

"Sure. Let's do it."

"We can all meet at my house," I said.

That night, twelve of us got together. It was a very tight deadline, with just two days to prepare. We found an old science-fair board, and we covered it with coloured paper, pasting on all the information I had found on child labour in the library, then drawing pictures to illustrate it.

We had determined that our first objective should be to inform people of the plight of child labourers. Armed with such knowledge, they might be willing to help. We decided to draw up a petition to present to the government, and called on the expertise of a couple of human-rights groups to refine the wording for us.

But we were still without a name for our group. For more than an hour we struggled to come up with something suitable. We flipped through the newspaper clippings for inspiration. One of them reported on a demonstration in Delhi, India, where 250 children had marched through the streets with placards, chanting, "We want an education," "We want freedom," "Free the children!"

"That's it!" someone shouted. "Free the Children!"

"Perfect," I said. "We're using their words. Children speaking for children."

"Exactly."

We had found a name. Marilyn Davis, the best artist among us, had earlier drawn a picture of children chained to a carpet loom. Before pasting the picture onto our information board, across the top she had written slogans, including "Break the Chains" and "Save the Children." Now we pasted a piece of paper over the word "SAVE" and wrote "FREE" in big letters.

Free the Children was born. We hoisted our board like a giant placard, in solidarity with the children who had marched through the streets of Delhi.

I remember lying awake that Thursday night, thinking about what we had gotten ourselves into. Here we were, just a group of friends, a ragtag lot compared to all the other organizations sure to be taking part in the youth fair. Yet we had worked hard, read all the information I had collected, and felt confident we could get our point across to anyone who was willing to listen.

As I slowly drifted off to sleep, I could only think, Ready or not, here we go. And the next morning, that's exactly what happened – off we went, the start of something that would take over my life and catch the world's attention to an extent that none of us could ever have imagined.

I am often asked where I found the confidence to start Free the Children and take on the responsibility of being its spokesperson. Was there something in my family background that prompted me to grab on to this issue and get so deeply involved in it? Others are more blunt about it. What were your parents like? Were you a *normal* kid?

"Normal" can mean a lot of things. If it means playing basketball, watching TV, listening to music, hanging out with my friends...sure, I did all those things. I still do. But to me it can also mean getting involved because you believe so deeply in a cause that you can't see yourself just standing on the sidelines, waiting for other people to act.

I can't honestly say that I remember my parents ever becoming involved in any social issues when I was young. But they did instil in my brother and me a sense that people should take care of one another. And they grew up in the Sixties, so perhaps the idealism of young people then had some effect on them. They never talked much about those days. It was only recently I discovered that before they were married my mother ran a drop-in centre for street kids in Toronto, and my father worked at L'Arche, a home for mentally challenged adults in France that had been started by Jean Vanier, a Canadian humanitarian.

My father's ancestry is German. His father arrived in Canada during the Great Depression, when he was just nineteen. My grandfather was a big man, and from the many stories he's told me, I know he earned money fighting boxers in Toronto, for what was considered suicide pay. Eventually he and my grandmother saved enough money to open a small grocery store close to the area of downtown Toronto known as Cabbagetown. His family worked in that store day and night. They closed the store only one day in twenty-three years, to take a trip to visit Niagara Falls.

My father worked in the store after school and on the weekends. He thought there was no chance for university, and never even discussed the possibility until his last year of high school. He was amazed when my grandparents told him they not only consented to the idea, but had saved up enough money to make it possible, with the understanding that he would still help out in the store.

My mother, the second youngest of four children, was born in Windsor, Ontario, just across the border from Detroit. She was only nine when her father passed away, and my grandmother was left to provide for the children. The family went through some difficult times, including one summer when their only shelter was a tent. Sometimes the family had to go without proper food. Often the simplest things, such as a bologna sandwich, became a treat. But my grandmother was a strong and determined woman, and with only a Grade Eight education she worked her way up from cleaning other people's homes to an office job at the Chrysler Corporation, where, eventually, she became head of her department. She instilled in her children the belief that they could do anything they wanted in life, and, working together as a team, their family life soon improved.

When my mother was ten years old, she began to work weekends with her older sister in a neighbourhood store, sorting pop bottles, waiting on customers, and delivering groceries. The whole family worked very hard, and in the years that followed, they could look with pride on the fact that every one of the children went on to university. My mother was always able to add a perspective on the issue of child labour from her own experience.

It was my parents' strong work ethic and belief that we must face challenges in life to achieve our goals that most influenced my brother and me. We grew up with the mottoes: "Go for it! The only failure in life is not trying."

My brother, Marc, is six years older than I am. He became, in many ways, my role model. Marc was good in everything – school, sports, public speaking – and I wanted to be just like him. He was a swimmer and a football player. Rugby was one of his favourite sports, and sometimes, horsing around in the backyard, he would tackle me. Just to toughen me up, he said!

When he was thirteen, Marc became interested in environmental issues. For a Grade Eight science project he set up a series of experiments to test the effects of various commercial home-cleaning

Here I am with my family on a trip to the Grand Canyon, Arizona. My brother and I didn't grow up with a list of rules or curfews. My parents believed in us and trusted us so much that we just never wanted to let them down. It was expected that we would live by certain standards. Basic to these was treating all people with respect, whatever their position in life.

products on the environment. He was able to prove that these cleansers had serious negative effects, including the pollution of the water system. The following year he took the project one step further. Using combinations of everyday kitchen items such as lemon juice, vinegar, baking soda, and water, he concocted recipes to make his own household cleansers. He demonstrated that not only were these cleansers environmentally friendly and cheaper, but they did the job just as well as – if not better than – the brand-name products.

Marc went on to prove that the paint used to decorate china plates and to label food wrappers often contained harmful amounts of lead. Food was exposed to this lead when the plates were scratched by cutlery or when it came in contact with the outside of the wrappers. As a result of his commitment, including the many speeches he gave, petitions he initiated, and the environmental clubs he helped to set up in schools, Marc won an environmental award from YTV, Canada's Youth Television Network, and he became the youngest person ever to receive the Ontario Citizenship Award.

I think it was from watching my brother's involvement in environmental issues that I realized children have power. And to this day my mother tells me that she would watch me as I listened to my brother practising his speeches, mimicking his words and expressions as I followed him, the whole time using my hands as if I were conducting an orchestra.

Sometimes when Marc was visiting high schools to get names on a petition, he would invite me along. Handing me a petition sheet and a pen, he would explain what it was all about. "Just go up to people," he would say, "and speak slowly and clearly." It was my first taste of activism. I was only seven years old. The high-school students towering over me thought I was so cute that they didn't hesitate to sign the petition.

It helped that I had a bit of a speech problem. When I went up to the first group of high-school girls and rattled off the lines Marc had taught me, I caused a sensation. "Oh, come and hear the way this kid talks. He's so cute!" Soon there was a crowd of students gathered around to hear me speak. That day I collected more names on the petition than all of Marc's friends put together.

"Someday I will give speeches," I would tell my mother.

"Don't worry," she would say. "You don't have to give speeches if you don't want to. You could be good in something else."

My speech problem was caused by chronic ear infections. These infections, and the ailments related to them, were a part of my childhood I had learned to live with. A loud cough caused by bronchitis, made me sound like a truck (to use my father's constant expression). I remember one schoolteacher getting angry with me because she thought I was trying to disrupt the class.

"Craig," she would say, "please don't do that! The other students are trying to study." I could never figure out why she thought anyone would make such a noise on purpose.

Because I wasn't hearing certain words or letter sounds correctly, my speech was sometimes slurred. Or I would drop letters, or mispronounce rs or certain vowels. Once a week my mother took me to the hospital for a session with a speech therapist. At first I saw no need of it. I thought I could go through life without using rs. But in the end, I took the therapist's advice and started to really concentrate on the program, including a daily session of practising a list of words with my mother in the car on the way to school. Before long, things were improving.

When I was ten years old, all of my speech problems disappeared. The ear infections that had plagued me for so long had stopped. One day my mother said to me, "You know, Craig, you are saying all your words clearly now." What a great feeling!

Now I could have fun in our backyard pool without the earplugs and the dreaded swim cap covering my ears. The weeklong camping trips I would take with my scout troop became less of a worry for my mother.

Those camping trips were one of the highlights of each year for me. I loved getting away from it all.

Some of my best scouting memories are the canoeing excursions we would take to Algonquin Park or Georgian Bay. Paddling and portaging through uninhabited country, through rain or shine, until, at the end of the day, we reached a spot to pitch our tents. As pack leader, I would be the one to organize setting up the tent and cooking the meal that followed. Macaroni and cheese was our specialty. In fact, we practically lived on the stuff.

After a long day of canoeing, there is nothing quite like sitting around a fire, devouring the evening meal, and then later, as it grows dark, watching the stars come out and listening for the sounds of nature far away from the commotion of city life.

The following spring, after my speech problems had cleared up, I found out about a public-speaking competition in our community. I was immediately interested, but I had little time to prepare, and it would be my first speech.

"You can't expect to win," my mother cautioned. "You will be a winner just for trying."

And so we decided the speech would be about "What It Means to Be a Winner."

The night before the competition, I had a coughing attack. My mother stayed up with me, feeding me hot tea and cough syrup. In the morning, my mother said that maybe it wasn't such a good idea for me to participate in the competition.

"No," I said, "I'll be fine. I want to go."

I spent the morning sitting up in bed learning my speech. But I still wasn't feeling well and couldn't seem to remember the words. When we arrived at the hall, we were told that the previous year's provincial winner was also competing in my group.

"Just do your best," my mother said to me. "That's all that matters."

When my name was called, I stood up and walked to the podium at the front of the room. I could feel the butterflies in my stomach. I looked at all the eyes staring at me. Suddenly I couldn't remember a word of what I had practised. And, unlike the other speakers, I didn't have any cue cards to refer to.

So I began to speak from my heart about the things I had learned about "winning." I spoke about sports coaches who scream at children and make them cry when they make a mistake. I told them about a note my mother had written to me when I lost a science-fair competition, which said I was still a winner to her. The more I talked, the more my confidence rose. I found my voice getting stronger and my hands come alive. I concluded by stressing the importance of fighting for the things we believe in, even when there are obstacles put in our way. That was what winning was all about.

I could hardly believe the applause as I returned to my seat. My mother gave me a hug. The previous year's provincial winner spoke next. She was excellent! Poised and articulate. You could tell she had a lot of experience. I thought she was clearly the best speaker of the group.

The judges returned a half-hour later. They reminded the speakers that we were all winners, making reference to what I had said in my speech. They began by announcing the third-place winner. Then in second place they named the girl who had won the provincial competition the year before. I was completely stunned. I had won the gold medal!

I learned something very important the day of my first public speech. There was no doubt that the girl who placed second gave a more articulate speech. I had won because I had spoken not from words on a piece of paper, but from my heart. It was a lesson I would never forget.

I had an entire week to practise my speech before the next competition. Over the following two months I won first place at the next four levels and ended up second in the province. That fall I represented my school at regional and school board-wide competitions and again won the gold medal for our school. My brother started to kid me that public speaking was in my blood.

I was now twelve years old and in Grade Seven. Boy Scouts remained a major part of my life, but I had also taken up tae kwon do. I continued my extracurricular activities at school, including teaching soccer to some of the younger students. On Sundays I went to church, and played floor hockey with the neighbourhood kids in the afternoon. I still found time now and then to read a good book.

One day I heard from a friend that the local library was being closed down, because the city councillors had decided it was too expensive to run. There was a meeting called to discuss the matter, and so a few of my friends and I decided to attend. We sat at the back and listened to the adults make their comments. When it came time for questions, again it was only adults speaking.

I raised my hand. I stood up and talked about the importance of the library to young people, how they depended on it for their research papers and science projects. I talked about how far away the other library would be – a twenty-five-minute bike ride, one way. When I was finished, other children stood up and began to speak.

One of the organizers of the fight to save the library phoned me a few days later, wondering if I would attend a second meeting. Eventually I was asked to speak on behalf of elementary-school students to a large gathering that included the mayor and our city councillor.

It was the first time I had become involved in an issue that was bigger than myself. In the end, we lost the fight to save the library, but I had learned a lot from the experience. I learned that children's opinions are seldom considered, even when it's an issue that affects them directly. I learned that many adults don't think of us as having a role to play in issues of social justice, assuming that we have little to contribute. But I also learned that, with enough determination, young people could be heard. And that what it required, first and foremost, was a sound understanding of an issue and the confidence to speak openly about it. Only then would we establish our credibility.

When Free the Children travelled to downtown Toronto for the youth fair that Saturday morning in April 1995, we hardly knew what to expect.

We proudly set up our makeshift information board on a table, and sat on the floor in a circle, where we stapled our information sheets together. As we did so, we couldn't help noticing the other organizations' impressive displays, their large, glossy panels, their professional brochures, their neat arrangements of videos and books. But the one thing the other groups didn't have was elementry-school children. A few high-school students took part, but mostly there were adults who spoke at the fair about what their organizations were doing "for" children. We were the only children speaking for themselves.

People flocked around our table to hear what we had to say. Twelve-year-old children working for other children? Children speaking for themselves about human rights? We were an oddity. That day the second goal of our group began to emerge – putting more power in the hands of young people. Children needed to have a voice and had to be able to participate in issues that affect them. Who best to understand children than other children? We realized that not only did children like Iqbal need to be freed from physical enslavement, but children like us needed to be freed from the misconception that we were not smart enough, old enough, or capable enough to contribute to social issues.

Over the next two months, we came to feel that our group had built a solid foundation. We had a name, we had definite goals, and soon we were to have an office.

My house seemed to be the ideal location. It had always been open to kids. Marc's friends and my friends had always used our house as a place to get together for fun, school projects, or parties. There were young people constantly coming and going.

Even better, there weren't a lot of doors separating one room from the next. One member of Free the Children (or FTC for short) could be working in the living room, stapling together information sheets, others could be in the dining room, discussing strategy, and another could be at the kitchen table, writing letters. As wonderful as this idea sounded, and as much as we all felt it would work, my parents weren't so thrilled.

"How about the den," my mother suggested. "I think that's a more reasonable possibility."

The den had once been a garage and, as my mother pointed out, had the great advantage of being close to the front door, so that people could come and go without much disturbance. We checked it out and, much to my parents' delight, decided it would be perfect. We retrieved an old filing cabinet from the basement, added a table and a bookcase, and we were in business.

Soon the filing cabinet started to fill with print material from the numerous organizations to whom we had sent letters requesting information. We cut out articles and compiled press clippings on the issue of child labour, and filled our shelves with books and videotapes and any other information we could find. We covered the walls with posters and moved in the family computer, which was soon in constant use. Before long we were putting together basic kits for distribution to schools and anyone else who might contact us for information about our organization and the issue of child labour.

One night my dad brought me into the room to remind me that I had left the lights on (something I did all the time). I remember standing there, with my hand on the light switch, looking around and thinking: It's amazing that with such a small group we can do all this. We had grown an incredible amount in the space of a few months – and in the months to come we could only grow bigger.

We were ready to take our campaign on the road. I drew up a letter in which I spoke about Free the Children and how we wanted to reach out and talk about the issue of child labour with young people. I gave it to my principal, and he arranged for it to be distributed to all the schools within our school district. The response was slow. It made us think that not many adults believed a group of twelve-year-olds could hold a class's attention for more than ten minutes.

Our first request came from a neighbouring school. With a date in place, we set to work preparing for our visit. We decided the best approach would be to tell stories of the children, the same stories that had affected us so deeply when we first heard them.

When the day came, we crowded aboard my family's minivan. At the school we piled out, clutching our posters and information sheets. We walked nervously, and almost in single file, towards the first classroom. Each of us was going over in our minds what we would say.

The teacher was very friendly. She explained to the students who we were and why we had come. We stood there – Ashley Stetts, Vance Ciaramella, and I – lined across the room in front of the blackboard, almost as if we were facing a firing squad. We all took a deep breath.

Vance spoke about Iqbal. Ashley told the story of a young girl named Easwaris who worked in a fireworks factory. Her job was loading the sulphur and charcoal into the fireworks tubes. There had been an explosion in which Easwaris's eight-year-old sister had been killed, and she herself now had scars lining her back and arms.

"According to the International Labour Organization, there are more than 250 million working children," I told the students. "That's equal to the entire population of the United States!"

By the end of the presentation, the students were just as shocked as we had been when we first heard about child labour. We left them with a challenge to take their first action and write a letter. It could be to a company, asking them to ensure that their products were child-labour free, or to a world leader, challenging them to put more money into education and the protection of children, or to the Pakistani government, demanding that Iqbal's killers be brought to justice.

We went from class to class, giving the same speech. And each time we had the same response. The students were eager to get involved.

They wanted to help. In fact, by the time we finished the fourth class, the teacher brought us back to the first, and the students presented us with a pile of letters.

These were the first of thousands of such letters we would receive from children in the years that followed.

Slowly but surely our campaign began to grow. Speaking at one school led to an invitation to speak at another, and then at another. We began to receive invitations from parent-teacher associations, local churches, and service groups. More and more letters filled our office files, and more and more information covered our walls.

We began to get a reputation as an organization that provided good speakers who were able to hold the attention of a crowd. In late May we received a request to speak to a world issues class at a high school, Brebeuf College. The presentation would be to a class of Grade Thirteen students, most of them six or seven years older than we were. It was certainly a big jump from speaking to those first Grade Five and Six classes.

The session took place in a portable classroom on a hot spring day. Despite every window being open, the place was stifling. The thirty students, in their white shirts and loosened ties, filled the room. It looked like a mini-United Nations; there were students from a dozen different ethnic backgrounds. One student was twirling a pencil, moving it from finger to finger and back again.

Marilyn Davis, Adam Fazzari, and I gave the presentation. Despite the age of our audience, we felt confident about what we had to say. After all, we had given the same presentation many times before. We each knew just where the other was going to stop, and where each of us would begin. We each took turns speaking, one perfectly synchronized with the other. When we wrapped up, we asked for questions.

"Well, don't all leap at us at once," I said to break the ice.

The first question was easy. A student asked if Iqbal's killers were ever brought to justice. I told the class that in fact someone had been arrested, but that it was widely suspected he did not commit the crime.

Then a student piped up, "If you eliminate child labour, won't you send local currencies plummeting, causing unemployment and economic chaos amongst the countries?"

Marilyn looked at me. I stared back at her. She glanced at Adam, then said, "Craig, you take this one."

An answer stumbled out. "I'm not really sure if that's the case. I can honestly say I don't really have an answer..."

Another student asked, "What gives you the right to go to these countries and tell them what to do? Aren't you simply white imperialists coming from a rich country, telling these people in the Third World how to raise their children?"

The questions came fast and furious. "What do you suppose happens to those children after they are taken out of child labour?"

"Wouldn't the World Trade Organization stop any chance of a boycott of products made by child labour on the grounds that it would affect international treaties?"

Marilyn, Adam, and I stood there and looked at each other after each and every question. Some of them we were able to answer, but most of our responses were simply lame and unconvincing. Often we had to say that we honestly didn't have an answer.

Through it all I found the room unbelievably warm. At times I thought I was going to faint. The three of us felt as if we were under attack, and shrinking more and more as the questions piled up.

I brought it all to an end and thanked the class. We walked outside for some fresh air. The teacher followed, asking if I was all right because I was sweating and had turned pale.

When the teacher had gone back inside, Marilyn turned to me and said, "That was torture."

Adam added, "I wouldn't want to have to go through that again."

We sat on the steps of the portable, out of view of the students, although with the windows open we could hear that they were already into their next topic – global trade. We sat there, holding our posters with the pictures of the child workers, thinking to ourselves that maybe we were getting in over our heads. If we were going to get seriously involved in this issue, then we would have to know what we were talking about.

Later that day, after soaking in a long bath and watching some TV, I went into the office and began looking through our information. I wrote down every question that had stumped us, and I went looking for the answers. I called Alam Rahman and asked if he would go to the

University of Toronto library and search out material for me on the issue. Our group did a systematic review of all the literature. Day by day, the answers began to build up.

I put together a three-page letter addressed to the class we had spoken to at Brebeuf College. It began: "Thank you very much for your challenging questions. We have undertaken research on the issues you raised and have found answers. If you have more questions we will be more than happy to respond to them."

And a few weeks later another invitation arrived from Brebeuf College, this time to speak to a class of Grade Twelve students. And this time, when we were confronted with the questions, we had our answers.

We had learned that knowledge was our key, that the only way adults and students would take us seriously was if we knew what we were talking about and had a good response for every question. We had to be able to defend our views.

Of course there was still an attitude from some adults we met that we were just a "cute bunch of kids" who had started a club. They wouldn't take us seriously, just flash that all-knowing smile of approval that usually comes before a pat on the head.

That didn't deter us. We just pressed ahead.

CHAPTER 2

Toronto

PINNED TO THE WALL OF OUR Free the Children office was a large map of the world. We had sent dozens of inquiries to organizations located all over that map, and with each response the world seemed to shrink. Our neighbours were no longer simply the young people down our street in Thornhill. They were the youth in India, in Africa, in Brazil. More than ever I thought of us – all of us – as the children of the world.

Human-rights organizations around the world sent us photographs of children released from bonded labour in carpet factories, newspaper reports of protest marches by children, and the ever-shocking statistics on child labour they had gathered from sources throughout their country.

It was through one such organization that we learned of an explosion in a fireworks factory in Rhotak, India, that killed twelve children and injured dozens of others. From our fax machine emerged the startling pictures and media reports. I immediately sent copies, with a covering letter, to Barbara Hall, the mayor of Toronto. Free the Children asked for permission to speak to the city council. Permission was granted, and the council members were obviously moved by the material we placed before them. They were uncertain whether any fireworks brought in by the City were being made by child labour, but they promised to investigate, and they passed a resolution not to purchase for City events any

25

fireworks made by children. There were no doubts in our minds about such a resolution. These were hazardous jobs. Many children had been killed, or scarred for life.

As school closed for the summer, I was more enthused than ever about what we were trying to do. Besides the fireworks issue, our other major concern was the news from India that Kailash Satyarthi, one of the leaders in the fight against child bonded labour, was being harassed by police and threatened with imprisonment. Later we learned that he had been detained.

Was there anything we could do? We decided to write a letter to the prime minister of India, insisting that Kailash be set free, and we organized a three-thousand-name petition. Both were put in a shoebox, which we wrapped in brown paper and mailed to the Indian government in Delhi. We had worked very hard, and it was an action we hoped would have some impact. A year later, when Kailash came to Canada to speak about his humanitarian work, he recalled the shoebox containing all those names of Canadian children. "It was one of the most powerful actions taken on my behalf," he said, "and, for me, definitely the most memorable."

A highlight of the summer was the community garage sale we undertook to raise money for Free the Children and help spread our message. About fifty of our friends signed up to help.

I don't think our parents knew what hit them! We had put out the word that FTC wanted to collect anything and everything we might be able to resell. Soon the donations started to arrive – old toys, books, furniture, clothes...you name it. They were heaped across our backyard and throughout our house.

We sat down and looked everything over.

"What we have," one of us concluded, "are countless piles of junk."

"Junk, but not useless junk."

"Some of it needs a little fixing up."

And for days we washed, cleaned, painted, sorted, and labelled. Of course, in between we played ball and cooled off in the swimming pool. The night before the sale, a couple of us slept outside in a tent with our dogs to protect all of the merchandise.

At five-thirty the next morning, the first customers arrived. We weren't quite prepared for what the following hours would bring; it was something a friend would later describe as "a character-building experience."

To every person who showed up, we explained our purpose for having the sale. Many of them congratulated us, and added a donation to the price of whatever they purchased. Others were just out for a bargain, including one guy who tried to walk off with a computer after paying only two bucks. My brother, Marc, the rugby player, put a stop to that.

But it was much more than just a sale. Older kids dressed up as clowns to entertain younger kids while their parents shopped. There were organized games, bead bracelet vendors, and a lemonade stand. We had FTC members with petitions on clipboards going through the crowds. TVO brought in a film crew.

As the crowds grew, so did the traffic problems. People we hadn't seen in a long time came by. Strangers became new friends. Whenever someone asked who was in charge, one of the FTC crew would step forward, much to the visitor's surprise.

That summer we learned more than what books or teachers could have taught us. We learned to take the initiative, and follow through. We learned a greater sense of self-worth. We discovered we could do more than talk about the world's problems. When we set our minds to it, we could make a difference.

When school was set to resume in September, my mother took me aside. There was a serious matter on her mind. Throughout the summer, our house had become a rather public place, with kids and parents coming and going non-stop. The telephone and fax machine rang all hours of the night with messages from our contacts around the world. Our house was in a constant state of turmoil. My parents had been very patient through it all, but the strain was starting to show.

"I think it's time for you to quit," my mother said. "You're about to begin Grade Eight. This is your last year of elementary school and it is an important year. Your dad and I have to go back to teaching. You have accomplished so much. But this can't go on. We have to live as a family. We have to get back to having a normal life."

I went to my room to think about what she had said.

More than fifty young people worked together to organize a garage sale to raise money for Free the Children. A lemonade stand was just one of the many attractions that day. Through this and similar activities, we learned how to plan and how to work as a team. We also discovered that helping others could be fun.

At first, when Free the Children began, we received as much as we gave – we enjoyed the feeling of self-worth, happiness, the new insights, and a sense of accomplishment. But now we had reached a whole new level of commitment, that point when real giving does not come without pain. Despite the pain, I knew in my heart that I could not quit, that our group had to at least try to do more. I had learned too much about the abuse of children. I was no longer the person I had been five months before.

But I also knew the toll it was taking on the family, how disrupted all our lives had become. I sat in my room a long time before coming out.

"I'm sorry, Mom. I know it's been hard for you and Dad with everything going on around here," I said. "But I just can't give up now. You always tell us that we have to fight for what we believe in. Well, I believe in this."

It was a turning point for my parents. Until that moment they had seen Free the Children as a phase, a group of kids with a noble purpose who would eventually go on to other pursuits. But now they realized for me it had become a mission.

My parents looked at me long and hard and saw the commitment in my face. "All right," my mother said. "If that is your decision, we'll support you."

And that support has never waned. Though not long after, it would be tested a great deal more than it had ever been before.

Earlier that summer I had met Dr. Panuddha Boonpala, a woman from the International Labour Organization in Geneva. She had worked with child labourers in the streets and factories of Thailand. I took to her right away. She was very bubbly and often broke into a wide grin, which made her look like a young girl. "If you really want to understand the issue of child labour," she told me, "then you should go to South Asia and meet the children yourself."

Her words never left me. The more I thought about what she had said, the more intense became my desire to make such a trip.

I felt my knowledge of the child-labour issue was comprehensive – as comprehensive as it could get, given the resources available to me. But one thing was lacking in almost all of the material I had collected. There was very little perspective provided by the children themselves, the actual workers, the ones the articles and research papers were all about.

There was, it seemed to me, a virtual industry of organizations speaking on behalf of young people. But where were the working kids in all this? What did *they* feel about their predicament? If they had a choice, would they want to go to school? Did they have to work to survive? Some of the publications I read suggested that the kids had no interest in going to school, that they didn't want to learn to read and write, that the work they did wasn't even exploitative. Were these kids, then, different from myself and my friends?

These questions swam through my mind, and I knew that if I really wanted to understand the situation of these children, I would have to meet them myself. When I spoke to students, they often asked, "Have you ever met any of these children?" and "How do you really know this is true?" I would always have to say no, that I hadn't actually seen the conditions myself. No, but I did hope to go see the children someday.

My answers lacked authority. The more I thought about it, the more I felt I really needed and wanted to go to South Asia. And, in fact, I had read so much on child labour and seen so much through other people's eyes that going to Asia myself was the logical next step.

Logical or not, my parents wouldn't even consider it. "It's another world. It's too dangerous. You're only twelve!"

I had discussed the idea on the telephone with Alam Rahman a number of times. Alam and I had gotten to know each other better. He was intrigued by the idea that people as young as myself would start a group to work on such a complex issue as child labour. And make a serious commitment to it.

At twenty-four years of age, Alam was a serious and committed person himself. I think that's what attracted my parents to him. They began to see him as a mentor for me. Over the months that we came to know him, my whole family grew to respect him as a person, as well as the depth of his knowledge and his willingness to spend long hours for the cause of social justice. In short, Alam was someone my parents admired and trusted.

One day, when I was working with a group of FTC friends at a food bank, I met Alam there. "Craig," he said, "I'm going to South Asia for a year. I'm visiting my family in Bangladesh and then travelling around. Do you want to come with me? You could meet some working children."

I almost passed out. I couldn't believe my ears. "Are you serious?"

Alam had travelled to Asia before. But now he had decided to take a year off from his studies at the University of Toronto to find out more about his Asian roots. Though he spoke Bengali fluently, he wanted the opportunity to learn Hindi and Tano.

The time had come for me to get serious with my parents about going to Asia. But I knew it would not be easy; my parents wouldn't even allow me to take the subway to downtown Toronto on my own – let alone go to Asia.

"Guess what, Mom. Great news! Alam is going to Asia and he asked me if I want to go."

"Is that right?" she answered, knowing full well what was coming next.

"I know how much you think of Alam. He could be my chaperone. You know he would take good care of me."

Silence. This is a good sign, I thought. At least it wasn't the instant "no" that had sprung back at me every other time.

I pleaded, "Mom, what do I have to do to change your mind?"

"Convince me that you would be safe," was the firm reply.

Convince her that I would be safe. Now, at last, I felt I was getting somewhere. Not an easy thing to do, I thought, but at least I know what I'm working with.

Looking back, I realize my mom was never totally against the idea of me going to Asia. She had definite and serious questions in her mind, and she was honestly looking for ways to answer them with me. She wanted to be supportive, as she had always been in the past, but at the same time her maternal instincts were welling up within her. If I could prove to her that I would be safe, that the trip would be well-organized, that the mountain of details that would come with such a trip could be taken care of, then I would be free to go. If not, then there was no way she was letting me out of her sight.

I immediately wrote to UNICEF in New York, telling them of my pending trip and asking for advice about the arrangements. I knew they had contacts in every country, and that my parents would trust them. I sent letters to organizations in South Asia and contacted people I had met through human-rights organizations in Canada.

"Convince me that you would be safe." Every night those words raced through my mind as I formed my plan. When my father set a second condition for going, that I would have to raise half the plane fare myself, I knew I was winning them over.

UNICEF in New York agreed to contact their offices in South Asia to see if they would help. PLAN International, a development agency formerly known in some countries as Foster Parents Plan, also went looking for contact people willing to take care of us. I faxed friends we had made over the past months in organizations throughout South Asia, hoping for offers of accommodation.

It was a very good start.

Of course, I was back at school, trying to concentrate on the work to be done there. And the day-to-day operations of FTC continued. Over the summer our members had drifted off with their own vacation plans. After the garage sale, we found it difficult to get together for meetings, and it seemed to me that the energy within FTC, which had been so high, had begun to subside.

I was worried that FTC would not regain its momentum. But after the first few days of September, it was clear there was no reason for concern. The phone started to ring, with kids checking in, anxious to discuss our plans for the fall, and offering their own ambitious ideas for new projects.

Free the Children was filling a gap in many kids' lives. At an age when we were constantly being told by adults what to do, FTC was something we took on voluntarily. It had our names on it. And it was our reputations that were at stake. FTC was almost revolutionary in allowing young people large amounts of responsibility. It seems to me that one of the consequences of a consumer-driven society is that many of today's youth are bored by life in the suburbs. How many games of Super Nintendo do they want to play? How many times do they want to go to the shopping mall? Young people are longing for something more meaningful in their lives, something more challenging, something that allows them to prove themselves. FTC answered that need, and we weren't about to give it up.

For many of them it wasn't an easy decision. Among our peer group they were being labelled by some as do-gooders and wimps. For the so-called "in-crowd," FTC just wasn't cool enough. The mere fact that we were doing something out of the ordinary made us targets. We were unusual. We didn't fit their mould.

Some of them taunted us. "Hey, man, like my shirt? Some kid made it. It's the latest thing to have clothes made by kids."

Many of their snide comments had to do with our stance against brand-name companies guilty of human-rights abuses. Some of us spoke out against such companies, and began wearing clothes without brand names. The fact that we were taking on popular culture, criticizing companies that made running shoes or baseball caps – the very symbols of youth culture – made us different. And no kid wants to be seen as different.

But an interesting phenomenon was developing. FTC was attracting some of the most popular girls in school. These were girls who did well academically and were very involved in extracurricular activities such as sports and school clubs.

Where girls go, of course, guys follow. And soon we were attracting not just the type of guys who regularly volunteer for things, but jock types, too – guys who never volunteered for anything in their lives. In other words, Free the Children was becoming cool. The fact that a TV crew was making a documentary about our work gave us credibility.

Many of the reporters who came to interview us could not believe that a group of kids could ever have achieved what we did on our own. Adult support was important to the organization, but in our formative years, when FTC could have gone either way, kids were (and still are) the heart and soul of the organization. Free the Children would be nowhere today if it were not for the original group of young people, some as young as ten and eleven, who believed in what we were doing, who didn't listen to the naysayers and the complainers, who resisted peer pressure and just said, "We want to get involved in this because we believe in it."

Free the Children reached another milestone that fall. I was invited to speak before two thousand delegates at the Ontario Federation of Labour (OFL) convention in Toronto. It was the largest group I had ever addressed.

When I entered the convention hall and weaved past table after table of union members, all I could think was, My God, this is a lot of people!

I was led to a seat at the back of the stage. I looked out at the audience but could see nothing because of the massive bank of lights shining in my eyes. I shuffled through my notes. My heart was pounding.

An organizer asked me how long I planned to speak, and I said, "Ten or fifteen minutes –"

Someone to my left interrupted, "You're booked for three minutes. You'd better cut down on that speech."

I looked again at my notes. I hardly knew what to cut. The person was staring at me, with eyes that suggested I was not to take one extra second.

I looked out at the lights, thinking, If they seem bored, then I'll cut it down.

Jane Armstrong, the person responsible for my being there, introduced me. It took all of forty-five seconds. Then she turned my way and said, "The stage is yours."

I began the walk to the rostrum, but someone put out a hand to stop me. A person came running up the stairs to the stage with a two-step ladder and set it in place.

I took one step up the ladder, then another. My head appeared in full view over the rostrum. I could hear a trail of laughter from the conference delegates. I smiled into the glare of lights, trusting that somewhere beyond them was the audience.

I started the way I had started just about all my speeches, with the story of Iqbal. I was nervous, but before long my words were interrupted by loud applause. It gave me new confidence. My voice grew stronger and stronger. I pushed aside my notes. Even though I couldn't see them, I could feel the energy of the audience. With each passing minute I took greater control of what I wanted to say.

Indeed, many minutes passed, several of them interrupted by applause. By the time I had finished, the audience was on its feet. I clasped my hands together and said, "Thank you very much." Fifteen minutes had gone by quickly.

A leader of the union, Ken Signoretti, took hold of my hand and raised it in the air. The applause hadn't stopped. He whispered in my ear that I was not to go anywhere.

"On behalf of the Ontario Federation of Labour and its steering committee," he said, "the OFL wishes to pledge five thousand dollars to your cause!" He presented me with an OFL T-shirt and helped me put it on. Again my hand was raised in the air.

It started a chain reaction. The Canadian Union of Public Employees, the Canadian Autoworkers Union, the Steelworkers Union, one union after another walked up to the mike and matched what the OFL had given, and challenged others to do the same. Most moving of all were the individuals who stood up and pledged thirty or forty, and sometimes a hundred, dollars on behalf of their families and children.

T-shirt after T-shirt arrived on the stage, and before long I was wearing eight layers of them. In all the heat and the bright lights and the tally of money rising higher and higher, I leaned into the mike and said, "I think I'm going to faint!"

After an hour and forty-five minutes, I left the stage. I walked past table after table, shaking hands, accepting their hugs and acknowledging their applause. Needless to say, my fellow Free the Children members were all smiles when I finally reached them at the back of the room.

"This is unbelievable!" I shouted to them over the noise.

It was more than unbelievable. A hundred and fifty thousand dollars had been pledged, to be put in a separate bank account and used for projects that would directly help the exploited working children of the developing world. The donation was hundreds of times bigger than any FTC had ever received. Never in our wildest dreams could we have expected it.

Free the Children had truly taken flight. And for all of us gathered at the back of the room, hardly able to contain our excitement, there was no turning back now.

We made our way to where we had set up a booth to gather names on a petition we had been circulating. There were no problems getting signatures. In fact, we ran out of pens and had to rush off to photocopy more petition sheets to keep up with the crowds of delegates stopping to sign. They stuffed our little donation box full of coins and bills, as well as notes of congratulation and encouragement. Among those present was Michele Landsberg, a columnist with the *Toronto Star*, who interviewed us for her newspaper. What she had just witnessed, she said, was extraordinary.

Soon it was all over. Two thousand people had walked through our midst. With our petitions piled high and our spirits in orbit, we loaded into the family van and headed home. That night, over pizza and pop, we recounted story after unbelievable story of what had happened that day.

On Sunday morning, my father left the house early, before the newspaper had been delivered. He returned a few minutes later and slowly made his way to the kitchen. He pulled out the *Toronto Star* and placed it in the middle of the table. There, on the front page, right below the masthead, was the headline "BOY, 12, TAKES OFL BY STORM WITH CHILD LABOUR PLEA," and next to it was a photo of our group and the long scroll of our petition. I read the story by Michele Landsberg out loud, turning to page two to complete it. We sent my father out to buy ten more copies for other FTC members.

Over cereal, and before the comics, I read the article again. It seemed such a short time since I had first seen the story of Iqbal in the very same paper.

All this came in the midst of preparations for the trip to Asia.

One of our first considerations was getting the many visas necessary for the trip. The Indian consulate wasn't so bad, but when my father and I arrived at the Pakistani consulate, the line-up was the longest I had ever seen, more than a two-hour wait just to submit a simple form. The official told us to come back in ten days to get the visa. When it came time to apply at the Nepalese consulate, I was very thankful my father volunteered to go by himself.

I wish he could have done the same when the day arrived for my vaccinations. I hate needles. The torture session commenced with the arrival of a stainless-steel tray bristling with syringes. And after injections for typhoid, yellow fever, diphtheria, and tetanus, the doctor announced that this was only the first round. "Come back in a week, and we'll take care of hepatitis B and meningitis." I was feeling like a pincushion.

Everything was moving ahead, but still I hadn't heard anything in response to all the faxes I had sent to organizations overseas. Without their input I couldn't put a schedule together, and without a schedule

This was the photo that appeared in the *Toronto Star*. Working hard together to gather the twenty thousand names on the petition was our first taste of activism.

I couldn't make plane reservations. Without reservations, I couldn't give Alam the information he needed. When I called to inquire about flights, the airlines wouldn't take me seriously, or they quoted fares that were out of the question, and I was due to report to the doctor for the second round of dreaded injections. Grade Eight math was beginning to look easy.

I retreated to the sanctuary of my bedroom.

Sometime later that day, there was a knock at my door. My mother walked in with a smile on her face and three faxes in her hand. She didn't say a word, just held out the faxes. They were all from Asia. They all asked, "When are you coming?"

The organizations I had contacted all thought the trip was a great idea. They raised none of the concerns that had been raised at home in Canada. They would work with me to develop a schedule that best met my needs, and they assured me I would meet lots of working children. One of the groups, SACCS (South Asian Coalition on Child Servitude), only now realized that the person with whom they had been corresponding over the past several months was twelve years old. They were particularly excited by the trip and what it could do for the profile of child labour.

Things were looking up!

Now I really needed to get down to raising enough money for the trip. Besides the money I had saved from doing jobs around the house, and those I landed around the neighbourhood (raking leaves, cat-sitting, and so on), I raided my bank account, sold my hockey cards, and hinted to my relatives that early birthday or Christmas presents of a monetary nature would be greatly appreciated.

My relatives came through wonderfully. They offered to do whatever it took. A few of them, I knew, had doubts about whether I should even be going, but that didn't stop them from supporting me as much as they possibly could.

Everything was coming together. A focal point for planning was something that came to be known as the Samosa Summit.

Alam had decided to go ahead of me to Bangladesh and spend some time with his relatives. I would meet him there, and then we would set out on our trip across South Asia. He arrived at our house just a few days before his departure for Bangladesh, bringing with him a brown paper bag filled with vegetarian samosas from his favourite Indian restaurant. We sat around the kitchen table and set the samosas on a plate in the centre. I had never eaten Indian food before. I didn't know what to expect from these triangles of pastry stuffed with minced vegetables and spices.

As we began to outline my itinerary, I quickly realized that the three weeks over the Christmas holidays my parents had first agreed to was just not going to be enough. We added another week.

"But what about Nepal?" I said. "It doesn't make sense to go all that way and not get to Nepal."

Another week was added, and another.

"We'll give you the seventh week on one condition: that's it. No more. Seven weeks, period. You can't miss any more school."

As it was, I had to make a solemn promise to do as much school work as I could on the trip. Fortunately, my teachers had not argued against me going. They considered it a good educational experience – but just to be sure, they outlined all the school work I was to try to cover.

My parents, of course, had a lot of questions for Alam about the trip. Did all the bus and train travel need to be organized in advance? If I fell ill, what would happen? Where would I be staying at each step? Were the places safe? How, in fact, would I meet working children? Could I even expect to get into the factories and sweatshops? Would it be safe to use the still and video cameras I was planning to bring?

Alam pointed out that there was only so much planning that could be done beforehand, but I think my parents were reassured by his calm, businesslike approach. They knew he had my best interests at heart and would do all he could to make it a worthwhile trip for me, without ever sacrificing my safety.

Through all our discussions, the samosas sat on the table uneaten. Finally, Alam reached for one, explaining that he had been careful to choose the mildest variety. "In India," he said, "they are ten times spicier." I could see that this would be a test of my ability to fit into Asian culture.

Without hesitation, I took one and bit into it, convinced that if I could handle a Canadian samosa, I could certainly handle India. All eyes were on me as I started chewing.

My mouth was on fire. I almost gagged. For someone to whom fast food meant pizza or fries, it was quite the mouthful.

But I was determined not to spit it out. I gulped down a glass of water, swallowing half the samosa in the process. My mouth was still on fire. I tried milk, then yoghurt. I gasped for breath and stubbornly smiled through teary eyes.

Alam shook his head. We all laughed. I had, for the moment at least, bitten off more than I could chew.

"I have a feeling," Alam said, "this is going to be a very long trip."

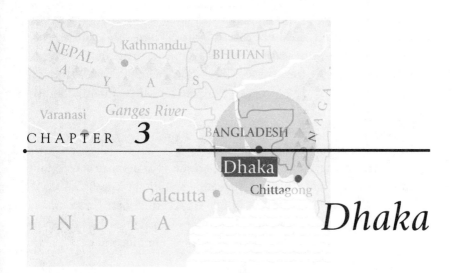

CHAPTER 3

Dhaka

I HAD BEEN ASSIGNED SEAT 3B. The KLM flight attendant checked the blue dog tag around my neck identifying me as an unaccompanied minor, and insisted on leading me by my hand to the seat. Slowly and deliberately, she went through all the emergency procedures. When she had finished, she leaned over and demonstrated how to buckle my seat belt. She was back in a few minutes, asking if everything was all right. Just before take-off she appeared again, this time with a colouring book and crayons. I politely declined.

I looked out the window as the 747 pulled away from the terminal buildings. Soon we were airborne, and below me was a steady stream of tiny cars. In one of those is my family, I thought – a family which I won't see for seven weeks. My mother probably still had tears in her eyes. I recalled my parents' final words: "Call us each time you change locations or when you arrive in a new city. We have to know where you are at all times."

The cars grew smaller and smaller. A strange feeling grew inside me, an uncertainty mixed with intense excitement. The cars below merged into the fabric of the sprawling city, a carpet of life, and then even that was gone.

It was dark when the plane landed in Amsterdam. After everyone else had deplaned, a flight attendant appeared, examined my charming dog tag, and escorted me off the plane. She directed me to one of the electric carts and we drove off, weaving a path through groups of passengers, honking the horn. I thought, This isn't so bad after all!

We pulled up to a door marked "UM."

"Unaccompanied minor," she noted.

She opened the door and led me inside. "Craig, you have eight hours until your flight departs." She smiled. "Enjoy yourself."

A virtual prisoner. For eight hours. I looked around the room. A five-year-old sat in the middle of the floor surrounded by Lego. *The Little Princess* was on the TV. I looked at the other videotapes: *The Lion King, Aladdin, Beverly Hills Cop II.*

In desperation I watched them all, and watched at least twenty kids come and go. One girl from Montreal recognized me from a television interview. She was close to my own age, so we talked and looked at bits of the movies until she left to catch her flight. There was nobody else, it seemed, going to Dhaka.

Finally I was escorted to the departure gate. The terminal was packed with travellers. At the gate I was taken straight to the front of the line, and was the first passenger to go aboard. As a kid alone, I really stood out. People probably assumed I was the son of some businessperson or foreign diplomat.

For the first time since leaving Toronto, I was feeling nervous. I was going to a strange and distant country where I certainly wouldn't be able to slip unnoticed into the crowd. I began to miss my parents, and hoped Alam would be there to meet me the minute I arrived.

A flight attendant came by and reviewed in detail all the safety procedures, including the operation of my seat belt. This time, however, my thick guidebook to Asia, open on my knees, seemed to ward off the colouring book and crayons.

The other passengers streamed aboard, and as soon as the plane was in the air, and the seat-belt sign went dark, they were up and out of their seats laughing with one another, walking around, introducing themselves to other passengers, chattering away as if they were old friends. This is definitely not Canada, I thought.

Dhaka

Two meals were served on the flight to Bangladesh. I decided to go for the Western-style meal the first time, since I wasn't sure when I would have that choice again. For the later meal, I decided to take the plunge and try the Asian selection. I ate it slowly, using my fork to sample a small bit at a time. To my delight, it was all interesting and tasty. In fact, I liked it a lot better than the first meal. I took that as a positive sign.

After ten hours we landed in Dhaka, Bangladesh. It was the morning of December 11; twenty-eight hours had passed since I left Toronto.

I had never seen such a place as the Dhaka airport. As I walked through the arrivals lounge, my eye caught a cockroach scurrying across the floor. Hundreds of mysterious faces rushed about, many shrouded in dark clothing. People were smoking everywhere, and the fans overhead had stopped dead. The sultry air smelled of sweat. I hadn't had a shower in over two days and I didn't smell any better myself.

The place was chaotic. Two 747s had just landed. People were pushing and shoving their way to the Immigration lines to present their passports and papers before any more planes arrived. When I reached the lines, they wound on ahead, almost forever. Fortunately, a KLM agent led me to the checkpoint reserved for the flight crew.

I placed my passport, visa, ticket, and boarding pass onto the counter in front of the Immigration official.

"Reason, time, and place that you will be staying while here?" he said in an accent so thick I could barely understand him.

Alam and the local organizations had instructed me not to say that I was here to do research on child labour. "Visiting friends," I told him.

He peered at me, but didn't bother to take issue with it. He handed back my documents and I was free to move on.

It took several minutes for my bags to arrive, and the flight attendant who had been standing by me all this time was getting a bit irritated. It was obvious she had other business to attend to. "Are you sure you checked *two* bags?" she asked.

I showed her my luggage tags. The area was crowded with people jostling each other to get to their bags, and there seemed to be a severe shortage of luggage carts. Arguments were breaking out all around me.

The whole idea of the unaccompanied-minor procedure is that young passengers are protected from abduction. The attendant was to leave me only when someone arrived with proper identification and

43

matched the description of Alam that my parents had provided. But as soon as my bags arrived, the attendant scribbled something on a clipboard, rushed me into the main airport lounge, and abandoned me. "Have a nice stay," she said, disappearing into the crowd.

I was on my own in the middle of Asia. Alam was nowhere to be seen. What was I to do now? I could feel my anxiety level rise several notches. I piled all my bags onto a luggage cart and looked around.

"Where is Alam?" I said out loud. Had he forgotten when my plane was due? Had he got into an accident? Should I call my parents?

I slowly scanned the crowd in the airport. The people were mostly Asian, a few of them in Western clothing, but no Alam.

One man asked me if I needed a hotel. Someone else kept asking if Lucinda was travelling with me.

"No." I shook my head. "There is no Lucinda with me."

He was insistent. "Where is Lucinda? Where is Lucinda?"

I got away from him, pushing the cart through a door to the outside. A wall of heat and humidity hit me. I was blinded by the intense sunlight.

I was immediately surrounded by a swarm of people, all wanting my attention. "You want hotel?" they asked in Bengali and broken English. "Taxi, you want taxi?" Others asked for money, or held things for sale in front of my face.

One person rushed up to me and started to take one of my suitcases. "No. No taxi," I said. I pulled it back from him. "Na!" I repeated again and again. With one hand I protected my bags as best I could, and with the other I pushed the cart away from them, along a walkway. There I found a little peace and time to recover.

When I left Canada, there was snow on the ground. Here, the heat was thick and overpowering, and I was very tired from the long trip. I felt sick.

But somehow, through it all, there surfaced the excitement of being in a totally foreign place. I caught sight of a vendor balancing a long rod on his shoulder. The rod was bent from the weight of the goods he carried. He was a walking store. Everything imaginable hung in bags from the rod – pots and pans, knives, cups, cigarettes, water, prayer mats. As he walked, he called out the names of the goods he had for sale.

Small food stands dotted the area outside the airport. As people left the airport they flocked to these stands, as if they'd been missing their favourite foods during their travels. The most popular food seemed to be a large leaf of some sort into which the customers piled a variety of fillings.

A massive palm tree towered over me. The air was sweet with the smell of spices and curries and charged with the rhythms of a strange, exotic language.

"I can't believe you brought so much stuff!"

It was Alam. He looked at me, a grin on his face. What a relief to see him.

"I made it," I said, smiling broadly. "Where were you?"

"I wasn't allowed inside. You have to have a ticket to get inside."

With Alam there to protect my luggage, I went to look for a phone to call home and tell my parents I was safe. Immediately I gathered an audience. A white child in Bangladesh making a phone call was far from a common sight.

"I stand out like a light bulb!" I said to my mother, after reassuring her I was safe.

For the first time in my life I experienced how it felt to be part of a very small minority. Alam told me that since his arrival two weeks earlier he had seen only six white people. Almost all of them would have been diplomats or businesspeople whose children are sent to schools abroad. When the children return to be with their parents, they are taken away by private cars to their homes and are never seen out on the city streets.

Alam told me to wait with my bags while he went to negotiate a price for a couple of rickshaws to carry us to his relatives' home. There must have been fifty rickshaws in front of the airport. They were painted in bright carnival colours and designs, as if each were trying to outdo the others in an attempt to get the customers' attention.

Eventually a price was set and Alam waved me over. When the drivers realized I was a foreigner, they became quite agitated. They had given Alam the local price instead of the tourist one, but they had no choice but to take us. The bags were loaded in one rickshaw, and Alam and I climbed aboard the other. And off we went through the streets of Dhaka.

Rickshaws were everywhere. I felt sorry for the drivers, having to carry such a heavy load. It took a great effort just to get them rolling.

The drivers weaved their way barefoot through narrow streets that were in desperate need of repair. Sweat glistened on their faces, which they wiped off with the bandannas tied around their necks.

Despite the blistering sun, I couldn't help but lose myself in the sights all around me. Children played with a beach ball along the roadside. Cows and dogs and rats roamed freely, sniffing the garbage that littered the streets. The poverty was overwhelming. I saw children sweeping and picking up garbage, others selling food or begging.

Dhaka is the capital of Bangladesh, with a population of four million people. I knew that the city, like many major cities in Southeast Asia, faced problems of poverty, overpopulation, and lack of living space. Over the years, Bangladesh's rural economy had been devastated by a series of droughts, tropical storms, and floods. Tens of thousands of people had left for the cities in search of a better life. But the cities could barely cope with the influx.

We passed many women doing laundry on the street in front of their homes. They had two tubs, one with soapy water, the other with clear. Using the pavement as a washing board, they pounded the clothes. We passed a man with a loudspeaker shouting in Bengali about a transit strike. The rickshaw drivers slowed down to catch what he was saying. And all around us were signs – most in Bengali, but a few in English – advertising clothes, movies, and countless brands of cigarettes.

Gradually, the poorer areas gave way to well-tended gardens and apartment buildings similar to those you would see in any North American city. Several of Alam's relatives lived together in one such apartment.

We arrived at the building to find the power out. Up four flights of stairs we trudged, dragging my bags. Partway there I stopped and looked out a window. Rows of low-rise buildings stretched to the horizon. The occasional plane landed at the airport not far away. There was very little green space. What trees and grass I could see were often on the roofs of the buildings. And dotting the hillsides around the city were the shanties, the homes of the poor.

Alam knocked loudly on the door and called out a few words in Bengali. The door was thrown open, and in he went to excited chatter and a great round of hugs.

"And this is Craig, my friend from Canada."

They looked at me. I think that were expecting someone older.

Throughout my trip I found that women are often treated as second-class citizens; they sometimes go without food, and their work in the home is deemed to be of little value. They have a strong spirit of cooperation, however, and seem to provide moral support for one another. Sometimes they even form partnerships in small businesses.

"Hello," I said.

No one moved. I tried again. "*Salam malekum,*" I said. Alam's uncle smiled warmly and welcomed me into the house. Soon I was being embraced by relative after relative, from the oldest to the youngest. "*Salam malekum, salam malekum*..." Within five minutes I was practically one of the family.

We sat down as Alam talked on, telling what I took to be stories of his recent travels. I was hot and sticky still. Overhead, a ceiling fan hung motionless.

Alam's aunt appeared with tall glasses of water. She passed one to me. Some parting words of my mother echoed in my head: Don't ever drink local water without treating it with chlorine. I retrieved some from my luggage and dutifully administered two drops into the glass. I forced myself to wait the fifteen minutes for the chlorine to do its job, then I downed the water with great relief.

Not long after, the ceiling fan came to life. The television flashed on and music from a Hindi movie filled the room. Two children reappeared and dropped themselves down in front of the TV. The plot was very simple: Man falls in love with woman, woman doesn't like man (but likes to sing, a lot), another man saves woman's life, two men fight for her hand (woman still singing), handsome man wins, two live happily ever after (now singing together).

Eventually Alam turned to me and announced above the racket, "We have to go through your luggage. We have to decide what goes back to Canada."

We found a place to inspect it all, and Alam dumped the contents of the first bag on the floor. He was impressed by the clothes I brought. "Perfect for the climate." He was pleased to find in another everything he had asked me to bring for him, including track pants, books on photography, and Nutrigrain bars, one of which he opened and started to chew.

Alam was less impressed when he came across my medical kit. He stared in disbelief at the contents. There were elastic bandages in case of sprains, syringes and blood-testing equipment, and drugs for worms and for at least a dozen different ailments. There were eye drops, painkillers, a toothache remedy, tweezers, tape, scissors, gauze, swabs, rubbing alcohol...the list went on and on.

48

"You're a walking medicine cabinet, for goodness sakes!" He picked up several bottles and read the labels, then turned to me and smiled. "Your mother packed this, didn't she?"

"She meant well." I smiled. "It's not *that* heavy."

Alam and I boxed up more than half the contents of the bags. We would be travelling light, with the bare necessities.

Soon it was time for dinner. I was looking forward to the meal, my first cooked in an Asian home. Alam even more so, especially when his aunt pointed out that she had cooked his favourite foods. We moved into the dining room and the dishes started to appear. First came steaming bowls of curried rice. Then something called *chokputi*, made from chickpeas, potatoes, and eggs. There was a pancake-flat bread, *roti*, followed by *dhal*, a mixture of different lentils in a sauce. It looked delicious. "And not too spicy," Alam's aunt said to him, who passed it on to me in English.

We all sat down. All the men, that is. I asked Alam whether the women would be joining us, but he shook his head and quickly turned the conversation back to the food.

After we had finished, the women settled in our places and had their meal from what we had left. I had to take a deep breath to stop myself from making a comment. I realized the custom was part of the Bangladeshi culture, yet it seemed very unfair.

That night I lay awake, thinking about what I had done, wondering if I had made the right decision to travel halfway around the world. I looked over at Alam asleep on the couch. The day before, when we had decided what items to send back to Canada, I placed my journal in the "send-home" pile. I got up, searched through the pile, and removed it. I flipped through the pages and saw the perfect blue lines still untouched by a pen. No matter how difficult the trip would become at times, I knew I would always want to remember it. I opened the journal and wrote, "Day One."

Well, I arrived at 8:26 their time. After getting my bags and going through customs I finally left to be met by Alam. There were coconut and banana trees! It was winter! We took a rickshaw rider from the airport to the home. The poverty is overwhelming; children are working in the street, picking up garbage, begging...

49

I thought that Alam might have scheduled a day to let me recuperate from all my travelling, but no such luck. First thing in the morning we were off, to visit a branch of PLAN International.

We met with several members of the PLAN staff, and soon my questioning turned to what their organization was doing for working children. They told me how some of their projects had significantly improved the lives of the poor.

"Would you like to see for yourself? Would you like to visit one of our projects?"

Of course. My purpose in coming to Asia was to be out with the children, to see for myself how they were living.

We were taken to one of Dhaka's largest slums. It was an experience I will never forget.

In the sweltering heat we piled out of our car onto the garbage-littered streets. The slum filled an entire valley, a maze of huts stretched away from us as far as the eye could see. It was an astonishing mass of poverty, like nothing I could ever have imagined. I stood for a moment, numbed by the sight before me.

The huts looked fragile, most of them made of panels of woven reed, framed by sticks that were tied together. We were told the people lived in constant threat of the government bulldozing their homes to the ground. It looked to me that a strong gust of wind would flatten them even faster.

I was hit with the smell of the place. Animal and human excrement lay in the gutters. The hot sun beat down on heaps of rotting garbage, intensifying the odour to the point that I could barely keep from covering my nose.

We walked down the alleyways between the huts, occasionally peering inside one to get a better idea of how the people lived. Most dwellings were a single room, in some cases no bigger than the bathrooms of some houses back home. In a few I noticed a small fire with a pot of water over it. No electricity or plumbing. The furniture was often simple crates. Frayed and tattered rugs were scattered over the dirt floors. The only decoration seemed to be woven cloths with the simplest of designs hung on the walls. The people had virtually no possessions.

The well is the centre of life in the slums. Clear, clean water is a valued gift that no one takes for granted. Every drop is precious.

As we walked, some children tagged along. What few clothes they wore were dirt-stained and ragged. Most of the boys wore only shorts, and the youngest children nothing at all. Most had bare feet.

But they were not without their laughter. Their attention quickly centred on me. With my blond hair and almost turquoise eyes, I certainly stood out from the crowd.

"*Salam malekum*," I said to them. "Hello."

They were surprised. They whispered and giggled, daring each other to come close to me. One brave fellow dashed up and poked my back. Before I could turn around to see his face, he had scurried away and disappeared between the shacks.

I doubt if any of them had ever seen a white child before. Certainly not one walking among their homes and wanting to talk to them. I decided to make a game out of their curiosity. I would crouch down, and when the younger children built up their courage to come within my reach, I would pounce on them and tickle them until they ran away. I did it again and again. Finally I was out of breath and sat down for a while. Some of the children came and sat next to me. We talked through an interpreter. They wanted me to come visit them again. Maybe I had more games they could play.

One young girl became our guide. She led us to a clearing. No refuse or garbage was to be seen anywhere. Standing in the centre of the clearing was her community's pride and joy – a hand pump built with the help of the local office of PLAN International. The people who lived in the slum absolutely cherished it.

The girl explained the operation of the pump, as if it were a miracle. "Once the hole had been dug, beautiful, clean, clear water rose from under the ground." She went on to show how it worked. "It is simple. You pump the handle like this, and after about ten pumps the water begins to flow." As if on cue, water appeared from the spout. "And then," she said, with excitement in her voice, "it gushes out!"

The people didn't want to lose a single drop. As soon as the pump filled one bucket, another appeared in its place. The full buckets were carried off in all directions. A team of men, we were told, was responsible for maintaining the pump and the site around it.

I tried to imagine what it must have been like before the pump was put in place. Water probably came from a great distance or, more likely, what was used was often contaminated. I couldn't help but compare it to how freely water was used in my own home. I thought of all the swimming pools back in Thornhill, each filled with thousands of gallons of water. In Canada we think nothing of letting water drain endlessly from our kitchen taps and garden hoses. Our country is filled with lakes and rivers. We take our fresh water so much for granted.

To these people, water was a gift. It was a treasure, as precious as life itself.

Our last stop was at the house of an elderly lady of seventy or more. She was slight and wrinkled and stiff with age. Her scarred hands told of a life of hard work. But in her old age she had taken on the responsibility of caring for babies who had been abandoned, infants left on her doorstep by girls and young women who had given birth to children they couldn't care for. We heard the babies crying in the background.

"Who will take her place once she is no longer able to care for them?" I asked.

There was no answer to my question. In such a place, people learn to cope as best they can. Amid the misery there is always hope. These people were not asking for hand-outs. No one asked me for money or food. They merely wanted the chance to make a better life for themselves.

As we were leaving, our driver said, "This is one of the largest slums in Dhaka, but it is certainly not the worst."

In the car, I quizzed our hosts from PLAN on the economic situation in the slums. Eighty per cent of the men who lived there made their living as rickshaw drivers. I knew from my ride from the airport that it had to be one of the most brutal and punishing jobs in the world. In exchange for his fourteen hours of work a day, a driver barely earned enough to feed his family. Most of the drivers had little hope of ever owning their own rickshaws. They were forced to rent them from a middleman, and it was to him that a large portion of their earnings went.

A rickshaw costs at least ninety dollars, an incredible amount of money in a country where the average yearly income is $220. I knew what ninety dollars meant for someone living in the West, the cost of a pair of running shoes. Many Canadian parents spend five times that amount just to outfit a child for hockey.

Seeing the slum was certainly a sobering experience. But even though the situation for these people was bleak, I could see evidence of an entrepreneurial spirit, especially among the women. I discovered women at the doorways of their huts selling baskets they had made and food they had cooked. A few were carrying drinking water to nearby construction sites to sell to the workers. My guide told me of the strong bond that existed among the women who lived in the slums. I understood why projects such as the Grameen Bank,* which gives them small loans to start their own businesses, were so successful.

My visit to the slums of Dhaka left me feeling that these people had a real spirit of cooperation and community, and caring for their neighbours. The visit had been, in a strange way, uplifting.

I had come to Asia to see as many child labourers as I could. I wanted to be there in their workplaces, seeing for myself their exact situations. The following morning I found myself at a train station, sitting on a ledge, my feet dangling over the side, simply observing everything around me.

There was a constant stream of activity. The dismal, decaying surroundings were alive with the surge of passengers pushing their way on and off trains filled to bursting. I spotted numerous children in the midst of it all, selling their services as porters for a few coins. As soon as a train pulled into the station, kids would rush aboard. They would hurry off again before the train left, and if they were lucky, they would be carrying someone's bags for them.

Later that morning we visited the docks on the river. Amid the bustle of the waterfront we found children loading and off-loading cargo. We found them also actively employed in the fishing trade – mending nets, cleaning fish, and scraping the debris from the hulls of boats.

There we discovered one of the informal schools that had been set up throughout the city by a Swiss-based organization. It was an impressive operation. Rather than try to get kids to come to one central location, this group was taking school directly to the children, at their

---

* The Grameen Bank, under the direction of its founder, Muhammad Yunus, has created a banking system to meet the needs of the poor throughout rural Bangladesh. Over 90 per cent of its loans go to women. Yanus has said, "These millions of small people with their millions of small pursuits can add up to create the biggest development wonder."

This group of kids in Bangladesh were happy to leave their work on the fishing docks for a few hours to learn to read and write at the travelling school. The teacher used a small portable blackboard, and the children enthusiastically shouted out the answers.

workplaces. The working children were given time from their jobs to join the teacher for a few hours each day to learn to read and write and to do basic math.

The children sat on mats under a tree or in a vacant shed, in groups of three or four, each group sharing a small textbook. The teacher, using a chalkboard set on an easel, conducted the lessons, then put questions to the children. The children shot back with their answers. It was simple and efficient, and, to judge by the eagerness of the children, it seemed to be working.

I particularly remember the face of one boy, and the deep gashes on his arms and legs. He had come to sit on the mat not for schooling, but for medical attention.

I sat down next to him. "How were you hurt?" I asked, through an interpreter.

"I was pushing a cart up a hill," he said. "It rolled backwards. The wheel ran over me."

The wound just above his ankle was jagged, and dirt had started to collect in it.

The teacher had brought some disinfectant and bandages. "I do the best I can for him," he said. "Much of my time is spent tending to the children's cuts and wounds."

"Shouldn't he go to a hospital?" I asked.

"They would only turn him away. He has no money."

The boy was in a great deal of pain. He tried to smile, but in his dark eyes was the deeper pain of someone who had known misery through much of his life.

"I hope it will heal soon, and you're feeling better," I said to him.

I knew my attempt at comforting him could be no more than a fleeting moment in a life marked by neglect and abuse.

During my four days in Bangladesh, I encountered many different attitudes toward child labour. Some of these were very disturbing, especially when it came to girls working as child domestics.

One woman who was working with an organization for children told me outright, "We see no problem with young girls working as domestics. Girls do not go to school, and this is a way for them to earn their keep."

She had to be aware, of course, that almost three-quarters of all females in Bangladesh are illiterate, that only 13 per cent of girls ever enrol in secondary school. Why was she not promoting education for girls, rather than trying to rationalize the present situation? If she had daughters of her own, would she be content to have them work as domestic servants?

These people were of the opinion that child domestic servitude was a tradition in Bangladeshi society that wasn't inherently wrong, that it just needed to be regulated to prevent abuse. They didn't feel it exploited children, because, in their opinion, unlike work in shops or industries, "the employer does not get any direct financial benefit from the child labour."

I think a poster on her office wall said it all. It showed a child domestic worker, and the caption read: "I am not a slave. This is my job."

In a study of child domestic work in Dhaka, it was found that "the majority of child domestics receive salaries less than 100 taka per month." That's $2.50 U.S. Is that not cheap labour?

On one occasion, we had arranged to pick up one of the coordinators of an education-video project developed to expose the discrimination against girls in South Asia. The video was titled *Meena*, referring to the central cartoon character, a highly spirited young girl. Our car came to a stop in front of the gates outside the coordinator's home. As we sat waiting for her to arrive, we looked past the partly open metal gates. We saw a child, a young girl, squatting on her legs and brushing the leaves and dust off the driveway. Alam, the driver, and I stepped out of the car and walked towards the girl.

When she looked up, we saw that she could be no more than ten years old. Her black hair was tied back and her face was marked with dirt. She was indeed one of the thousands of child domestic servants we had heard about.

The woman we were waiting for appeared. On seeing us with the girl, she immediately became very agitated.

"Is she not going to school?" we asked.

"I know nothing about this girl. She has been hired by the landlord."

The purpose of the film we later watched was to help girls realize they are capable of more than serving others, that they have a right to an education and a right to fulfil their own dreams. Throughout the screening, my mind couldn't help returning back to the young girl behind the metal gates. I was left to wonder what was stopping the coordinator from making the connection between the girl in the film and the one at her home.

This episode was just one of several in Bangladesh that took me by surprise. Most of my correspondence with human-rights organizations in South Asia had been with India, where there was a strong movement against child labour. I was not prepared for what I found in Bangladesh – a strong movement that condoned it.

Again and again we were told that the income children earned from employment was essential for their family's survival. They pointed directly to what happened with the country's garment industry as an example of where attempts to change the situation had made matters worse for children, not better.

Bangladesh's garment industry had been the fastest-growing source of foreign money and employment, with 52 per cent of its exports going to the American market. More than fifty thousand children worked in the industry, often for long hours in cramped conditions, and for wages of no more than a dollar a day.

In August, four months before my visit, a fire had raged through a Bangladeshi garment factory, resulting in nine people being trampled to death while trying to escape. Four of them were under the age of fourteen. Reports concluded that a gate at the exit was locked and escape routes were blocked. Firefighting equipment was absent or inaccessible.

Yet allowing children to work in textile factories was defended as essential. Many were quick to bring up what had happened as a result of the bill introduced by Tom Harkin* in the U.S. Senate in 1993. The bill would prohibit the importation of goods made by child labour.

---

* As a result of the Harkin Bill, a "Memorandum of Understanding" was proposed to Bangladesh's garment manufacturers by the American ambassador to Bangladesh and other U.S. officials. It included a monitoring program that would prevent child workers from being suddenly dismissed, and would instead allow them to be gradually phased out of the garment industry over a three-year period to September 1, 1997. Adult relatives of the dismissed children would be given preference for their jobs. Education would be made available for the children.

The members of the Bangladesh garment manufacturers voted against the plan. They did not feel it was their responsibility to provide rehabilitation programs for the children.

Consequently, many children were dismissed without alternative opportunities being in place for them. Seeing that many of the children were worse off, the International Labour Organization, UNICEF, and the Bangladesh Manufacturers and Exporters Association

D h a k a

Although it has never been passed, it caused great concern in Bangladesh's garment industry. Fearing the loss of their market, industry officials quickly removed all children from their factories. Without access to any other source of income or better schooling, some children ended up in jobs that were far more dangerous than work in the garment factories – breaking bricks, making fireworks, selling goods on the street.

I met with numerous organizations that used this situation as a reason to promote the need for child labour in Bangladesh. "Work in the garment industry is better than anywhere else. What would you have these children do? Let themselves be scarred making fireworks? Allow them to become prostitutes?"

These organizations, composed entirely of adults, appeared to exist for the sole purpose of writing and distributing literature to promote the need for child labour. One such pamphlet, which was distributed around the world, showed a series of pictures of a child breaking bricks, taking money, eating, and smiling, as if to justify child labour.

I was getting a quick education in the world of human-rights organizations. Some seemed more interested in giving themselves jobs than in actually helping children. It was another brand of exploitation, a more elaborate and sophisticated kind, but exploitation nevertheless.

I couldn't understand why anyone would be satisfied to see kids working long hours in any type of dangerous job. How would the lives of child labourers change if people put all of their energy into justifying it? Couldn't there be other options for these children – improved social programs, schooling? I couldn't help but feel that the ones who attempt to justify child labour are never the ones who are suffering the most.

(BGMEA) signed an agreement to provide schooling and a stipend for children under fourteen who had lost their jobs in garment factories. Over two hundred schools were opened.

Many people in developing countries see the sudden concern about child labour in the rich countries, especially the United States, as hypocritical, a self-serving way to block out imports. Others say they recognize that minimum standards must be attained, but they resent the use of pressure.

On the positive side, the Harkin Bill helped to raise greater awareness of the issue of child labour. Governments and business leaders in developing countries, concerned about their exports and financial markets, have begun to take action against child labour in all sectors, not only the export market.

The negative effects, however, are on the children themselves. There is the risk of the children ending up in worse situations, unless programs and alternative sources of income are set up for them before they are dismissed from the factories.

59

In fact, I didn't meet a single child in any of the organizations we met. And no one seemed to agree on a solution.

This was particularly evident in one meeting we had. It brought together Alam and me, a representative of UNICEF, and three "experts" in the field of child labour, two of whom were professors. I asked one basic question: What must be done to eliminate child labour in Bangladesh?

"Good primary education must be available to all children," said one.

"No," interrupted another. "These children must have vocational training if they are to find jobs."

The third broke in quickly: "Primary education and vocational training are both useless, my friends, if we don't have more economic growth and foreign investment."

The three of them began to argue among themselves. At first they politely debated their colleagues' opinions, and attempted to elaborate on their own. Gradually the tension grew, however, and the politeness gave way to bickering. And amplified into a full-fledged war of words.

Then the most incredible thing happened. The man who had driven us to the meeting, a chauffeur employed by UNICEF, became so frustrated with the academics that he turned away from them and began to explain to us his own ideas on what should be done to end child labour. As the three experts continued to argue, Alam and I listened to the chauffeur with great interest. He knew working children because he lived and worked with them every day.

I caught the eye of the UNICEF representative, and she began to chuckle. It was enough to touch off the same response from Alam. Soon both of them broke out laughing. Even the driver threw his head back and joined in. I placed my hand over my face to cover the smile that was spreading from ear to ear.

The academics finally stopped their arguing and turned to us in bewilderment. I did my best to apologize for the outburst, and the others gained control of themselves, though we were careful not to look at each other. The meeting continued and we took the discussions in a new direction, all of us now listening to the chauffeur.

I did see some good work done on behalf of child workers. Underprivileged Children's Education Programme (UCEP), for example, had set up a huge skills-training centre. There I encountered young people hard at work learning a wide variety of trades, including carpentry, metal work, sewing, and weaving. They had been given a stipend of 325 taka a month to substitute for the money they would have earned as child labourers.

Another group, the Bangladesh Rural Advancement Committee (BRAC), operates over thirty thousand primary schools throughout the country with close to a million children taking part. To its great credit, BRAC has made a strong effort to bring young girls into its programs, with the result that at least 70 per cent of the students (ages eight to sixteen) are female.

Still, sometimes the enormity of the problem of child labour overwhelmed me. Was there, in fact, anything that young people in other countries could do that would really make a difference?

It was a question I asked the representative of UNICEF, an impressive man from the Netherlands, who saw clearly the responsibility of all people to help exploited children. "The very best thing you and the other young people in Free the Children can do is spend your time and the money you raise to educate your own people on the importance of international aid. Help them understand what is happening in poor countries. People in rich countries have to learn to share, to learn how to do with less. They have a psychological need to buy, buy, buy. They are consumed with the idea that they need more, more, more."

I thought about some of my friends at school, of how important it was to have the newest style of basketball shoes, or the sweatshirt with the right logo. And I thought of my bedroom at home. The video games piled high. All the clothes that filled the closet, all the toys stuffed under my bed. Did I really need all those things? Was it fair that I had so much and the kids I had seen in the slums had nothing?

"Do you really think it makes people happy to have so many possessions?" he asked.

I didn't have an answer for him.

"If anyone looked seriously at the poor nations, they would see how it is absolutely unacceptable for people in a country like Bangladesh to be living the way they are."

It left me with a lot to think about. I realized that it's not enough to look at these people and condemn their child-labour practices. The truth is – we are part of the problem, too.

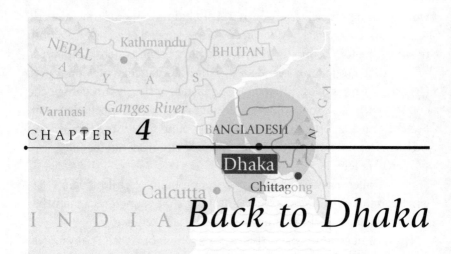

CHAPTER **4**

Back to Dhaka

FOLLOWING OUR STAY IN Bangladesh, we planned to go to Thailand. We would travel by a combination of rickshaw, bus, and ferry to Calcutta, India, then take a flight from there to Bangkok, Thailand. We had already purchased tickets for this leg of our journey before leaving Canada. But getting out of Dhaka proved to be a major challenge. The transit dispute had spread, and now the city was gradually being shut down by a general strike. All public services were affected. On the advice of Alam's relatives, we decided to leave early, before everything ground to a halt.

We packed our bags and headed to the bus station by rickshaw. The line-up for tickets to get out of the city was already long, with every seat in the waiting room taken and mounds of luggage everywhere. We lined up for our tickets, then found a spot on the waiting-room floor. There were no signs of a bus anywhere, and no one had information about when we could expect one. There was nothing we could do but wait. I strapped myself to the luggage and fell asleep.

At about eleven at night I was awakened by Alam's gentle prodding. A bus had finally arrived. It was not our scheduled bus, which was lost en route somewhere, but a bus substituted to transport people to the Indian border. The bulkier pieces of luggage were thrown up onto the bus's roof rack. Whatever was left was stuffed inside. Off we went

62

into the night, a herd of humanity, draped over our possessions, all longing for sleep.

At about two or three in the morning, after two hours of weaving a route through the maze of vehicles in a constant lurching line of stop-and-go traffic, we came to a dead and final stop.

"What's going on?" I mumbled sleepily to Alam.

"It doesn't look good," he said.

In the blackness, we had little idea what was happening. The bus driver shouted back at us the dreaded details. The trucks and buses were coming off the ferry at the other end. In their hurry to get to Dhaka, they were using both lanes of the two-lane road. We had met them head-on, with a ditch on either side of the road. We were going nowhere.

There was only one thing to do. We would walk the twelve kilometres to the ferry terminal, dragging our possessions with us.

"I said you'd have to be prepared for anything in this country," Alam said to me, strapping on his backpack and helping me with mine. He was smiling, but just barely.

We trekked off into the dead of night, pressing our way single file through the mass of stalled vehicles. We wormed a route past the dense clumps of people held motionless on either side. Occasionally there would be enough light, often only from the end of a cigarette, to see a darkened face as we passed. There were thousands of people aboard these buses, yet very little noise broke the night air. Most people had probably given up hope of moving and had fallen asleep. Alam, in his quest to record as much of the trip as possible, switched on the video-camera for a while. The people we passed, some crouched on the ground, dark clothing draped over their heads, must have been thoroughly bewildered by the sight of a floodlit kid passing among them.

All our separate bits of luggage were proving to be a nuisance. I didn't seem to have hands enough, or shoulders strong enough, to lug it all.

"Just be thankful we got rid of most of what you brought," Alam said. It was meant to be a comforting thought.

"You mean you don't wish my mother had packed a few more medicine bottles?" I joked. We both laughed.

Two men we had met on the bus came to our rescue. They offered to carry the extra bags of supplies I had brought from Canada for our hosts in Bangkok. I felt uneasy handing over any of our bags to strangers. Weren't we taking a big chance? But given our situation, we just had to trust them.

After seven kilometres, the odyssey through the Bangladeshi night was getting to me. The two good Samaritans carrying our bags had disappeared. We had been up most of the night. I was exhausted.

Dawn was starting to break, light slowly returning the world to us. We had walked through the night into a sunrise sky of orange and pink. The world around us was coming more alive with each step, drivers and passengers easing themselves out of the stupor of the night.

Finally, we encountered a rickshaw driver who, for a fee, agreed to take us the rest of the way to the ferry. We piled our bags aboard the rickshaw, and I climbed in and collapsed onto the seat. I glanced over my shoulder and there was Alam running behind the rickshaw.

The bewildered driver said a few words in Bengali, which I knew had to be something like, "What is that crazy guy doing?"

"He is out for his morning jog," I said, laughing. Early every morning for years Alam had made a point of exercising. He could see no reason to change his routine.

We arrived at the ferry just as it was about to leave. The two men who had been carrying our bags were there, waiting for us.

"We lost you in the crowd," one said in his heavily accented English, as they handed us the bags.

I was very relieved, and thanked them several times. I wished I had been more trusting, but instead had assumed our bags had vanished forever.

"You are welcome. You are very brave boy to come alone to our country. Very strong. We wish you much happiness in your journey."

They travelled with us on the ferry, but then they were gone. It would not be the last time I would encounter the generosity of perfect strangers.

Once we arrived on the other side of the river, we loaded our belongings into another rickshaw, a bicycle-powered one, and headed towards the Indian border. Twelve hours had passed since we left Dhaka. All I wanted to do was sleep, but given what we had gone through to get here, I could wait another while until we cleared customs.

At the checkpoint, we passed our papers to two officials. They looked through our bags for weapons and illegal substances.

"Passport? Ah, yes, Canada. I have cousin in Ed-mon-ton."

"Very nice city." I smiled. Everything was going smoothly.

He shuffled through the papers, looking for something more. "Route pass? Where is your change-of-route pass?"

A more stern-faced Bangladeshi official appeared, looking overworked from the influx of people caused by the strike. "You have no route pass?"

"Route pass? What is that?" Alam said.

"You entered Bangladesh by air," the fellow replied impatiently. "You must leave by air. If you want to leave the country by another way, you must have a change-of-route pass."

"Where do I get a change-of-route pass?"

"Dhaka. You must go back to Dhaka!" He waved us aside and reached for the papers of the man standing behind us.

I couldn't believe my ears. "Back to Dhaka," I muttered. "He must be kidding."

We had made every conceivable effort just to get here. How could we even think of going back to Dhaka? Besides, with the strike we couldn't possibly make it to Calcutta in time to catch our flight.

"This is ridiculous," said Alam. He decided we had to try again to get through the border crossing. "There's no way we're going back to Dhaka."

We would go to another line-up. Maybe another customs official would let us through.

We tried it. The new official examined our papers. I held my breath and prayed. He quickly checked our visas, closed the passports, and pointed to the Indian border. I quickly passed him a couple of the maple-leaf pins given to me by the office of the Canadian ambassador in Dhaka.

We had made it! All that remained was for our passports to be stamped by Indian Immigration and we would be on our way to the airport.

It was a strange sight, no doubt, a white child travelling by ordinary bus to a rural, middle-of-nowhere border crossing where tourists seldom travelled. That was the reason the Indian Immigration official now examined my papers in such detail, peering at me, then at my passport photo. He read the letter my parents had written, giving Alam authorization to travel with me.

We waited patiently. We were in India now. Our papers were all in order.

"How did you enter Bangladesh?" he asked, knowing full well by the stamp on my passport what the answer should be.

"By air."

"Good. Now, where is your change-of-route pass?"

We hesitated. Finally Alam said, "We don't have one."

"Then how did you get this far?"

It was not his responsibility to be concerned about any change-of-route pass. He was an Indian official. But I was a child from Canada and travelling with an Asian adult. He wasn't taking any chances. We were not entering India.

He led us back across the Bangladeshi border, yelling at the Customs officials who had allowed us into his country without the proper papers.

We were given over to the Bangladeshi official who had first dealt with us, the stern-faced one who had told us to return to Dhaka. I started to worry. "We're in big trouble, Alam."

My face was pale. There was no hiding the dread I felt. The official led us into his office and closed the door. We felt like two criminals. Perhaps we *were* two criminals, and would soon be under arrest. I imagined my parents flying from Canada to argue for my release. Not a pretty sight.

He slouched behind a desk and lit a cigarette. That practically confirmed it in my mind.

He looked at us and began to speak in a fatherly tone, as if we were very young children. "You don't understand, do you? That is why you got into line again and crossed the border without proper papers."

This was one time I was not about to question an adult underestimating the intelligence of a kid.

We would play dumb. And play it really well. "No, we do not understand. Why can we not cross the border?"

He drew on his cigarette, mustering up great patience. He explained in slow and deliberate detail the need for a change-of-route pass. He pointed to the map on the wall, tracing with the tip of his cigarette the route back to Dhaka.

"Back to Dhaka," he said. "Back to Dhaka. You must go back to Dhaka!"

It was hopeless. We were not crossing the border. That was quite evident.

"You mean," said Alam, "we must go back to Dhaka to get a change-of-route pass?"

"Yes! Yes. That is it!" shouted the official ecstatically.

I let a smile of recognition slowly cross my face. "Ahhh," I said. "Back to Dhaka."

We would have to retrace our steps. First a bus to the docks, then the ferry, and finally another bus back to where we had started. But all hope of a simple return journey evaporated when we were told that the next bus to the ferry terminal was not for another seven hours.

We bought some bananas and mangoes from a vendor outside the station and then sat down in the waiting room. Alam took out his knife and began peeling a mango. He cut off a thick slice and passed it to me on the end of his knife.

It was one of those situations where you laugh or cry. And we were almost too tired to do either.

"Back to Dhaka!" Alam exclaimed, mimicking the Bangladeshi official. We both burst out laughing. The juice of the fruit dribbled down our chins.

"Ahhh," I said, turning on an imaginary light bulb in my head. "Back to Dhaka."

We burst out laughing again.

It attracted the attention of a young boy. He looked to be no more than eight, and worked as an errand boy at the station. He came over and sat down next to us as we ate. Alam passed him a piece of the mango. His dark eyes sparkled. With both hands he brought the juicy fruit to his lips and grinned from ear to ear.

He made short work of the fruit. We chatted for a while, finding out as much as we could about the work he did at the station. We had quickly become friends. When Hindi music was turned on in the waiting room, he stood up and began to dance! We were intrigued, of course, by this spontaneous outpouring. As we watched his intricate moves, he chatted away to Alam, telling him how he loved music and movies and knew all of the latest dances. He offered to teach us one.

We stood up and followed his lead. He laughed when we stumbled over our feet. He stopped us and showed us the same move again and again until we got it right. Gradually, all eyes in the terminal turned to us. We were a strange sight indeed – two foreigners following the swaying arm and hip movements of a young local boy.

We were in a crazy mood, laughing as we danced. Alam and I eventually gave in to our tiredness and slumped back in the seats. But not our new young friend. On he danced, his moves more intricate than ever.

It was seven o'clock in the morning when we arrived at Dhaka airport. We had been on the road for thirty-six hours, and still no further ahead. Our only hope was to get on a flight to Calcutta – an expense we had originally hoped to avoid.

The airport was in complete chaos. There were stacks of luggage everywhere. Flights had been cancelled, leaving passengers marooned. They were now lying about all over the place, practically camping out. It was so hot the air was barely breathable. We forced a path to the ticket counter.

"We need two tickets on the next flight to Calcutta."

The ticket agent tried hard not to show his amusement. "All our flights to Calcutta are booked for the next ten days."

"You mean there's no chance whatsoever?"

"Sorry," he smiled. "You might try buying tickets from confirmed passengers."

We looked at each other. It was worth the effort.

"Good luck," the agent said.

For the next hour we worked the floor in search of anyone with a boarding pass to Calcutta. It was an absurd scene: the two of us dragging our luggage through the crowds, Alam calling out our request, punctuating it with personal pleas for understanding. I'm sure he expected me to look the part of the homeless waif, with big, watery eyes. I was so tired I could easily have done it.

Nobody bought our offer. With the strike on, a boarding pass to Calcutta was pure gold.

Then Alam had a brainwave. We dragged our luggage up the steps of a broken escalator to the office of Thai Airways. He thought we might have better luck there than at their ticket counter. The person we encountered was very friendly and very efficient. Maybe they had seats to Calcutta?

She checked the flights. "Sorry," she said, almost as discouraged as we were.

We retreated and went off again. We scouted out the terminal until we found a place to store our bags. We piled them up under a set of stairs, with the most important ones at the bottom and out of sight. One of us would sleep while the other kept watch.

Suddenly we heard someone call our names. The Thai official was looking for us, waving frantically for us to come quickly. Two passengers had just cancelled their seats to Calcutta! The plane was leaving in forty-five minutes.

We ran like mad, with me struggling to find a way through the wall of people and to keep up with the jogging Alam. We arrived breathless at the Thai check-in gate. The red light above the counter flashed "Now Boarding." We were the last passengers. We had made it!

A hand went up in front of us. "Sorry, gentlemen, you are too late to board the aircraft."

There were still twelve minutes before departure. "Too late?" Alam shouted. "There are at least another fifteen minutes..." I had never seen him so agitated.

"Sorry, sir, but that's the regulations."

We had been trying for forty-eight hours to leave Dhaka. We had travelled by rickshaw, bus, and ferry, and walked miles with our backpacks. We had spent the entire day on a hunt for tickets, and now the plane to Calcutta was taking off with two empty seats.

"You can't do this!" Alam said to him. "You have to let us on this flight." Now he had the attention of everyone around him. "You have to realize how urgent this is."

A supervisor stepped into the fray. "Is there some problem?"

"Yes, yes, there's a big problem. There are ten minutes left to board this flight and we absolutely must get on it." Alam's tactic was to stir up the crowd at the check-in counter, and he had succeeded.

The manager looked at our passports and boarding passes. With a sweep of his hand he pointed in the direction of the loading tunnel. "Have a nice flight."

Aboard the aircraft we sank, absolutely exhausted, into the seats. Within minutes we were in the air and on our way to Calcutta.

Partway into the flight, Alam turned to me and said, "It's December seventeenth."

In all the commotion, we both had forgotten.

"Happy birthday," he said to me.

"Happy birthday," I said to him.

Alam and I have our birthdays on the same day of the year. He had turned twenty-five, and I had turned thirteen.

We ordered a cold drink and toasted each other.

"One thing for sure. You'll never forget the day you turned into a teenager."

Alam was right. For days I hadn't been able to get the images of the slums of Dhaka out of my mind. The children with not enough food. The shacks without any toilets. The rags that hung over windows without any glass. As I sat there, drinking pop with Alam, I wondered how those children spent their birthdays.

We finished our drinks, and I settled into a much-needed nap. I woke only minutes before landing. It was eleven o'clock at night. We were shepherded into the transit lounge. It was completed deserted. We had fifteen hours until our flight to Bangkok.

Just after dawn, an airport official opened up a complimentary local phone booth. We decided to call Swapam Mukherjee, a representative of the Centre for Communication and Development with whom we had been corresponding. He was the one making arrangements for our visit when we returned to Calcutta.

"Where are you? What happened? Your parents are frantic!"

We had been expected to pass through Calcutta three days earlier. Swapam had even organized a press conference. When we didn't show up, he telephoned my mother. It threw everyone into a panic. Swapam contacted the mounted police in Calcutta. They issued an all-out alert and faxed my description to all police stations and border crossings. I was a wanted man.

And my mother was a wreck. "Call her right away," I said. "I can't call long distance from here." I could picture what she must have been going through.

We explained all the problems we had getting out of Dhaka. We apologized for not making it to the press conference and set a time to reschedule it.

"And make sure you tell my parents how sorry I am."

We told Swapam we'd see him in a week, and hung up.

Our flight for Thailand left on schedule. I closed my eyes and dreamed of Bangkok, the Pearl of the Orient, the Great City of Angels . . .

CHAPTER **5**

Bangkok

BANGKOK IS A CITY OF PRO-
found contrasts.

It has hundreds of Buddhist temples, incredibly beautiful and serene. It is also home to a gaudy nightlife district, one of the world's most notorious, where child prostitution is rampant.

It is a place where people greet each other by demurely putting their palms together and gently bowing. And where drivers scream at each other over the fury of some of the worst traffic to be found anywhere.

My first encounter with that traffic was driving from the airport with our host in Thailand, Ian Hamilton. It took us more than ninety minutes to travel the five kilometres to his house. Traffic in this city is so bad and so slow that vendors walk between cars selling the use of portable toilets.

Ian had become Free the Children's major contact in Bangkok. He worked for Canadian University Services Overseas (CUSO) and had sent us a great deal of information about child labour in Thailand, and had volunteered to be our host. His wife, Sue, who was seven and a half months pregnant, met us at the door of the house they were renting in a pleasant section of Bangkok. We had our own bedrooms and a hot shower. After what we had gone through to get to Bangkok, it was pure bliss!

72

The Grand Palace in Bangkok is a city within a city, similar to the Vatican in Rome or the Forbidden City in Beijing. I noticed many people laying incense, fruit, and other small offerings before this impressive statue. Someone told me that the previous week's winner of the biggest lottery in Bangkok believed he had won because he had left an offering of incense in front of this statue only minutes before buying the ticket.

Sue saw right away that I was exhausted. "You definitely could do with some sleep," she said, and sent me off to bed.

I woke at six that evening, my sleep patterns totally wrecked and my stomach in desperate need of food. We decided to visit the open-air market near Ian and Sue's home. The stalls were lit with small lanterns that lent a magical, near-carnival atmosphere to the place. Each stall displayed an array of food, most of which I didn't recognize, with more cooking on open-air stoves inside. The pungent, spicy smells were strange, but fascinating.

We found a comfortable table in an area in the midst of it all, and sat down to what was the best meal I've had in my entire life! In the space of a few unforgettable hours, Thai food became my absolute favourite. The meal turned into a birthday celebration and stretched long into the night.

The restaurant had no kitchen, as such. Our waiter acted as a middle-man, finding out what we wished to eat, then going off to the various vendors and bargaining for it. He spoke perfect English and quoted outrageous prices, until he found out that our hosts were not tourists but were living in Bangkok. The prices dropped to a fraction of the original figure. He still, of course, expected a large tip at the end of the meal.

We started with lemon-grass soup, hot and spicy, with huge shrimp and mushrooms. We feasted on deep-fried squid and gingered crab, *pad thai* noodles, and a dozen different vegetables with their assortment of dipping sauces, from the fiery hot to the cool of cucumber and lime. And we ended with a lavish platter of exotic fruit – lychees, mangosteens, jackfruit, papayas, and more. I can still taste it.

Our first meeting the next day was with one of the leading and most tireless opponents of child labour, Child Workers in Asia (CWA). They run projects for working children, and the literature they distribute is among the best to be found anywhere. I had heard lots of good things about this organization, and I went with great anticipation into the room where the meeting was to be held.

I was stopped right away by someone speaking Thai and pointing to my feet. I was to remove my shoes as a sign of respect. It was one of many customs I learned on my trip. I took off my shoes, then held my hands together in the prayer position and bowed to my hosts.

I had much to learn, and as we sat around a table, a bowl of cut-up fruit in its centre, I listened intently to every word.

The fight to eliminate child labour did not begin in the West, but rather began with organizations such as CWA, made up of parents, neighbours, and friends of child labourers and the children themselves. The head of the organization, in fact, had once been a child labourer. I was pleased to hear, however, that they thought developed countries could play just as important a role in the elimination of child labour as did the countries that faced the problem day to day. "What we need is not money or hand-outs. We need to share experiences. We need technology and we need moral support."

I was looking for solutions. Any they were about to offer came with a warning: "Change will not come overnight. It has to be fundamental, and that may take generations. It is not simply a question of economics, it is a change in attitude as well. The government must give greater priority to education and social programs."

We agreed there was no single solution to the problem. But we quickly saw that we had a basic common ground: the belief that children have rights that have to be respected, regardless of the economic situation that surrounds them. Children have the inalienable right to go to school and to be protected from abuse. The people in CWA did not see child labour as a necessary evil. They saw it as something to be eradicated. I was very much at home with these people. Their efforts, I felt, were ones FTC must strongly support, and I left the meeting sure that our relationship would continue.

Outside, to celebrate our arrival in Bangkok, and the feeling that our trip was back on track, Alam and I bought a *dhabrapani*, a fresh coconut with one end chopped off that still contained its milk. We drank it with a straw. It was the natural nectar of the coconut – cool, sweet, and delicious.

We hopped aboard a river ferry, not knowing which direction it would take. We got lost in the canals of Bangkok, but we loved it. It was a terrific way to see the city – free of cars, congestion, and pollution. The sun was beginning to set. It was spectacular.

With its canals and palaces, some people compare Bangkok to Venice. It is no longer the mystic, ageless, unblemished city it was even a generation ago. It has given itself over to Western influences, to commercialization in its most vulgar form. As the sun turned to an orange ball low on the horizon, its glow left to outline the magnificent towers and palaces, I could imagine that city of long ago, where one could get lost in another world, another time. My stay in Bangkok would allow me time to seek out those places, and I was determined to find that culture and soak it up as much as I could.

We made our way back to the open-air market and found the very same table. Already we were becoming regulars!

I think Alam was gaining new respect for my eating habits. The gagging-on-the-samosa days were long gone. We skipped saying *Mai phet farang* ("not spicy, foreigner"), as we had been instructed to do. I genuinely relished what the spices did to my taste buds. Pizza and burgers were a bland and distant memory. I even learned how to use a spoon and fork in the Thai manner. The fork is used only to break apart the food and push it onto the spoon. Putting the fork into your mouth is as frowned upon as putting the knife into your mouth in Western culture.

While Alam and I ate, I took the opportunity to go over all the customs I had learned so far. I didn't want to embarrass myself and repeat the mistake I had made at the CWA office.

"Never place your feet on a chair or desk or rest one foot across your knee," Alam informed me. "Feet are the lowest part of the body, spiritually as well as physically. You mustn't even point at your feet or point at things with your feet."

I would have my feet planted firmly on the ground at all times. "And the head is considered the highest part of the body. So never touch a person on the head, even a little kid. Very disrespectful."

"Feet on the ground. Hands by the side," I said smartly.

"Except when you *wai*, when you are greeting people."

He had seen me *wai*; I was very good at it.

"The higher the hands are in front of you," he said, "the more respect you have for the person."

I looked at Alam and raised my hands over my head, palms together. He grinned.

"Thanks for asking me to come to Asia, Alam. If not for you I would be in Thornhill right now, shovelling snow."

We chuckled into our spicy feast, relishing every morsel.

Seeing first hand the lives of working children was my main reason for journeying to South Asia. But even I was not prepared for the abuse I would find in the back alleys of Bangkok. I don't think most adults would have been either.

I came to Thailand having read much about the so-called "sex trade" involving children. I was curious to know more, to venture near the places where it was occurring, yet at the same time I was not sure I could stomach even that. I was of two minds. Intellectually, I thought I could handle it. But emotionally, I wasn't sure I ever wanted to go near such places.

Alam, perhaps because he was older, felt more confident. He had this grand scheme of concealing a videocamera on his person and secretly filming inside a brothel. He wanted the solid evidence that no one could dispute. When Alam proposed this to one of the local human-rights organizations, the Centre for the Protection of Children's Rights (CPCR), they said it would be impossible and too dangerous.

"Besides, no one would be willing to take you."

Our conversation was interrupted by a tall, blond fellow with an Australian accent. He looked to be in his mid-thirties. "I would," he said.

He introduced himself. His name was Mick, and he had been a police officer in Australia, but had been so troubled by the abuse of children from sexual predators coming to Thailand from Australia that he had decided to quit his job and take up residence in Bangkok. Here he was doing undercover work for a human-rights organization in order to gather evidence that could lead to the prosecution of individuals sexually exploiting children.

Slowly, as we got to know Mick, our trust of each other grew, and there developed a plan that could lead Alam to the exact place he wanted to go. And yes, if the two of them were careful and took precautions, they might well be able to do some filming.

It had all the excitement of a spy operation, with the added thrill that this one involved a kid from Canada whose biggest covert plot to date had been a failed attempt to slip past an Indian border guard.

The final plans were made at Mick's apartment. When we left the office of CPCR, Mick led us down one of Bangkok's main streets, then away from the bright lights and the traffic. It was well past dark, and venturing down a narrow alleyway behind some run-down shops was an eerie experience. The path suddenly met a series of steps that took us up to a wooden walkway a few feet above the ground and over a marshy area. The buildings looked old and not very well cared for.

Mick lived in a four-storey building, in what, by Canadian standards, was a tiny apartment. Surfing pictures and posters covered the walls. Surfing magazines and wilderness books were scattered across the floor. And a surfboard, with the scars from numerous beaches, leaned against the wall behind the door. Next to the mattress where he slept was a book about Africa. He had a small stove and a bucket with water in it that held bottles of pop. Rummaging through his belongings he came up with three glasses. He washed and dried them in a tiny bathroom off to the side. He handed one to each of us and filled them with pop. We toasted our plans for the following night.

Around nine, the three of us would head down to the area of Bangkok called Patpong, perhaps the world's most notorious sex district. There, Mick would look for a pimp who was willing to take him and Alam to a club that used child prostitutes. They would set a time to return later that night, then leave me at Sue and Ian's place before the two of them headed back for the rendezvous.

We left Mick's that night feeling an intense excitement, yet with great apprehension at what lay ahead. In the space of a few hours we had become fast friends with someone who was willing to lead us to the edge of a nightmare, where children were being exploited in ways that I had found hard even to contemplate.

I would go because I was curious to see things for myself – I wanted to know the life these children were living – and because my confidence in Mick had never wavered from the moment we met. He was like no other person I had ever known, fiercely dedicated to a cause, yet a free spirit and a man of the world. I admired him a lot.

Most of the following day was taken up with meetings. But in the back of my mind the whole time was what that night would bring. Our day ended with a meeting with a local programmer from the International Labour Organization office. As it wrapped up, I felt I was closing my notebook on one type of learning and opening a much bigger one on a very different type.

I donned my backpack and we headed to Mick's apartment that evening, eventually finding our way there after taking several wrong turns. We knocked on his door, and found him in T-shirt and jeans, ready to go. He handed Alam a waist-pack for the videocamera, which was compact enough to fit comfortably inside without appearing too bulky and giving the game away.

"Now you both look perfect," he said.

"What do you mean?"

"You look just like tourists!"

We boarded a taxi to the market on the edge of Patpong. When we told the driver where we wanted to go, he didn't give it a second thought. To him it was an everyday occurrence, nothing out of the ordinary, even for a young boy like myself.

The sun had long set, but the lanterns and fluorescent signs and neon lights, flashing Sony, Kodak, Pepsi, Panasonic..., made it as bright as a midway. A huge neon Coke bottle moved side to side. The market was lined with stalls selling everything from food to clothes to electronics to the latest CDs. As we made our way along, checking out the stalls, we were constantly having to squeeze past other people. We caught snippets of conversations in dozens of languages. Everyone was on the lookout for a bargain.

"Are you sure this is genuine leather?" one American woman was saying, sounding like she was straight from Brooklyn.

"Of course! Genuine leather."

"Are you sure?" She ran her hand over the grain of a purse. "Can you prove it? Are you sure?"

We moved on. Mick leaned over to me. "And of course it's not genuine leather."

I was enjoying Mick's guided tour. He was comfortable in this city. He knew the game the vendors played, and threw us insider comments that made it all the more interesting. At one stall he picked up a Rolling Stones CD. For the price the guy was charging, it looked like a terrific deal. "A very good knock-off," Mick said. "One of the better ones, as a matter of fact." He picked up a T-shirt with Calvin Klein stitched across the front. It was a fraction of the price someone would pay in Toronto. "Not bad," he said, winking at me. "Could almost fool me if I didn't know the difference." I decided not to bring up the matter of the five-dollar Armani watches.

We continued on our walk through the markets, Alam a little behind us, concentrating on his camera. When he wanted to shoot something, he would simply slip the camera lens out of the waist-pack. He was very good at playing the casual tourist. I was thinking we had a potential 007 in our midst.

It was now past nine o'clock. Many of the stores were closing, as the market scene gave way to the nightlife of the district. The farther we walked, the more seedy it became. The remaining stalls were now wedged between doorways leading to bars and clubs and shops selling all types of sex paraphernalia. Signs flashed "Topless" and "XXX." Hawkers held out five-dollar coupons for exotic dance shows and bars with all-nude waitresses.

I was beginning to feel very uncomfortable. For a moment my attention was diverted to a boxing match inside one of the bars. There was a wide-open view of the ring from the street. Thai boxing differs from Western boxing, as the opponents are allowed to use their feet. The fighters, their thick bodies dripping sweat, pounded each other fiercely. A wild crowd of gamblers surrounded the ring, shouting at the fighters, goading them into turning even more ruthless. I'm not a fan of any form of boxing, but in this case I watched with some interest. I was avoiding the inevitable.

We moved on. The narrow lane was packed with tourists, some giving me odd looks, perhaps surprised to see a foreign kid so late at night in Patpong. I saw one American couple, probably in their seventies, holding hands and kissing, then moving off – he to a massage parlour, she to a nude dance club. Soon there were bars everywhere, dance music throbbing from every one. Men at their doorways shouted what they had to offer to the passers-by. "All nude!" "Go all the way!" "Prices very cheap! You like, you like!" It was a fair, an amusement park. The go-go dancers, the men and women flashing their wares to the people inside, were out of view of those crowding the street. But the pounding music and hawkers' sex-talk was plenty to lure a steady stream of customers.

I was out of place, even scared at what was surrounding me. I couldn't believe how casual people were about it all – walking in and out of sex clubs as if they were at a shopping centre. Even Mick seemed cool and collected. I knew he had been to Patpong many times, but I was still amazed at how calm he was. I could hardly believe people could get used to such a thing.

I thought I was pretty wise to the ways of the world. But nothing had prepared me for this. As we walked, Mick told me more.

"People come to Thailand from all over the world in search of sex. Half of the passengers on some flights are single males. Travel agencies offer 'sex tours.' Hotels give them special deals. Sex drives this economy, even though over a half-million people are HIV-positive, many of them prostitutes."

"That's appalling."

"Girls are stolen from the hill tribes in northern Thailand and brought here to work in the brothels. In some Thai villages, if there is a bride who is particularly attractive, pimps will make a down payment for female offspring before a child is even born."

"Sick." It was all I could think of to say.

It got worse. "Then there are the paedophiles. Their sexual desire is for children. They come here, too, from all over the world. And here they find it. For a price, of course. And the more they are willing to pay, the younger the child they get. The pimps set the highest prices for the youngest children, promising they are free of AIDS.

"Many of those involved in the sex trade try to justify what they do. They would say they are helping the children out financially, helping them pay for an education. Some even say they give them extra tips and gifts, so they will have a better future. But the truth is, every one of them is doing wrong, and they know it. They're sick. They need help."

I would call them more than sick. The word "evil" came to my mind.

The thought was reinforced by what happened next.

A tall, slender man interrupted Mick's conversation with me and asked if Mick wanted to attend a show. He reached into his shirt pocket and pulled out a series of pictures, in what looked like a plastic credit-card case that folded together. It was what Mick had called a "menu."

I was standing at one of the stalls nearby, pretending to examine some clothes, but not completely out of hearing range.

"How old are they?" Mick asked him, looking through the pictures.

"Sixteen, seventeen." The fellow pointed to one. "She very nice girl. She do anything you want."

"How much?" Mick said.

"One and a half hour. Full body massage. Eighty dollar."

"A little high," Mick said. "A little high."

The vendor at the stall where I was standing came over to me. "You try on belt," she said. "Very nice. Genuine leather."

I had been standing for so long in the same spot that she thought I must be interested in buying something. "Just looking," I said, trying to put her off, but at the same time not wanting to move. It was getting very awkward. Even when I stood a little away from the stall, all I could see were coupons from the sex clubs littering the ground.

I heard Mick say to the fellow, "You have boys?"

"Yes, boys."

I glanced at Alam. By the way he was standing I could see he had the videocamera running. What if he got caught? Our only choice would be to run like mad away from there.

"My friend likes younger," Mick said, pointing to Alam. "Boys – ten, eleven?"

The man shook his head.

"I like your girls," Mick said. "Maybe we'll come back. We have to bring my nephew back to the hotel."

I was the nephew. And right now I was standing, still looking at the belts, trying to play the part of the tourist. My insides were in a knot.

"You know where I can get young boys for my friend?" Mick asked.

He nodded. "I tell you where to go."

He directed Mick and Alam to a street a short distance away. Mick shook his hand and said maybe he would see him later, when it was just him and Alam.

We headed in the direction the pimp had indicated. We hadn't walked more than a few metres when Mick was approached again. The scene was much the same: the clubs and their music, a few market stalls nearby, the fellow with his menu in his pocket.

The guy flipped through his pictures – girls barely clothed, in provocative poses, pictures from the shows.

Mick looked at them as if he might be interested. Then he shook his head. "Younger," he told him. "Twelve."

"No problem."

"And for my friend. Young boy."

I was standing away from them at a stall that sold candy and chewing gum. And soon I discovered I had positioned myself near the back entrance of a massage parlour. This was even more awkward. People were coming and going constantly. Now I was too frightened to move.

The fellow looked around a bit, to see if he was being watched. He leaned closer to Mick. "How old you want?"

"Eight."

He nodded. "You come back later."

I was astonished by what had happened. It was as if they were negotiating for a taxi fare or to buy a pair of running shoes. Mick shook his hand. The guy told him he would see them later that night and show them to a club called "Astro Boy."

Mick and Alam came and collected me. "We got what we wanted. Let's get you home."

I was glad to be leaving Patpong. I had known there was no chance I would ever get inside a club to speak to children. Nor did I want to. I'd had more than enough of this place.

They took me to Ian and Sue's. Then they returned to Patpong alone.

I lay awake waiting for Alam to return, my mind whirling from all I had seen and heard. I felt filthy from just having been there. Disgust churned inside me. Some of the children were even younger than I was.

What I heard later that night from Alam confirmed my worst thoughts. They had witnessed the scum of the world exploiting children in the worst possible way.

It was about four in the morning when Alam returned. He was physically and mentally exhausted. He and Mick had carried out their plan. They met up with the same fellow and were put into a taxi. The ride took so long that Alam began to get worried. Maybe they were being taken to some side alley where they would be robbed and left in the gutter? Eventually they drove up to a building with a brightly lit sign that read "Astro Boy." In an upstairs lounge were lots of men, sitting around in groups, talking and drinking. Smoke hung in the air. Dance music pounded out its rhythm. Mick and Alam were directed to a table and offered drinks.

On a stage, lit by spotlights, were boys in a line, kids probably twelve to sixteen years old. They were practically naked, wearing nothing but skimpy white thongs, a number pinned to each. The boys danced awkwardly to the music.

A boy was ordered like a customer would order a drink, brought to the table by a manager to be checked out. If the customer liked what he saw, arrangements would be made for the boy to accompany him to his place, or to a place arranged by the manager.

Mick played along to find out as much as he could about the operation. A boy was brought to their table. They talked. Mick found out the boy was a student in a local high school. He needed the money, he said, to help pay for his school books.

When the manager returned, Mick shook his head. "My friend would like someone younger. An eight-year-old boy. And I would like a girl. Eleven."

He was told it could be arranged. Tomorrow night, he said, no problem.

But Mick didn't stop there. They talked at length and, to earn the manager's confidence, Mick told him he and Alam could arrange to bring men from Australia and Canada for a sex tour. In exchange for their work in setting it up, they would get a cut of the profits.

The manager liked the idea. They settled on a time for another meeting the following night.

"What about the police?" Mick eventually asked.

The managerer chuckled. "Trust me, the police are no problem. This place is owned by a three-star general."

Mick and Alam left, a deal in the making.

Alam, at least, would not be going back. I'm not sure if Mick did. His undercover work would continue, as he told us over lunch the next day. But he knew that in a few months club owners would start to recognize him, and what he was doing would be even more dangerous. As he left us that day, his unkempt blond hair making it easy to picture him on a beach, surfboard under his arm, I wished him luck.

Our time exploring the sex trade in Thailand gave me much to think about. I have never been so repulsed in my life. I couldn't help but compare the lives of myself and my friends with the tortured lives of so many young people in underdeveloped countries.

Besides the visit to Patpong, we had been given the opportunity to talk with some of the young girls who had been rescued from life in the brothels. CPCR had set up a network of group homes where such girls and boys could go through rehabilitation for the abuse they suffered and, hopefully, move on to a better life.

We spoke to about fifteen girls. They all had black hair flowing just past their shoulders. Their faces, like those of many Thai people, had a natural golden glow, like a perfect tan. I knew teenage girls in North America who would spend long, idle hours in the sun trying to get such a look.

But the lives of these girls were far less privileged. We were asked not to mention anything about their past when we talked to them. It would prove too painful. When I looked at these girls, I hardly knew what to say. I could only think of what they must have suffered, the damage to their dignity and self-respect.

None of the girls had families to go to. And I was struck by the fact that practically every one of them said they would never want to be married, or have children of their own. In fact, several of them spoke out fiercely against the idea. Later I learned that they had learned not to trust any man. The mothers of these girls had been abused by their husbands, most of the girls themselves had been sold to brothels by a man in their family, and the girls feared any child they might have would get caught up in such a cycle of abuse.

I found it hard to get to know these girls without upsetting them in some way. I was treading a very thin line in talking to them. At other times, when I had talked with child labourers, I could ask about the work they did and how they came to be in that situation. Here I could only speak about school, how they liked where they were living, and their hopes for the future. It was strange and awkward at times. They all probably knew I was aware of their past, and here I was, barely thirteen, and already with so much more in life. What could the youth of Canada do to help them? It hardly seemed a meaningful question.

Alam and I met with other groups. We kept a tight agenda, but following our confrontation with the sex trade, we also had to have time away. Visits to some of Bangkok's monumental buildings would provide a much-needed break. I wanted time to deal with recent experiences and how they had changed my view of the world.

Alam, never one for tourist sights, was willing to go along, if somewhat reluctantly. He had a camera he could play with if he was bored.

Bangkok is very much a mixture of the old and the new. Seven-Elevens and Pizza Huts stood next door to restaurants serving the best of Thai cuisine. Temple spires shared the skyline with office towers. The architecture of the wealthy residential sections of the city was no different than that found in a thousand other cities around the world. In Thai homes – such as that of Ian's landlord, whom we visited several times – "Baywatch" was a TV program not to be missed.

Sometimes the variety in living conditions took some getting used to, as when I encountered my first South Asian–style toilet. It was a hole in the middle of a concrete floor, with a gutter angled away from it. You plant your feet on either side and crouch. Flushing consists of pouring water from a bucket into the gutter. Luckily my camping days as a Boy Scout, of digging a pit and covering it with dirt, proved to be good training. The Scout motto, "Be Prepared," rang truer than ever.

Another thing that struck me was the immense number of stray dogs roaming the city. They seemed to be everywhere. The religion of Thailand, Buddhism, forbids the killing of any animal. We were told many of the dogs had rabies, an especially eerie thought while we walked to and from the market after dark with bags of food.

In the markets I was attracted by the intense colours of the flowers and the sweet smell of spices. Children were scattered among the stalls offering birds for sale. Thai people love birds, and they would buy birds and liberate them as a way of gaining favour in their religion. Such good deeds were considered to be "merit points." After freeing a bird they would record their merit points in a small black book. They believed it stood them in good stead for their return in the next life.

It was all a goldmine for street kids. As soon as a bird was released, another child hiding in the crowd chased after it and tempted it with treats until he was able to recapture it. Then it would be released again by some new unsuspecting buyer. I couldn't help but laugh at the kids' ingenuity. They were releasing the same birds over and over again to earn money for their families.

It was the historic parts of the city that appealed to me the most. The first stop was the Grand Palace. It is really a city within a city, in the way that the Forbidden City is part of Beijing, or the Vatican is part of Rome.

It consists of several immense temples encircled by a high wall. Before you step inside the entrance gate, you see only the golden peaks of the temples reaching for the sky. Once past the gate, you enter a far-off century. Ancient trees, like huge bonsai, stand before the temples. The exteriors of these temples are elaborate almost beyond belief. Their walls of mosaic stretch high above you, and their pillars, with designs thickly outlined with gold, support multi-layered roofs edged with golden ornamentation.

At the core of the Grand Palace is the temple of the Emerald Buddha. We removed our shoes some distance away and began the long walk up the steps leading to the altar inside. We noted the signs telling us it was forbidden to point your feet in the direction of the statue of Buddha, or to take pictures of it.

The walls leading to the altar were covered in murals, humans fighting lizards and monkeys, depicting the battle between good and evil. At the end was the Buddha, wearing a mantle of gold and seated on a high golden altar. The immense altar was inlaid with diamonds, emeralds, rubies, and other gems and precious metals.

If there was any doubt that my trip was a powerful educational experience, this surely erased it. I learned more about religion and Asian art that day than I would have if I had studied at a desk in Canada for a year. The paintings on the temple walls explained the various wars, famines, and voyages that brought Buddha around South Asia. In the shadows of the temples we saw young monks in their orange robes, their bodies bent in prayer. Some held items towards the Buddha, as an offering. Others kept their heads low, as a sign of respect. Incense wafted through the temple, caught in the shafts of light, surrounding us all like a cloak.

I was fascinated by these monks and watched them for a long time. There seemed to be monks everywhere in Thailand. There are, in fact, over 200,000 of them. Every Thai male is expected to become a monk for a short period of his life, usually about three months. I saw many boys in Thailand who were monks at thirteen and fourteen. I thought of how, if I were part of this culture, I would have to have my head shaved and learn to be quiet all day.

It was the whole sense of spirituality in Thailand that intrigued me. Buddhists believe the effects of a good or bad action will come back to you in your next life. That is one reason why you see many of them doing deeds of charity, or spending short periods of time in monasteries. I would have loved to have spent a few days at a monastery, meditating and studying more about Buddhism. I was drawn by the solitude, the sense of quietly coming to an understanding of the world and the goodness that should be at the core of us all.

Even the unauthorized visit we made to Wat Pho, the temple of the Reclining Buddha, left me in awe of the peace and tranquillity amid the bustle of everyday Bangkok. We arrived to discover the door of the temple closed, the building shut to tourists for the day. But then we noticed a construction crew making its way inside. We mingled with them and managed to enter undetected. In the darkened interior, we took our own private tour. Several times we stopped and hid to avoid being found out by the security guards. At some points I felt like a detective in a mystery novel. After forty-five minutes, our game was up. We were escorted outside by an irritated guard waving a flashlight, and the gates were securely shut behind us.

Our visit to the Golden Mount was just as thrilling, but in a different way. At sunset we started the climb from its base, past the catacombs that lined the winding path practically all the way to the top. We stopped occasionally at a gravesite to look at the incense burning and the offerings of fruit laid out in front of small statues of Buddha. At the top of the hill, the highest in Bangkok, was a Buddhist temple. In front of it were ten large bells, which monks play on the hour.

We arrived just before the temple gates were being shut. The monks had abandoned the bells for the day. Alam and I took over and quietly played for a while. It must have been some of the strangest music ever to come from them.

The view all around us was astounding. Buildings stretched as far as the eye could see, bathed in the golden light of the setting sun, tinged with red and pink and orange.

It was Christmas Eve. Here I was in Bangkok, so far away from my family and friends, and yet I felt strangely fulfilled. I could not have received a greater Christmas gift than to be where I stood, atop the Pearl of the Orient, the Great City of Angels. I tapped out "Jingle Bells" on the temple bells.

"Nobody would know the tune," Alam said, "even if they *could* hear it."

"It's a call to my family in Canada."

I knew my parents and brother were in Windsor, spending Christmas with my grandmother. My aunt and uncle would be arriving from Brantford to join them. The next day, they all would be phoning me, but for now I pictured them around the Christmas tree, humming carols as my grandmother played the piano, or getting ready for midnight mass. And no doubt they were thinking about me, wondering if I needed anything, wondering what I could be doing at that very moment.

There were a few monks, stragglers, in the distance, no one else. The temple itself had closed. If we had our way, we would have stayed the whole night, sleeping on the temple floor. But eventually a security guard approached us and led us to the gate. Spending time with local security guards was becoming a habit.

There were more memories to be had that Christmas Eve. We went by bus to a party for street kids, held by a Jesuit priest from Quebec. Word of the party had spread across the city. Children came from everywhere to a huge room decorated with balloons and streamers, laid out with free food and drink, and ringing with music.

We arrived to find the children dancing and singing. Not many of them knew or really cared that it was Christmas Eve, but it was a chance to forget their lives of hard work and for the moment be wild and free and full of joy.

A long row of bells was hung along a temple wall at the Golden Mount, overlooking Bangkok. On Christmas Eve I played "Jingle Bells" and sent my season's greeting echoing home to Canada.

Many of the kids worked in the train stations. There were also children who worked as metal pounders, or in fabric factories, children who made shoes, others in the sex trade. I talked with one fourteen-year-old boy who spent all day hauling ice. He was allowed only one day off, Sunday, a day he attended a school run by the same Jesuit priest.

The party went on for several hours. At one point the priest announced that the kids, if they wanted, could perform plays, and that prizes would be awarded to the best performances. A simple stage had been erected. Some kids wore costumes. The stories they acted out were often elaborate, mimicking the soap operas they watched on television. I couldn't understand a word, but it was still great fun. They howled with delight at times, jumping up and down, slapping their thighs. Their enthusiasm was contagious, and I laughed along with them.

As the party ended, they wandered off into the night, some still laughing with their friends, others disappearing into the darkness alone. I wondered how these kids, some as young as nine or ten, could fend for themselves in such a difficult and hostile environment. These children were remarkable people.

I saw in their eyes that night, and in the work of the priest, a truer meaning of Christmas than I had ever known before.

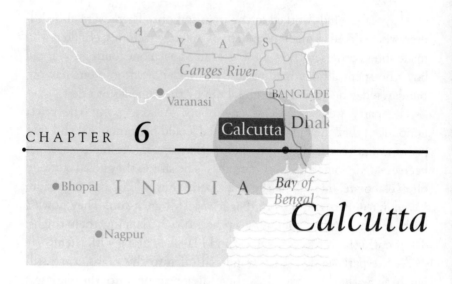

CHAPTER **6**

Calcutta

CHRISTMAS DAY, 1995 – NOT one I'll soon forget. Palm trees instead of mistletoe and holly. Coconut milk instead of eggnog. The morning brought a bout of Bangkok traffic and another mad dash through an airport.

We had risen early, with the best of intentions. Just as we were ready to head for the airport, two phone calls came in from Canada. Christmas cheer from family members across the seas.

"Last night I played 'Jingle Bells' for you on these gigantic iron bells," I told my grandmother.

"And I played it for you on the piano," she said. "We all wish you were here, dear."

It was so good to hear from home, yet I couldn't resist getting in a dig about the snow. "Must be beautiful," I said to my parents, as I smiled at Alam. "Poor us, all we can do is pick bananas."

After saying our goodbyes, we hurried off to the waiting taxi. Christmas Day is a regular workday in Bangkok, and the only things flashing red and green were the traffic lights. Mostly red, it appeared to me. But we eventually made it to the airport.

We arrived in Calcutta to masses of people in too small an airport with too few facilities. With elbows locked in position, we retrieved our bags. Swapan Mukherjee, our main contact in Calcutta, met us, and off we went aboard a Jeep to his office. The door at the rear of the Jeep had no glass in its window. The traffic, which rivalled what we had left a few hours before in Bangkok, was practically on top of us. I could have easily reached out and touched the passengers crowded in the open steps of the buses honking their way past. Christmas Day was definitely a workday in Calcutta as well.

Swapan talked the whole way from the airport. I could finally put a face to all the correspondence we had received from his office – round features, jet-black hair, and animated brown eyes that were rarely without their touch of good humour.

The Centre for Communication and Development, where Swapan works, has its offices in a basic block of a building, just a nondescript structure with crumbling brick, surrounded by coconut trees. In the spartan interior was evidence of an organization hard at work – books scattered over the desks, posters and press clippings pinned to the walls.

"Welcome to Calcutta," Swapan began. "This time we've not had to ask the police to put on a search for you. This is a very good omen."

We all laughed.

Then it was down to business. A press conference had been set for the following day and a protest march for the day after that. Kailash Satyarthi, the head of SACCS (South Asian Coalition on Child Servitude), had come by train from Delhi especially for them. I would be sitting at the press conference next to him.

It would be a major media event, and I was expected to write a press release on behalf of Canada. I was a little taken aback at what had been thrust my way, never having even been to a press conference before.

"I'm not sure I can answer all their questions."

"Don't worry," Swapan assured me. "Your role is to show the press there is international solidarity on this issue, that people in other countries care, and the eye of the world is on us. You know what you've done in Canada. The press is just looking for your own perspective."

"Will they understand me?" I wondered out loud, thinking of the eighteen languages in India, and the sixteen hundred minor dialects.

"Don't worry. The press all speak English."

Tea was brought in to the meeting – Indian tea, with the tea leaves, water, and milk all boiled together. Definitely not my mother's Tetley.

It was my first experience with the local drink, and I quickly discovered how incredibly strong they make it. I had some trouble swallowing it at first, but I was not about to insult my host. Alam's smile edged towards a smirk.

The meeting went on for several hours, finally breaking up about seven. I was tired and hungry, but there was much work still to be done. Alam sat at a computer in a corner of the office and I began to dictate the press release to him. He felt strongly that Free the Children was a children's group and that I should be the one coming up with the wording. However, both he and Swapan studied my first draft and took friendly aim with a red pen. It was back to the drawing board.

After a second try, then a third, I came up with a statement that worked for all of us. I printed a final copy. It would be distributed at nine o'clock the following morning.

We shut off the computers, turned out the lights, and headed to Swapan's apartment, twenty minutes' drive away. He lived with his wife and family in a very ordinary section of Calcutta.

We walked up a dark staircase to the apartment. I was amazed at the security precautions. There was a metal grate, then a metal door, then a solid wood door with two deadbolt locks. As he unlocked them, he explained that over the years two human-rights activists he knew had been murdered by people opposed to their efforts to end child labour, and that he himself had received numerous threats. He wasn't so worried about his own protection as he was about that of his family.

The apartment consisted of a main living area, which was more or less a hallway with several small rooms off it. One was a storage room, converted for the moment to a bedroom for myself and Alam. The main living area served many functions, including a bedroom for some of the family. In fact, Swapan's two children were asleep there when we arrived. His wife was in a tiny room at the end of the hallway, preparing a meal for us.

She wheeled out a table and unfolded it into the hallway. Within minutes there was a meal laid on it – chapattis, rice, dhal, and mutton curry. Alam, being vegetarian, passed on the mutton, but I savoured every bite.

It had been a long Christmas Day. After dinner, and more anxious questions from me about the press conference, I unrolled my sleeping bag in the storage room, atop the makeshift bed that had been constructed from a packing crate. I slipped some blankets under it for padding. I looked over at Alam, about to ask him another question, but he was already fast asleep.

I lay in my sleeping bag, thinking of what tomorrow would bring. If there was one thing I was looking forward to it was meeting Kailash Satyarthi. I greatly admired the man. He was the one who had been arrested the previous summer and for whom FTC had sent the three-thousand-name petition to the Indian government.

"Have you prepared an opening statement?" Swapan said to me the next morning as we were driving to the hotel where the press conference was being held.

It seemed to come out of nowhere. I had thought I would be there just to answer questions.

"I didn't say anything last night because I knew you had so much on your mind."

"Now I have a lot more," I said, a little panic in my voice.

"Five minutes," he told me. "That's all."

I looked at my watch. Less than an hour to go. I started scribbling notes as the Jeep bumped along through the traffic. My pen flew all over the page. The words made no sense.

We arrived at the hotel and I still had no notes. I would have to speak from the heart. The way my heart was pounding at this point, however, I thought I might have to shout over it to be heard.

There were about twenty people in the meeting room when we arrived. One television camera was already filming. A long table had been set up with a line of chairs on one side, and filling much of the wall behind the table was a large banner reading, "South Asian Coalition on Child Servitude, West Bengal Unit."

I looked around as Swapan positioned the microphone in front of himself. There must have been a party in the room the night before. Streamers and balloons hung from the ceiling. The back wall was covered in posters, all the same advertisement for some liquor, picturing a bottle and the face of a woman, dark and mysterious. An odd place for a press conference, I thought.

The mood in the room changed dramatically as Swapan began the opening remarks. He had chosen to speak in Bengali and I didn't understand a word, but I could see that all eyes were focused on him. I sat upright and tried to settle my mind on what I would say when my turn came.

Kailash spoke in English. There was no ranting or rhetoric. He spoke slowly and precisely. The words said it all.

We are trying to raise the voice of all children who are forced to work day in and day out to earn their bread in this state.

Laws were made in 1976 against bonded labour, and in 1986 against child labour. But not a single employer has been put in jail. It shows the serious lack of political will.

On the fifteenth of August last year, the prime minister announced a scheme for the elimination of child labour. Almost one and a half years later, nothing concrete has been achieved. Not a single child has been liberated. For the victims, nothing has happened.

Absence of social concern is one of the biggest causes of child labour. People believe that children are working because of poverty. Poverty and unemployment are not the causes behind child labour; child labour and child servitude perpetuate poverty and unemployment.

Today in India, we have fifty-five million children in child servitude on one hand, and sixty million adults jobless – and the statistics state that most of the children who work come from those families with parents unemployed. Every single child in India who is working takes the place of one adult – an adult who could be his own father or mother or other family member.

Nor is it true that poverty is the cause of child labour. All of the children who are working earn less than fifteen rupees a day. Adults who are employed in the same occupation are getting close to four or five times more. If you continue employing children, you are creating the biggest hurdle to the distribution of profit, of wealth. Poverty cannot be eradicated until money is distributed, until it comes down to be spread among all of the people.

So not only is this a legal question, a humanitarian question, and a violation of human rights, it is a serious question of economics.

That is why we are demanding one thing that is very clear. We do not want to hear an excuse for child labour. We are saying simply there should be a law to ban it in all its forms.

His speech continued. When he ended, he moved the microphone in front of me. I know my remarks could never rival his in intensity.

Coming from outside the country, what I could do was bring a different perspective to the issue of child labour. I needed to show that people in other countries were concerned and wanted to do what they could to help. I stressed the fact that I came to South Asia to observe, not to tell people how to deal with their problems. I ended with these words:

We support the children in India in their march and in their demands. Child labour is an issue of grave importance. It must become a top priority for all governments of the world. How can the world move into the twenty-first century with children still being exploited for their labour and denied their basic right to an education?

The opening statements were complete. It was time for the reporters to ask their questions. The tone of the press conference suddenly changed. It was quickly apparent the media had come with an agenda. They knew something we did not.

Swapan and his group had led a fight to get compensation for the families of victims in a recent fireworks explosion in West Bengal. Family members of an injured child were supposed to be at the press conference, but they had not shown up. The press wanted to know why. "Is it not because the compensation promised those people is going to your organization's bank account and not to the families?"

"Rumours and lies spread by the fireworks company," came the reply. "They have done everything in their power to discredit our organization, for the simple reason they do not want to pay compensation."

One journalist stood up, saying he demanded to know the truth. The whole press conference was coming dangerously close to falling apart.

But out of the chaos came the calming voice of Swapan. He quietly but firmly declared that they were on the side of the victims and their families. "Over one and a half million children work in the fireworks factories in this country. Many of them suffer from lung and kidney diseases because of the sulphur, phosphorus, and other chemicals they inhale every day. We must put pressure on the government if it is to change."

There would be no argument with that. There could be no defence of companies that so unashamedly abuse children.

The press eventually turned their attention to other matters. I answered their questions about Free the Children and why I had come to South Asia. I listed the places I would be travelling to and how my primary objective was to meet with children themselves.

We left the room with the feeling that much had been accomplished. I felt good about the role I had played, and I was now much wiser about the influence of the media. I had discovered just how key a component they are in the struggle for human rights.

"Hundreds of our workers may see and hear the abuse," Kailash said to me when we were back in his hotel room, "but millions will respond to it if they see it in the newspaper or on television. You must have the media on your side if you are to bring about change."

I nodded, thinking back to the morning I had first read Iqbal's story. It was all because of a newspaper article that I had become involved in child labour and was standing at that very moment with one of the most prominent figures in the whole movement.

"But, as you saw today," continued Kailash, "a good turnout at a press conference is not always a good thing. The media can show up with their own agenda, one that can work against you. The people who control the press are very powerful. They have friends and relatives in high places who embrace the status quo. This is not the first time the press has tried to discredit us. You must know how to make the most of your relationship with these people. You can't alienate them. You have your truth, but it also has to be the truth they want to tell."

It was an incredible feeling to be taken into the confidence of this group of people, to be treated as a partner in their effort to oppose child labour. Like other members of SACCS, Kailash had been threatened many times. Some of the factory owners who employed children were his sworn enemies.

It was an honour to be in the presence of such dedicated men as Kailash and Swapan, and a greater honour to be helping their cause.

They had cancelled the original press conference and rescheduled it to a day when they were sure I could attend. It showed great confidence in what I could bring to the event. I hoped I had lived up to their trust.

And as that day drew to a close, I could look forward to playing another role. Swapan asked if I would help them lead the protest march against child labour through the streets of Calcutta the following day. I was thrilled to say yes.

Most people imagine Calcutta as a desperately poor city, which it certainly is in some areas. But it is also a vibrant metropolis, with a colourful past showing through in the stately architecture. I loved the energy in its streets. It throbs with life, and doesn't try to hide the struggles of its people in the way that North American cities often do.

We passed Calcutta's famous Victoria Memorial, the vast marble monument to Queen Victoria and the era of British rule in India. It is grand and pompous, and glories in the achievements of the colonial past. I couldn't help but think that the colonial masters did very little for the ordinary citizens of India.

I preferred the people of Calcutta to its monuments. Their humour is well known throughout the country. The people we met always took the opportunity to laugh and enjoy themselves. They were passionate about their struggle to make a better world for future generations, but they embraced life and made the best of it. They were a spirited people who immediately made strangers to their city feel at home.

I saw many facets of Calcutta as we took to the streets the next day. I was struck first by the sheer number of people. Yet they all seemed to have carved out space for themselves. They made use of every inch of the city. The businesses swelled onto the streets and sidewalks, where you could get a haircut or have a letter written for you just as easily as you could buy a piece of fruit or pump a bucket of water.

The march began in an open field near a highway leading into the centre of the city. Most of the marchers arrived in buses, as did the piles of signs for them to carry. Only a few of the signs were in English, but it was no problem to imagine what they said, for many were illustrated with drawings depicting the cruel results of child labour in fireworks factories. The sign I was given showed the bloodied remains of young children.

Kailash took the lead, with a ten-year-old boy and me on one side of him, and more children on the other. Behind us, two men held high a SACCS banner, and beyond that was a trail of people, three hundred strong – parents, university students, activists, and many, many children.

From the first few steps the chanting began, and it didn't waver for a single moment throughout the march.

"*Aatishbaazi band karo, bal majdoori band karo!*" a marcher shouted.

"*Band karo! Band karo!*" we echoed.

One of the children translated for me. "Stop using firecrackers! Ban child labour!"

I shouted all the louder.

It was the first time I had ever been involved in a political demonstration. Many times during the months I had worked on the issue of child labour, I had wanted to yell at world governments for allowing the injustice to continue. Now I had the opportunity. My rage cut the air in unity with hundreds more protesters. "Down with child labour! We want an education! Never again!" Our voices bellowed up and down the line.

I recalled that it was reading about such a march that had led to the naming of Free the Children. I wished those who had been there in Thornhill when we came up with the name – Katie, Marilyn, Ryan, Elizabeth, Andrew, and all the others – could have been with me at that moment in India.

I looked over my shoulder at the people marching behind me. I was tremendously moved by the mothers in their saris, holding their signs for all to see. Many had come from villages outside Calcutta; many had lost children in the explosions at fireworks factories. It took tremendous courage to march in protest against the factory owners, often the only employer in their small villages. They had made enemies among their own people for doing so. I was overwhelmed by the strength of their conviction, and that of the children who marched along at their sides. I felt it was not my place to lead; *they* should be the people in front. I took up a position near the rear of the line.

As we marched through the streets of Calcutta, we chanted, "We want an education!" and "Stop child labour!" Many children on the march had seen their friends, or their own brothers and sisters, killed or severely injured in explosions at fireworks factories.

One mother on the march had been cooking chapattis when the force of an explosion at the local fireworks factory rocked her tiny home. She collapsed in shock, and remained unconscious for twelve hours. The blast had killed both her boys. Their bodies were unrecognizable.

In another case, the owner of the same factory had convinced one young boy to quit school and come work for him, over the desperate pleas of his mother. On the very first day of his job, he was killed by the same devastating blast.

The tragedy of that day remained in the downcast eyes of these women. I had the feeling it would never go away.

I studied the faces of some of the children and could see that the march was not a game or a diversion for the afternoon. Their futures were at stake here. In the West we are always talking about what the future will bring, about our hopes for it, and our dreams of a better day ahead. For many of the children in the march, their future was set from the day they were born. With little education to pull them out of the cycle of dependency on the factory owners, their future was labour, the same labour that in many cases had killed or maimed their brothers or sisters. They knew that if they wanted a brighter future, they would have to fight for it.

The march moved into the centre of the city. Our chants vied with the vehicle horns for attention. Sometimes the traffic forced us to a stop. Some of the men in the group would run ahead and clear a path for us, waving cars out of the way to let us through. Besides the TV crews and newspaper reporters, we had another audience for our efforts. Ordinary people on the streets stopped what they were doing to read our signs and ask questions of one another. Some shouted encouragement. Others saw us as potential customers for their wares, everything from sunglasses to keychains to magazines. One young girl ran after us with a tray of roti. How ironic, I thought: a child labourer working to sell food to people protesting child labour.

Alam was managing to capture much of the march with the video-camera. I was amazed to see the lengths to which he was going to get good camera angles. He climbed onto walls, lay on the ground, jumped on the back of a van. "Keep this up," I said to him as he passed by, "and you'll soon be making Hindi movies."

The march slowed to a stop in front of the government offices of West Bengal. All entrances to the building were blocked by a chain of police. The protesters sat down, still chanting. As our voices subsided, those of our leaders took up the call. Kailash addressed the rally in English, his message of protest filling the air. Other messages quickly followed, ringing out in a half-dozen languages and dialects. As one speaker finished, another stood up, to the sight of hundreds of fists raised in protest and our call to action resounding again. It was my hope that the government workers had their windows open and were feverishly feeding reports to the heads of their departments.

A small delegation went inside the building and presented the protestors' demands: an end to child labour, and free and compulsory primary education. It had been the first such demonstration in the history of West Bengal.

"This is something to tell my grandchildren," I told Alam as the protest came to an end and I piled my sign with the others.

As we were getting ready to leave, I noticed a group of street children rushing in to gather up the signs. They tore off the cardboard and separated it and the wood into two piles. There was money to be made here, and they were not about to miss out. Yet it was a sad commentary on just how much child labour pervaded this society.

Alam and I returned with Swapan to his apartment. It was a time to relax and reflect on the extraordinary events of the last couple of days.

Swapan's young son of nine or ten, Suprio, who had taken a strong liking to me, had other ideas. He wanted to play badminton. I couldn't imagine where. In the hallway of the apartment, of course, where the night before we had eaten dinner. The table was rolled away, the chairs put aside, and a net set up. The boy teamed up with his father and challenged Alam and me to a match. It wasn't your regulation-size court, but no matter: in India you improvise.

The Indian people have a passion for badminton, and needless to say, Alam and I were soundly defeated. Later that night, we sat around the table where the net had been and played cards by candlelight. I was then introduced to "carom," a game that is almost a miniature version of pool. It is played on a small board about two feet square, with corner pockets. Instead of a pool cue, the player uses his finger to flick a round white disc against coloured discs, in an attempt to knock them into the pockets. It was a game I would encounter again and again in my travels through South Asia. In fact, it became a favourite pastime. But I would break no world records at carom either.

The following morning I opened my eyes to find Suprio patiently standing over the bed waiting for me to wake up. He had the carom board in one hand and a cricket bat in the other!

"Cricket? In the hallway?"

He nodded, staring at me with his big brown eyes and impish smile. I thought we'd better not, for the sake of the walls and furniture. But there was no escaping a game of carom.

Suprio stuck to me like glue whenever we were in the same room. He had found a friend, one willing to indulge his passion for games. At one point I tried to explain to him some games he would play if he lived in Canada, but he couldn't quite imagine the concept of skating on ice.

In India I never knew what to expect, even from a stroll down a street.

One day we stopped to sample a fresh coconut. The vendor used a large curved knife, one that looked to me as if it could slice off a finger with no effort. He shaved away the hairy outer husk, then with an expert flick of the blade he broke open the nut and drained the milk into a glass. I drank it with great pleasure.

Tea stalls in India are as numerous as coffee shops in North America. They are the places where people go to socialize, talk politics, or just enjoy a favourite blend of tea. In one I met a boy my own age hard at work. I watched in amazement as he placed the huge teapot on red-hot coals and poured boiling milk into it from a cauldron. I wanted to find out more. The translator who was with us helped me to speak to him as he prepared our tea.

"What hours do you work?"

"From four in the morning to nine o'clock at night," he said.

"Every day?"

"Yes."

I did a quick calculation. "That's seventeen hours a day!"

He didn't seem to understand why I should be surprised.

"Do you have time to spend with other young people your age?" I asked.

"No."

"Have you gone to school?"

"I quit six months ago," he replied. "My father needs me to help at the tea stall."

They were simple answers to direct questions, but I could easily see that, although the two of us were the same age, our attitudes and expectations were worlds apart. Just as he couldn't understand my surprise at his long hours of work, young people where I came from could never understand his acceptance of not having time for anything else.

I told him what people our age in my country would do with their time when they weren't going to school or working at part-time jobs. "Watch television, play sports, go to movies." I avoided saying hang out at shopping malls, in part because I would have to explain what a shopping mall was, and because in India it would have sounded even dumber than it is. Nor did I say that in my country most young people my age are only expected to do a few odd jobs around the house, such as putting out garbage.

Still, I could see the bewilderment in his eyes. "You are treated like little children," he said. "Here, you are expected to be a man."

I wasn't sure either was right.

I encountered a similar attitude a little later when we visited a market, the largest in Calcutta. Vendors rented space in a warehouse and set up their produce, often just on the bare ground, with their stock piled high behind them. Dozens of sombre men, darkened by the dirt and dust of the place, moved about with bulging sacks of produce, often balancing them on their heads. The warehouse was very dimly lit. Indeed, it was too dark really to see the faces of the children we wanted to talk to. We were finally able to find a spot in one corner of the market, filming with the light from a single overhead bulb.

There were kids working everywhere. Many helped to offload the produce, others sold it in the stalls, others worked with butchers as they prepared meat for sale. One boy, only six years old, worked at picking up produce that had fallen to the ground as it was being transported. He was especially good at retrieving the prized green chili peppers that had slipped out of burlap bags either torn open or chewed through by mice. The boy would polish them up and resell

The slums of Calcutta can bring a person to tears. It was not the poverty, however, but the incredible welcome that moved me the most. These people accepted me into their lives, brought me into their homes, and offered to share what little food they had with me.

them to customers just outside the market at a reduced price. Such opportunists were often hassled by the police for selling without a permit, or by stall owners who accused them of stealing the produce. The boy told us he made just a few rupees a day and used it to buy food for his family.

"I work here until ten at night, then I go to eat with my mother," he said, through a translator.

"Do you go to school?"

A crowd of adults and children was gathering around us. The boy, obviously a little overwhelmed by the videocamera and all the attention he was getting, said simply, "No."

"Why don't you go to school?"

"The teachers beat me," he replied.

"Why do they beat you?"

"Because I come to school late or I don't do my homework. I work at the market every night, and when I get home I am too tired to do my homework. If I stay up to do it, I am tired in the morning, and that is why I am sometimes late for school."

It was a situation I was to encounter again and again: schools staffed by underpaid teachers who were often rigid and unable to adapt to the needs of the poor and underprivileged. They demanded children have proper identification and birth certificates, things that these children often don't possess. In many cases the parents could not afford the school uniforms or to help pay the teachers' salaries, as many of the schools required.

I asked one of the children in the market what he wanted to do in the future when he was older. I got a blank stare. We waited, but there was not a word. To him it was a strange, unanswerable question. The future seemed to have no meaning. It would come, and he would do what he had to do to survive. That look, that stare into a future without the promise of anything better, is the most depressing look ever to see in the eyes of a child.

The opinions on a solution to the many problems of the working child in India seemed endless. Alam and I would sometimes stop people in the street and ask them what they thought should be done. It was not a very sophisticated technique, but it was one that certainly brought a wide range of responses.

Small vendors' stalls dot the streets of Calcutta, with children working in many of them. Entire families work together in family businesses.

Some people were annoyed that we even raised the issue. "Don't you have enough problems in your own country? If I go to Canada, do I question the way you treat your native people?" They told us we should let India deal with the problem on its own. They hated it when foreigners showed up and saw only the negative side of their country. Why even come to India, others asked, when in Pakistan child labour is so much worse?

Some we questioned dismissed child labour as a necessary evil. I noticed these people were most often the more well-to-do.

One group of four young men on a street corner were very keen to talk to us. The walls around them were plastered with posters depicting the clenched-fist symbol of some political party. The young men looked like university types out to challenge the status quo.

"Indian government doesn't care about children," one said. "If they care, they work harder to fix the problem. Many politicians are bad. They want money for themselves." I was hardly surprised. India is the largest democracy in the world, but this view of politicians was no less cynical than anywhere in the West.

I was more surprised by what followed. In their opinion, government officials were not the only offenders. "Charities are worse. They fight each other. They do not agree on what to do. Don't share ideas. They fight for money, then waste it. How much gets to children?"

I was sometimes left to wonder that myself. During my trip I had come to see that aid agencies in many countries, whether their funding comes from within the country or outside, were often regarded with distrust by the people they were set up to help. Many times they were seen as a big bureaucracy that used up its donations in maintaining offices and wages and didn't help people to the extent that donors were led to believe. Because I was seeing so much poverty, that conclusion would lie heavily on my mind throughout much of my trip to Asia.

For one charity in Calcutta, however, there was never any such doubt. Its workers had earned the absolute respect of everyone in the city. They were the Sisters of Charity, the order of nuns set up to help the poor and destitute, founded in Calcutta by Mother Teresa.

I had grown up with a great admiration for Mother Teresa. I had read about her work and seen her on television many times. I had given no thought to ever meeting her while in Calcutta, but the day before we were due to leave the city for Nepal, we found ourselves in the neighbourhood of the Mission of the Sisters of Charity.

It was evening and already dark outside. Suddenly we saw a sign with an arrow pointing in the direction of the mission house.

"Do we have time to go there?" I asked.

"It's seven o'clock. Even if Mother Teresa is in, I doubt if she is still receiving visitors," said our guide for that day.

"But we could try," I said, hopefully.

We followed the sign to a large but plain building. The main door was slightly ajar, so we walked in. We found ourselves in a central courtyard, surrounded by a balcony on the upper level. The stone floor of the courtyard was worn smooth by the footsteps of visitors from around the world. Along the walls were plants in colourful bloom. Several sisters and volunteers, dressed in the white-and-blue cotton saris of the order, were sitting on benches, resting and chatting after a long day.

We weren't sure what to do. There appeared to be some activity on the upper level. We looked at each other. "We might be disturbing people. Do you think we should go upstairs?" Alam asked.

We decided we would. As we walked past, the women looked up, smiling, then clasped their hands together and bowed slightly. We repeated the gesture.

Upstairs we came to a wooden door with the imprint of a cross in its centre. A small sign said simply, "Mother Teresa."

This door, too, was slightly ajar. We stepped inside, into a prayer room. We knelt silently. I prayed as I would when I attended church at home.

The room where we knelt led to a smaller room set aside for prayers. We could see several nuns kneeling on mats before a simple altar.

Among them was Mother Teresa. I could hardly believe that it was really her.

A young nun approached us. "May I help you?"

"Good evening, sister," our guide said. "We realize it is late...we must apologize. We were wondering if it might be possible to meet Mother Teresa."

"Mother Teresa is very tired. I suggest you return tomorrow."

"These people are from Canada, and tomorrow they leave for Nepal."

"Mother Teresa needs her rest."

At that moment a group of sisters walked out of the inner room. In the centre of the group was Mother Teresa. She had overheard the last part of our conversation. She walked slowly towards us.

She was a small woman, shorter even than the thirteen-year-old boy standing before her. She was eighty-six, and looking frail in her sari. Her face was wrinkled. But through the wrinkles was a warm and caring smile.

"You are from Canada?" she said. "What brings you all the way to Calcutta?"

It took a moment to get past the fact that she had spoken to me. "We have come to meet working children. We have come to learn about their lives and how we might help them."

"This is good," she said. "The poor will teach you many things."

She took my hands in hers and looked into my eyes. She listened closely to every word I spoke. I told her about Free the Children and how children in many countries were concerned with the issue of child labour. She smiled and held my hands tighter, nodding at my words and following my eyes with hers.

"The youth of the world needs to be part of the solution to the world's problems," I said to her.

She nodded. "I am happy to hear this. It pleases God to know that young people wish to help the poor."

"I have a favour to ask of you," I confided. "Could you please include in your prayers the children who live on the streets and work every day?"

She led me by the hand to the entrance of the prayer room. There was a blackboard with the words "Issues To Pray For" written on it. She pressed a piece of chalk into my hand.

I wrote: *Please pray for child labourers.*

She smiled and blessed me and said all the nuns and visitors would keep these children in their prayers.

We were interrupted by a nun who said there was an urgent call from a priest in Bombay.

"Please don't leave," Mother Teresa said, "I will be back in a moment."

Leaving was the last thing on my mind. She returned a short while later. We talked for a few moments more about my trip to Asia. Then she presented me with three religious medals.

Mother Teresa asked me to write a message on a blackboard outside the chapel to remind the sisters to pray for labouring children. She moved me like no other person I have ever met. She held my hands in hers and looked into my eyes as if she were searching for my soul. "The poor will teach you many things," she said.

As she departed to her room for the night, she blessed me once again. "May God look over you and protect you in your work. We will remember the world's labouring children in our prayers."

I had tears in my eyes. I had been wrapped in her good will and generous spirit. I felt a peacefulness, an inner calm that returns every time I think of our meeting.

As we made our way back to the streets of Calcutta that evening, I realized how extraordinary the moment had been. I knew I would never meet a more inspiring person. I knew that her blessing and prayers for any work I did on child labour would make a difference.

I now wear one of the medals she gave me on a silver chain given to me by my mother. When I find myself frustrated with the work for Free the Children, I remember Mother Teresa and her message that one person can make a difference. She once said, "We can do no great things in life. We can only do small things with great love."

There are some people who question Mother Teresa's ways of dealing with poverty, people who feel there is a need to take a definite political stance if poverty is ever to be abolished. But no one can be all things to all people. I feel strongly that Mother Teresa's life has a great message for young people. We so often feel powerless to do anything about the many problems in the world around us. We are so often left to wonder whether one person can possibly make a difference. Mother Teresa said yes we can. Her life was resounding proof that it is possible.

What I remember most about Mother Teresa was the simplicity by which she lived. For her and her sister nuns it was not complicated. There are people who are hungry; they need to be fed. There are people who are dying; they need to be comforted. There are street children; they need shelter and an education.

She lived in the middle of the slums with the poorest of the poor. There were no plush buildings or material possessions. She lived simply. She had no ego. The work she did was for the poor, and never for any personal gain. She remained true to her beliefs all her life.

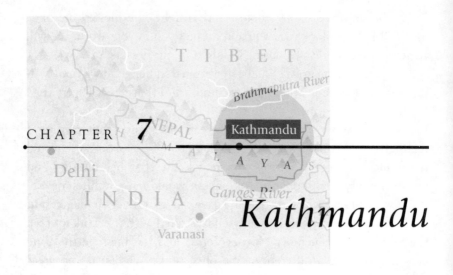

CHAPTER 7

Kathmandu

THE FLIGHT TO NEPAL WAS
the most spectacular of our whole Asian trip. The Himalayan Mountains were incredibly beautiful – sheer faces of rock and snow-covered peaks capped with the golden light of late afternoon. Nepal has eight of the ten highest mountains on Earth. Even though our route didn't take us over Mount Everest, we had the feeling we were flying over the roof of the world.

There were climbers down there, we speculated, slowly trekking their way through the mountain passes. The view from the airplane window made me think of the struggle they had undertaken to reach their goals. Occasionally we were able to trace the line of a mountain pass and pinpoint villages.

Boarding the flight had not been without incident. I was beginning to think there was no such thing as routine travel in Asia. As we were walking towards the aircraft on the tarmac in Calcutta, Alam decided to record the scene on videotape. I smiled for the camera and waved, with the aircraft in the background. Immediately we were set upon by a security officer.

"It is against the law to take pictures of aircraft when travelling in this country. I'm afraid I must confiscate your videotape."

We were astounded. We knew of no such law. And we were not about to give up the tape. It had several segments on Calcutta, including our meeting with Mother Teresa.

"We had no idea about this law," Alam pleaded. "It was merely a few seconds of my friend. The aircraft was probably not even in the frame."

"There should be a sign," I interjected, "if people are expected to know about this."

"There is a sign. Obviously, neither of you read it." He had his hand out for the tape.

"We've done nothing wrong," Alam said. "And I swear there is nothing on this tape."

"We can judge for ourselves. The tape, please."

"Sir," I begged, "we cannot give you the tape. You must understand – it is of great importance to us."

The fellow shook his head. He wasn't buying it. We would have to try another tactic.

"It's our whole visit to this wonderful city," Alam told him with sudden charm. "I'm sure your tourist department wouldn't want us to go back to Canada with a story of how we were not even allowed to bring back a videotape! Imagine if word were to get to the Indian embassy in Canada that two innocent people had had their memories of Calcutta confiscated just as they were about to leave the country. I would say your boss would hear about it rather quickly, don't you think?"

"Well, it *is* the law."

"But we have not broken the law. We merely made an innocent mistake." Alam took out a pen and a piece of paper. "Could I have the name of the director of your department, please? I would like to pass it on to the Indian embassy when I get home."

"Are you sure there is nothing on the tape?"

"Absolutely."

"And you won't use the camera again until you reach your destination?"

"Scout's honour," I said.

"What?"

"I mean no, definitely not."

He backed away and waved us on.

By the time we took our seats aboard the aircraft, we were cracking up.

"And for the best performance in a lead role," I said between the laughter, "the Oscar goes to...Alam Rahman."

"Thank you. Thank you. I must thank all the little people." He pointed to me.

I ignored his weak attempt at an insult.

As the plane neared the mountains, I peered out the window. "Look, snow."

Alam leaned over and shared my view of the snow-capped peaks. "Hey, a white Christmas after all."

"You don't think it could be cold in Kathmandu?"

Alam shrugged.

For some reason we had not counted on winter. Some people in Calcutta wore light sweaters or vests, but the days were no colder than a warm spring day in Canada, and a T-shirt was all I had needed. In fact, I could easily have worn shorts if it had been acceptable. Now, as we neared touchdown in Kathmandu, which sits at an elevation of 1,336 metres, I began to wonder if we should not have brought warmer clothes.

I also wondered whether we were coming to a land of giants. The airplane was filled with tall people, all at least six-foot-two in height. Even the flight attendant seemed much taller than average. We had to find out if, indeed, we would look abnormally short in this country. We made an inquiry to one of the lofty passengers.

"Volleyball team," he said.

Alam and I looked at each other and nodded.

"We won South Asian competition."

"Congratulations," we said together with relief.

As soon as we cleared Immigration, we were spotted by someone from PLAN International, our host while in Kathmandu.

"Welcome to Nepal," she said, shaking our hands. "I hope you had a smooth flight."

"Very smooth," Alam said. "The mountains were beautiful."

I suddenly noticed that my T-shirt felt rather thin.

"It gets cold here, then?" I said.

"A little cold, especially at night. Nothing like Canada, of course."

"Of course." I smiled, only partially relieved. Just how cold at night we were soon to find out. Our host drove us to the hotel where we planned to stay during our three-night visit to Nepal.

Where possible, we avoided hotels. After one night, this one gave us good reason to continue that trend. It was expensive and it was cold. We were kept awake half the night by our efforts to stay warm, including taking every piece of clothing from our backpacks and piling it on top of us.

"Are you still cold?" I called across the room to Alam for about the fiftieth time.

"Hear that?" he said.

I listened. "A definite chattering of teeth," I concluded.

We had learned the hard way that at night during this time of the year Kathmandu's temperature often hovers around the freezing mark. We had also learned that most hotels see no reason to include heat on their list of amenities.

Our friends at PLAN came to our rescue the next day, kindly proposing we use their office as a place to sleep. After they left at the end of each day, we would clear a section of their conference room and unroll our sleeping bags. They even brought in two fold-up beds and a couple of heaters.

Alam unwound the few metres of twine he had brought from Canada and set up a clothesline. We would wash our clothes in the sink at night, then hang them up to dry while we slept. Early in the morning it was off to a local market for some fresh fruit and bread. Then down would come the clothesline and back in place would go the furniture, so there was no trace of us when the office opened at eight. We nicknamed our five-star accommodations "Hotel PLAN."

Kathmandu, like many Asian cities, is a blend of a rich past and the commercial grime of modern life. Vehicles sometimes share the streets with monkeys and elephants. One day, while we were driving along a main street, all of the cars suddenly swerved to one side and jerked to a stop. Through the ocean of vehicles an elephant was manoeuvring its massive feet, taking care not to step on a car or a person. With a load of sugar cane strapped to its back, the mighty beast had made the long trek from a rural village, carrying the farmer's produce to the city market.

The ancient architecture of Kathmandu was impressive. In the city centre we found the narrow streets of Durbar Square with its temples and shrines, some dating back to the twelfth century. An earthquake devastated much of Kathmandu in 1933, but these buildings remained, their beautiful exteriors a reminder of the richness of the city's past. One of them was called the "Monkey Temple," after the hundreds of monkeys that had made it their home. Alam had to put his videocamera away after one of them tried to grab it from him.

On a clear day in December, if you can escape the traffic pollution of the city's core, the mountains that ring Kathmandu can draw even the most well-travelled tourist like a magnet. We, however, were not typical visitors. Though we were inspired to draw deep breaths and speak of the potential beauty of a hike through the mountains, our feet were planted firmly on the ground. We had people to meet and work to do. Tourist destinations would have to wait for another time.

The first official meeting was with Child Workers in Nepal (CWIN). Headed by Gauri Pradhan, an outspoken advocate of children's rights, CWIN has worked throughout Nepal to oppose the widespread exploitation of children. It estimates that in a country of 18 million, there are close to four million children under the age of fourteen involved in full-time or part-time labour. This ranges from farm labour to work in carpet and garment factories, to domestic servitude, to the trafficking of young girls out of the country to the brothels of India and Thailand. Of those who attend primary school, more than half drop out.

The statistics are staggering. But CWIN is making a difference, especially since the establishment of democracy in the country in 1991. I spoke with Gauri and was impressed by the depth of his knowledge. He had worked long and hard on the issue of child labour and had obviously gained a far-reaching insight into the situation in his country.

"Lack of political will," he said, "that's the main obstacle to reform."

"Isn't the public on your side?"

"Yes, but they have to *demand* change. The politicians shout in favour of it at election time, but when it comes to the crunch of making a law, it's all too easy to sidestep the issue."

"Even in a democracy?"

He smiled. "Bribes paid to cover up child-labour practices have never really gone away."

We spent much of our time in Nepal with CWIN's project to help the street children of Kathmandu. When we walked at night, we had seen these children hanging out near the hotels, restaurants, and the other spots that tourists frequent. Most of them were nine to fifteen years old, but some were as young as six. We knew them by their appearance – unruly hair, dirty clothes covering their thin bodies, faces often scarred or bearing sores. We knew them by their cheeky actions to draw attention to themselves. I found their pleas for money hard to ignore, though many tourists and most locals found it easy enough. For most it was no more difficult than for the residents of Toronto to pass by the street people begging along Yonge Street.

These kids, known as *kathe* in Nepal, had made the streets their home. They tucked themselves away late at night in whatever bit of vacant space they could find. I was told many of them were abandoned by their parents. In some cases they had been orphaned, or had run away from abusive families. In others, they were on the street begging for money to support their parents, the very people who had sent them out.

CWIN estimates there are fifteen hundred kids on the streets of Kathmandu.

CWIN is one of the few organizations that these street kids can turn to for help. They have set up centres across Kathmandu where kids can go for relief from life on the street. They provide health care and a chance for the children to play together in a safe and friendly environment.

In addition, CWIN has established a series of "halfway homes." Here, children come to stay for several months and are encouraged to fit into a routine of keeping themselves and their rooms clean, attending school, eating regular meals. It teaches them self-discipline and habits that with luck will stay with them once they leave. In some instances, the program has been able to reunite kids with their families, or set up adoptions.

I dropped in at several of their projects. Most of the buildings follow the same basic floor plan. A paved area surrounds the building, a place where kids can hang out and play games. By far the most popular was carom, the game Swapan's son had taught me when I was in Calcutta. I joined in a game and flicked around a few discs. They blew me away. It would take a lot more practice to get as good as these guys.

Kids have to be tough to survive on the streets of Kathmandu, where older gang members often beat and rob them. They face cold winters, hunger, homelessness, and unsympathetic police. But under each hardened shell there is still a child.

Street children love to play carom, a game in which small discs are flicked into the corner pockets of a board. These boys were very happy to teach me the game and would cheer every time I scored a goal.

One boy took me on a tour of their facility. There are washrooms with showers and a cooking area, which the kids themselves are responsible for keeping clean. We headed into the main building.

"Here are the bedrooms. Ten beds to a room. A noisy place sometimes."

By nine o'clock at night these rooms would be filled with whoever had come in off the street. If the staff ran out of beds, space would be found somewhere in the building. No kid was ever turned away.

"And now for the sick room." Here, the kids come with their many cuts and burns and lesions, often as a result of attacks from older kids. "We don't go to the hospital," the boy said. "They would just turn us away."

"Unless they are really sick," one of the staff added, "then we take them to the hospital and make sure they are attended to."

I noticed that many of the staff were in their early twenties. Often they were former street kids had come to work for CWIN. These young men and women were proof to the kids that it *was* possible to pull themselves out of their miserable circumstances on the street and settle into a new life.

The next stop was a small room that was used as a library. "And we've even got a bank," the boy told me proudly. "We can open an account and keep our money safe from the gangs."

"These kids make maybe one or two U.S. dollars a day," one of the staff told me. "That is a lot of money in Nepal. Lots of times it will get stolen from them. That is why you see kids coming in here with broken bones and knife wounds. Last year a boy was slashed across his temple by an older boy trying to rob him."

"Did he die?" I asked.

The CWIN worker nodded.

"And sometimes the police will load them in a truck and dump them by the side of the highway miles out of the city, just to get them off the streets. Other times, they arrest them and send them to jail. Guards and older inmates abuse them, sometimes sexually. AIDS is a very real possibility for some of these kids.

"And when they do have money, a lot waste it. To get away from their troubles they gamble, they buy drugs and alcohol, they sniff glue, they go to prostitution houses."

"At their age?"

He nodded.

"But they know that if they hope to stay here they must stop their bad habits. They are not allowed even to swear." He smiled. "That's a difficult one to enforce, but we do our best.

"Many don't like the discipline at first. But they see it is a place where they can get fed for free and are safe. They change. They take pride in this place. The worst possible punishment any of them can receive is to be asked to leave the centre."

I had seen evidence of just how much pride they took in what CWIN had provided for them. I had watched a boy that morning with a bucket of red paint and a brush, painting a stone wall. I had seen others sweeping the floors. It was the only home many of them had ever known, a place where they were loved.

We chatted to dozens of kids as we strolled about the centre, but one boy in particular stood out. He looked to be no more than eight, and he was playing by himself with a few pieces of Lego in a corner of a roof area. I sat near him, and for a long time neither of us said a word.

He was making a car from the blocks. Now and then I would pick up a loose piece that I thought might be useful and hand it to him. He would take it and try it out. If it didn't work, or he didn't care to use it, he would put it back in the pile.

I could feel a trust slowly developing between us. It took a while, but eventually he spoke to me, just mumbling a few words at first. He continued working with the Lego, and quietly, one tortured sentence after another, he told his story.

He was born in a small village in the hills of Nepal. When he was a baby, his father deserted him and his mother. Over time his mother remarried and had another child. The new husband turned out to be a drug addict, however, and he eventually passed along the habit to his wife.

One day a stranger showed up in the village. He had come looking for children to buy and take away with him, children he would then resell as labourers. The boy's parents, willing to do anything to support their drug habit, took the man's money and gave him their son.

"I was taken to a tea shop," the boy told us. "My job was to wash the cups and glasses. If I broke one, my master would yell at me and call me stupid, and then beat me up."

After several months, he managed to escape. He ended up on the streets of Kathmandu. The only skill he had was washing teacups. He found a job in another tea shop, but this man turned out to be worse than the first one. Again he was forced into working for nothing but his food.

"I tried to escape, many times," he said, his words broken by the painful memories. "Every time, the man beat me. Then I became sick. The man thought I was dying, so he dumped me in the street."

He was discovered by street kids, who told a worker from CWIN they had found a dead boy in a back alley. When the worker showed up, the boy was still alive, though barely. They managed to get him to the hospital, and in time he recovered. A few physical scars remained, and many emotional ones.

"They all thought I would die. But I didn't," the boy said proudly. In those words I detected a conviction to fight off the pain he had suffered in the past, to find a way to a better future.

Our translator cautioned us not to be too optimistic. He told us the boy had built a shell around himself. He wouldn't let anyone too close for fear of being hurt again. Any rehabilitation would take a long time.

That afternoon CWIN threw a party to celebrate its ninth anniversary, and invited all the street kids who came to their centres. A tent had been set up with a stage and a microphone. There was music and dancing, and lots of food.

The kids loved it. Each centre had written a play to be performed by the kids. Some were comic, some serious. They were all big on costumes and props, making great use of what few materials were available to them. There was no shortage of talent, and little stage fright. A favourite scenario was a chase between a policeman and a robber. Of course, the robber always managed to outsmart the cop, much to the delight of an audience who'd experienced more than their share of run-ins with the law.

In one play, a big box was brought on the stage. The robber kept outwitting the cop by disappearing into the box. It was a simple plot, but the audience loved it, laughing uproariously each time the cop was left scratching his head. When it was over, the boy who played the robber bowed to the loudest applause of the afternoon.

When we returned to the relative comfort of "Hotel PLAN," I looked around and saw how trivial were the inconveniences I sometimes had to deal with in my life. I was surprised that some of these heroic young people could laugh and smile as much as they did.

It was New Year's Eve. Tomorrow would be the first day of 1996. A time for celebration? A wild party late into the night? Not for Alam. He ended the year with a bad stomachache. He figured it was all because of some condiments he'd had with his curry that night. According to our guidebook, Nepal is not known for its cuisine. But there were lots of places to indulge in foreign food, so Alam decided to go for an old favourite. The local condiment on the side of his plate seemed innocent enough, but there must have been some bacteria crawling through it, because his normally iron stomach took a beating. Off he went to bed, and slept his way into the new year.

I was left to party by myself. I washed and scrubbed – socks, turtle-neck, underwear, everything – and then hung my laundry out to dry, like party banners through "Hotel PLAN." I rocked the place past mid-night. It was no Times Square, and I skipped the champagne, but I made the most of it.

The next morning Alam was already up and dressed when I awoke. He had even gone off to the market and returned with breakfast.

"Looks like you've made a miraculous recovery," I said sleepily.

"Happy New Year!" He was rather more lively than when he went to bed. "How did you celebrate?"

"I kept it quiet. You know, just some good, clean fun."

Soon we were all set to go. We met up with someone from CWIN who had offered to be our guide and translator for the day.

All through Nepal we had seen a type of vehicle that the local people called "tempos." Many of them had a young boy standing on the back bumper as they made their way through the city.

"It would be great if we could talk to some of these children," I said to our guide.

He took us to a street in the centre of Kathmandu. It was here that many of the tempos came to be refuelled. We strolled over to where five or six were gathered.

A tempo looks like a cross between a taxi and a minibus, with room to squeeze in eight or ten people. The passengers get on and off through an open doorway at the back. Tempo owners hire young boys (because they are lightweight and cheap labour) to announce the stops, direct the passengers, collect the fares, and stop anyone from jumping off without paying. When the tempos are in motion, the boys stand on the back step and hang on to the frame of the open doorway.

It's not an easy job, or a safe one. Choking gas fumes and black smoke spew out from the tailpipes, even when the tempos are idling. And if one comes to a quick stop or has to swerve suddenly in traffic, the boy could easily be thrown to the street. Stories of legs being run over and bones being broken were common. Boys had been maimed for life and even struck down and killed, all for the sake of a few rupees.

Hanging around the tempos, waiting for his workday to begin, was a twelve-year-old boy. The corners of his mouth were raw with infection. On his chin, a section of skin the size of a small coin had been torn away.

"How long have you worked as a tempo helper?" our translator asked.

The boy shifted about uncomfortably, his dirty and hardened feet slipping out of their sandals. He couldn't remember.

"How many hours do you work a day?"

"Twelve."

"For how much money?"

"Thirty rupees."

It was less than one U.S. dollar.

"What do you want to do in the future?"

"Buy a tempo," he was quick to answer.

"Won't it take a very long time to save that much money?"

"Yes. But I will make more when I am sixteen."

By law, children had to be sixteen to work as tempo helpers, but like a lot of child-labour laws in South Asia, this one was never enforced. In the meantime, because the boy was underage, the driver paid him a lower wage.

His dream of owning a tempo seemed very remote to us. What would become of him? I wondered. I hoped his ambition stayed with him, and that somehow his life as an adult would become better than what he faced as a child.

Farther down the same street, we came upon a young girl sitting on the ground at the roadside, selling oranges and small candies from a broad, flat basket. She was shy at first and reluctant to talk to us, but she whispered to our translator that her parents sent her out each morning with the basket and a collection of items. Whenever cars stopped, perhaps caught in traffic, she would brave the exhaust fumes and hurry from window to window, her basket held high. I could see that in mid-summer her work must have been even more torturous. Long hours in the blazing sun, breathing smoke and carbon monoxide, would be a hellish way to spend a childhood. It was a heartbreaking contrast to the carefree summers of most North American children her age.

The unfortunate girl also had to take care of her baby sister. The child, less than a year old, squirmed about next to her, whining and trying to get away. The girl kept trying to entertain her, with the hope that she would sit still. She herself was only ten.

We discovered she had gone to school for only two months in her whole life. Like a lot of girls her age, she was expected to take care of younger children in the family. Often girls are kept at home for that reason, and to do household chores. More than 88 per cent of Nepalese girls fourteen and under (and more than 60 per cent of boys) are illiterate. They are denied an education, because parents see no value in it; girls are expected to marry and take care of the home and raise children.

But that, at least, was better than the fate of many young girls in Nepal, who were being sold by their families and ending up as prostitutes. Up to seven thousand young Nepalese girls are trafficked each year, many sent to the brothels of Bombay and Bangkok and other cities in countries nearby.

I learned that loan sharks arrive in the villages of Nepal to secure girls by lending money to their families. The loan sharks deceive the girls and their parents by telling them they will become waitresses or factory workers, but often they are never seen by their parents again. Those who do manage to escape life in the brothels are shunned and ignored. Many find themselves infected with the AIDS virus.

It is a cruel and hideous crime. Only recently has there been any active campaign to stop it, with some governments being shamed into action. In some cases, raids have been undertaken on the brothels of Bombay, and girls returned to Nepal. The girls are brought to rehabilitation centres where they undergo counselling in an effort to integrate them back into society.

Not only was this young girl expected to sell produce on the streets, but also to take care of her baby sister every day. In many developing countries, little emphasis is placed on education for girls.

We continued a little farther along the street. Before long, we came upon another working child, again a girl, again not yet a teenager. This girl was seated on the ground beside a stone slab, using a hammer to break up pieces of old brick to be used in the manufacture of new ones. We discovered she worked from dawn to dusk, and earned only food and shelter.

"I have no choice," she said. "I ran away from home. I was beaten. Before this I lived on the street."

"How did you get this job?"

"The lady who owns the quarry gave it to me."

When the owner came out to see why a crowd had gathered, she had a different story.

"The girl was dumped here by her parents. I took pity on her. I could have tossed her out on the street. She works a few hours a day, and for her work I provide food and a place to sleep."

As we were leaving, one of the people who had stopped to listen had yet another explanation. "She was a street child," he said. "That is true. But she escaped from a brothel. This is how she got here."

Three different stories, or perhaps the same story with different details. The fact remained that the girl worked long hours breaking bricks for food and shelter, and received not a cent for her labour.

She told our guide that she wanted to be a teacher when she was older. When I looked at her, I could almost picture it. In her eyes was the faraway look of someone who dreamed of a life much better than her own. In her manner was the pride of someone who knew what she was capable of. Perhaps she would find a way to be free of this miserable existence. The chances seemed very slim, but what is anyone's world without hope?

Before leaving Canada I had always assumed that child labour was something hidden, kept out of the public eye, something I would find only in dark alleyways and back streets. I thought we would have to break down doors to get to these children. But within the space of an hour, walking down one street, I had come upon three different instances of child labour, all of them in full view of everyone, including the police and government officials. Yet it continued.

Later that day, Alam and I were picked up by a driver to visit a school that PLAN had set up in a village about one hour outside Kathmandu.

No one I talked to was certain how this child ended up on the streets. Some suggested she had been taken in by a family that was now taking the earnings she made breaking bricks every day. Others said she had been saved from the brothels of Bombay, to which many girls from Nepal are trafficked every year.

It was a rough ride, often along narrow roads through mountainous terrain. The village was nestled into thickly forested mountains.

We arrived at the school to find a line of fifty students, each clutching wildflowers to present to us. In some cases they had woven the flowers into chains, and these they hung around our necks. It was a magical welcome.

It was a school holiday, in honour of the King of Nepal's birthday, and many of the students had made long trips on foot to be there. They performed some of their traditional songs and dances for us, then took us on a tour of their schoolroom, stopping to show us the drawings they had done in their art classes – animals, birds, village scenes.

The students obviously took a lot of pride in what they had accomplished. Many of them came from poor farming families, and such opportunities for education, especially for girls, were rare in Nepal. The students had formed clubs, one for boys and one for girls, and had taken their message of the value of education into the communities, going door to door, explaining to parents about what it meant for the futures of the children. They wrote letters to the government, asking that education be given a higher priority. They also did community service, such as explaining to families the importance of good nutrition and how to prevent the spread of disease. In many ways they reminded me of some of my friends back in Canada.

We ended our travel day with a visit to another village not far away. By that time it was almost dusk, and as we walked into the village we were met with a sea of dark faces, many of them children, all with wide, welcoming smiles. We met children amongst them sponsored by people overseas.

As long as I could remember, my parents had also sponsored children in other countries. It was a moving experience to meet children like the ones in the pictures and letters that came to our home in Canada.

The families tended gardens along the mountainsides and lived in simple thatched dwellings they call *durahs*. We were guests for supper in one of these homes. The meat dish placed before me was a strange pink mixture that made my eyes widen in dread. I was sure if I stared long enough I would see it twitch. Yet I could not offend our hosts. I ate, and somehow persuaded my stomach to cooperate. Immediately after the meal, I made a quick exit into the fresh air.

When we visited a village school in the mountains outside Kathmandu, the children greeted Alam and me with garlands of flowers. They were eager to perform plays and sing and dance for us, and to show us their school.

We left the village with the sun well below the horizon, and I walked back to our vehicle with a trail of kids tagging behind me.

"I live in Canada," I said, "far, far away." I swooped my hand in the air, making the motions of an airplane. "But first I go back to India."

They laughed and chattered among themselves, probably not understanding a word I had said. But they had made friends with me, and that was the important thing. As our vehicle moved away, the older kids raced after it, slowing to a stop only when they saw there was no chance of catching up.

"*Namasto*," I called for a final time. "Goodbye".

"*Namasto*," several of them chanted in reply.

When we flew out of Nepal the next day, the flight took us over many similar mountain villages. I wished the children in them were all as hopeful as the ones we had visited.

I knew they probably weren't. As I looked down over the mountain peaks, I realized that the struggles of these children were far more critical than the struggles of tourists I had pictured earlier trekking through the mountains.

It was not mountain climbers I pictured now; it was young girls and boys burdened with the struggles of everyday life.

133

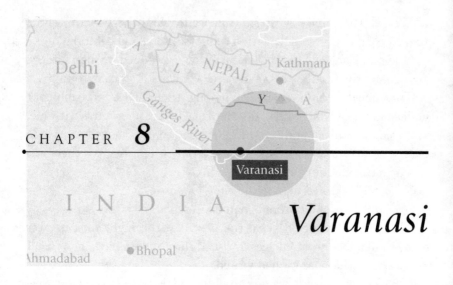

CHAPTER **8**

Varanasi

Our flight was bound for Varanasi, in northern India. And we were sorely disappointed it wasn't Delhi.

While in Calcutta we had made plans with Kailash Satyarthi to meet him in Delhi. We were then to take a train together to a secret destination where we would participate in a raid on a carpet factory to release children held in bondage there. This was one of my greatest hopes in coming to South Asia. And now it looked like we might never make it to Delhi in time to meet with Kailash as planned.

We had arrived in Kathmandu's airport to discover the airport crowded with people heading home to India from the celebrations for the Nepalese king's birthday. Every flight to Delhi was full. We waited for hours, hoping that a seat would become available. There was nothing. We were becoming desperate.

"Maybe what we should do," said Alam, "is fly to some city *close* to Delhi. Then catch a train from there."

"Would we make it in time to meet up with Kailash?"

"It's worth a try. It's better than sitting here, going nowhere."

Faint as it was, it was our only hope.

We stood in front of the departure schedule with a map.

"Let's see," I said, "Bombay, Madras, Patna, Varanasi..."

134

We pinpointed Varanasi, 250 kilometres from Delhi. It was our best bet.

We caught the next flight. When we landed, we headed directly to the train station.

"Nothing, sir," was the word from the ticket agent. "The trains to Delhi are all booked."

"Not even first class?"

"Sorry, sir."

We phoned the Air India office. Nothing until the next day. Too late to meet up with Kailash.

We had no choice but to resign ourselves to missing the raid.

Later that day, from a hotel in Varanasi, we made a telephone call to Kailash's office in Delhi and explained our situation.

"Kailash has already left for his destination," the SACCS official told us.

"Where is his destination?"

"I'm afraid we cannot tell you."

We understood. We knew the raid had to be carried out with the utmost secrecy. We left the phone number of our hotel in case Kailash wanted to get in touch with us.

That evening, over a meal of soup and cheese bread, we tried to recover from our disappointment.

"Tomorrow is January third," said Alam. "That's the halfway point of your trip."

"Really?"

"And here you are, polishing off a bowl of spicy curried soup."

"It only seems like yesterday that you had me sweating buckets in Dhaka airport, thinking you'd never show up."

"You must be homesick by now," Alam said, although he knew better.

"Actually . . . no."

We chuckled.

"We've been so busy," I said, "there's no time to be homesick!"

"More soup?"

"Why not? Ask them to make it a little spicier, would you?"

I lay in bed that night thinking that if the second half of the trip was as interesting as the first, then I would never want to go home.

The city of Varanasi is at least three thousand years old. Built at a bend in the Ganges River, it is the spiritual capital of Hinduism. Thousands of pilgrims pour into the city daily to bathe in the river's sacred waters. And from all over India, people arrive with their dead, to have them cremated and the ashes delivered into the waters of the Ganges.

We rose early, with the hope of taking a boat along the river to watch the rituals of its people. It was raining heavily, however, and we were told such a trip would be too dangerous, that the rain would flood the boats.

I had never seen such rain. It struck the skin like pellets. Out on the streets we pressed our backs against buildings and watched the deluge from under the cover of their eaves. It flowed through the city, down cement stairs to join other streams, past the moored boats, and into the Ganges.

My eye caught a girl walking along the riverbank selling flowers. Her black hair was plastered to her face, her clothes soaked to her skin. She was making no attempt to escape the downpour. In fact, she seemed to relish it. A man with an umbrella came by. He gave her a few coins for a flower, then walked to the river's edge and laid it on the water. The flower drifted from the shore, its petals dancing in the splash of rain. The girl chanted a few words in Hindi to people as they passed by. Most paid no heed to her. She walked on, her chanting blending into the rhythm of the rain.

I got it in my head to catch up with her. I dashed out, letting the water splash against me. It soaked through to my skin, too long dried with the sun and dust of the weeks past. I bought a flower from the girl. I didn't understand her words, and perhaps she did not understand my "thank you," but we caught each other's smile through the rain. I laid the flower at the river's edge, then caught up with Alam and walked back with him to the hotel, not caring about the downpour. Loving it, in fact, and how it had transformed the city.

We were hardly back in the hotel when there was a call from Kailash.

"What? You must be kidding!" Alam said into the receiver.

The secret destination turned out to be, of all places, Varanasi. The raid was scheduled for that very afternoon, at a carpet factory less than two hours from where we were standing.

Alam and I were to go to the home of one of the SACCS agents and wait for Kailash. He would let him know we were coming.

We were amazed at our good fortune, yet again. Was it fate that sent us to the very city we needed to reach? The Hindu gods must have been watching over us, I thought. Perhaps it was the rain, washing all our disappointments away.

We immediately took a taxi to the address Kailash had given us. We knocked on the back door of a small shop. A man answered and looked us over, head to toe. He took a quick glance into the alleyway to reassure himself we weren't being followed, then motioned for us to be quiet and ushered us inside.

We didn't speak until we were spoken to.

"Was there anybody with you? You're certain you weren't followed?"

Alam and I looked at each other. We felt like KGB agents.

"We saw no one," Alam said.

The fellow checked outside the door again, then finally relaxed a little and sat down. He informed us the raid had been postponed, but that it should take place that evening.

When Kailash arrived a few hours later, it was with discouraging news. The raid could not take place that evening. The magistrate who was to accompany them had cancelled at the last minute.

"Because of an important meeting," Kailash told us. I could hear the doubt in his voice.

Any raids on factories suspected of using child labour had to be conducted with a magistrate in attendance, and there had to be a police escort, for the magistrate's protection. The magistrate who had been assigned to this particular raid was stalling. Kailash believed it was because he was newly appointed to his position and didn't want to get involved in anything controversial. With any more delays, Kailash feared, the factory owner would get wind of what was going on and disappear with the children.

Alam and I checked into the hotel where Kailash and the SACCS workers were staying. That night we sat around and discussed how the raid – if it ever did take place – would unfold. One thing became immediately clear: I would not be going along on the raid.

I was so disappointed. I was desperate to be part of the raid to free these children.

Once these children were freed from bondage, Kailash Satyarthi accompanied them to the police station, where they gave their testimonies. It was important for the local magistrate and the police to participate in the carpet factory raid to guarantee the freed children placement in a government rehabilitation program and school.

"A white boy travelling in a rural area of India, it would not look good," a SACCS worker explained. "It would raise too many suspicions. Besides, it is too dangerous. The police will have guns. Others might too."

There was nothing I could do about the colour of my skin. And I didn't mind a little danger. But, of course, because there was a possibility that the raid would backfire, and the children would lose their chance at freedom, I accepted their decision.

Even in the hallways of our hotel I was attracting attention. Heads turned as I walked by. Who was this white boy with all these Asians who spoke English? What were they planning to do? Whenever anyone sat near us at a restaurant, we immediately stopped any talk that might be suspicious. In fact, it was decided I should remain out of sight as much as possible.

The good sense of this was confirmed the following morning, when I noticed two strange men leaning against the wall outside the door to Kailash's room.

As I walked past, they said a few words to me in Hindi. I looked over my shoulder. They had begun to follow me. The room where Alam and I were staying was the second-to-last at the end of the hallway, and I quickly figured that unless these guys were in the very last room, then something was up. I looked back again. They were gaining fast. I jogged the last few metres to our door. I knocked. It stopped them in their tracks.

Alam wasn't answering. "Hurry up," I muttered between clenched teeth.

The men had started towards me again. There was no more than three metres between us. I pounded on the door.

Finally Alam opened it and I slipped inside and set the deadbolt.

I blew out a lungful of air in relief.

Then I spewed out the story to Alam and a human-rights worker who was in the room.

"They just wanted to scare you," the worker said. "If they really wanted to hurt you, they could easily have overpowered a thirteen-year-old boy."

They were not exactly words of comfort.

Upon hearing my story, Kailash decided he and the SACCS people should move out of the hotel and into the home of one of their local contacts. Alam and I were to remain in the hotel, but join them the following day.

Plans for the raid still hadn't been finalized. SACCS was in touch with the magistrate's office again, but still they weren't getting a commitment. Kailash threatened to go on a hunger strike, starting the next day.

There was one phone call that evening that we hadn't been expecting. My mother called to tell me there was another Canadian who was going to be in Delhi the following week, at the exact same time I would be there.

"Alam?" I hadn't lost my sense of humour.

"The prime minister."

"Of Canada? Jean Chrétien?"

"He's coming with eight provincial premiers and 250 business-people. They're starting a tour of four South Asian countries to promote trade. No mention of human rights. No mention of child labour."

"That's ridiculous!"

"The FTC kids are really upset. They're going to the airport when the business delegation is leaving so they can hand out information on child labour."

"Perfect! That will at least get them thinking about the issue."

"The kids said to tell you that you should try to meet with the prime minister while he's in India."

"You're kidding."

"I know. There's no chance he would ever meet with you. But they really want to send a letter to his office on your behalf requesting a meeting."

"Sure, if they want. I've already written to him once about child labour."

After I hung up, I told Alam what the kids had said. "The prime minister of Canada and me, in the same room, discussing the issue of child labour? No chance," I said.

"I wouldn't be so sure."

I stared at him. "C'mon, be serious."

"I am serious. He shouldn't be allowed to just ignore the issue. Someone's got to press him on it. And who better to do it than you?

You've researched the topic thoroughly, and for the past month you've been on the road seeing it firsthand, day after day. Plus, you're a kid yourself. Plus, you're Canadian!"

There was no doubt, it would be the best possible way to bring child labour to the attention of people in my own country's government.

"I can see it now," he said. "You and the PM. Face-to-face. Man-to-boy."

"Maybe it's worth a try," I concluded. The prime minister *should* be dealing with the issue. I wished I could just take him down some of the same streets I had walked, and have him sit down with some of the same kids I had talked to. Then there would be no need for me to try to convince him that child labour was an important issue for his government. The kids would do that. One look at their world and the work they are forced to do, and he would be convinced. If he was human at all, he would have to see that child labour was something that deserved his immediate attention. That trade was more than making money. That profit had to take second place to the basic rights of children.

The new day brought great news. The raid on the carpet factory was going ahead. Kailash's threat of a hunger strike seemed to have done the trick. The local magistrate had agreed to meet the SACCS members that morning and, accompanied by some police from another district, proceed to the village where the carpet factory was located.

Kailash and the SACCS workers, together with Alam and a BBC reporter from England, piled into two Jeeps. Left to await their return, I waved from the doorway as they disappeared from sight, then I retreated inside. But my excitement was just as high as theirs.

I have never been good at waiting. In fact, I would place it at the very top of the list of things that drive me crazy. This time it was especially tough. A thousand and one questions were swirling through my head. What if it didn't go according to plan? What if the owner had been tipped off? What if there was a confrontation with the police?

But all I could do was wait. In the end they returned, though they were late by several anxious hours. Alam's first words as he came through the door were "Mission accomplished." And gradually, as we all sat down to tea, the whole story emerged.

They drove first to the appointed spot where they were to meet the magistrate. They had waited an hour for the magistrate and the police assigned to protect him. They boarded two more Jeeps, and the group was on its way again. There was one additional stop – to pick up three fathers of boys they were hoping to free. It was these parents who had first contacted SACCS with the stories of their children being taken away.

In the days leading up to the raid, some SACCS workers had gone undercover to the village and were able to supply the raiding party with a detailed map. This was brought out at the last possible moment, and only then shared with the magistrate and the police. They were told precisely where the raiding party was going and the exact layout of the land and the buildings. Perfect timing was essential. And not a second could be wasted once they arrived on the scene.

The carpet factory was hidden away in an isolated village. They passed over numerous dirt roads and raced through a string of villages. The rush to their destination was met with a stream of curious looks. Where was this line of Jeeps going in such a hurry? Who were these people?

The lead driver gave no warning they were nearing the village. Only when he ground to a halt did everyone realize they had arrived. They leaped from the vehicles and began a mad dash on foot along narrow paths, through fields, past trees and bushes and villagers at work, to the factory – a single-storey structure of decaying red bricks.

As the police broke through the trees into the clearing, their guns in full view, SACCS workers rushed past the open doors of the factory. "We have come to free you!" they shouted to the children. "We're taking you back to your parents!"

There were children huddled together. The SACCS workers hurried to them and tried to calm their fears. "You're safe now. Everything will be okay."

Somehow word had reached the factory owner minutes before the raid. He had escaped, though it all happened too quickly for him

Children working in the carpet industry often suffer from many health problems. These include breathing difficulties from inhaling the carpet fibres, arthritis in their fingers from tying the tiny knots, and growth deformities from working hunched over their looms for so long every day.

to hide the boys. He had thrown open the doors and shouted at them to run away, that some evil men were about to capture them. It scared three of the boys into running off, though sometime later they wandered out of the forest and made their way back to the factory.

The fathers who had joined in the raid rushed onto the scene just behind the leaders of the raiding party. They found their sons as they emerged from the factory and hugged them tightly. It was the first affection these children had known for a very long time.

There were twenty-two children rescued, many of them between the ages of eight and twelve. It was a great victory. Alam and the BBC reporter had quietly captured much of it on videotape, though the magistrate was adamant that no cameras be used. He was worried that evidence of the raid would reflect badly on his district.

I viewed the footage Alam had shot inside the factory. On its dirt floor sat several looms. They stood silent now, but they bore the stories of boys enslaved by brutish men. It was at these looms the boys began each day, endless hours hardly moving from their task. It was on this factory floor they ate what little food was given them. And it was here they slept, until the early hours of morning brought another day, no different from the last.

Normally the looms were hidden from view, as were the boys. Now their stories emerged for everyone to hear.

"Sometimes we were given only one meal a day," one boy said. "And then only watery lentils."

"The master kept us hungry so the pains would take away our sleep," another boy added. "The longer he could keep us awake, the more work he would make us do."

Many of them suffered from the lack of ventilation inside the factory walls. Wool dust had collected in their lungs. Coughs broke their raspy breathing.

Skin infections had been left untreated. Their hands were callused and pitted from constant tying of the knots.

If the owner was anxious to have a carpet completed, he would force the children to work through the night.

"I fell asleep at the loom," one boy said. He pushed aside his hair to show a scar left by a gash. "He struck me with the sharp prongs of the *panja* fork."

The children collected their few pieces of clothing and left the hell that had buried their childhood. They walked away and never looked back. They boarded the Jeeps to be driven to the police station, where each of them would give his statement. Then the boys would be free to go, and I would get to join them all on the trip back to their parents.

It was a moment I was looking forward to with excitement. It was the culmination of many days of preparation on the part of Kailash and the SACCS workers. For me, it was a dream come true, one I'd had since the earliest days of Free the Children.

We left early the next morning, thirty of us piling into two Jeeps to begin the eleven-hour trip to the boys' village. We were so tightly packed that moving a limb was a major undertaking. In fact, many of the limbs were out windows, and for most of the trip, one whole body was on the roof. Alam had escaped up there, and partway along the route, I joined him.

For most of it, though, I was half in the Jeep, half clinging to the side. The sides and roof were actually just a metal frame with canvas stretched over it. The canvas flapped constantly, and we had to shout to be heard. Our vehicle reminded me of the kind you see in old army movies. Always dependable, able to make its way through anything, but not big on comfort.

We hadn't gone far when one of the boys started to sing. The others quickly joined in, their voices soaring above the noise, their hands clapping a steady rhythm. Even Alam picked up on the words and chanted along.

"Free!" were the Hindi words they sang. "We are free! Free!"

The joy that had so long been dormant erupted to the open skies. I could not tell where they had learned the song; maybe it was one they remembered from days before they were sold to the carpet trade. Their short taste of freedom had stirred old ways, when life was good enough to clap for joy and sing out loud.

They grew excited at everything we passed, and several times we had to stop so they could get a closer look. My excitement was equal to theirs, for there were elephants tramping through a landscape

Bringing these freed children home after a carpet factory raid was the high-light of my trip. My spirits were as high as theirs as they clapped their hands and chanted, "We are free! We are free!" It was a song of celebration and of new hope for the future.

wilder than any I had ever seen, and bands of monkeys, their long tails curled the length of their backs and hanging just above their heads.

Next to me sat Ramatha, and on his lap, Munnilal. Munnilal was eight and wore an old, faded tank top, pink and full of holes, and a pair of plaid pants, much too big for his undernourished body. I handed him the videocamera and showed him what magic could be worked by pressing its buttons. I showed him how to film all the kids in the Jeep. We played the tape back and no one could believe his eyes.

Munnilal's words were few at first, but gradually his shyness fell away. We shared stories of two lives that were, for a few hours, no longer worlds apart.

"Munnilal, did you ever go to school?" I asked through a translator.

"Yes. Every day I used to walk to school with Mikindre, my friend. We had lots of fun. We hid in the fields and played tricks on the other boys." Munnilal smiled at the thought of it.

"Your parents, did they want you to go to school?"

"Yes, yes. They cannot read or write. They wanted me to learn."

"Were you a good student?"

"Sometimes." He hesitated. "Every time I made a mistake, the teacher would strike me with a stick. It hurt so much." His eyes tightened with the pain of the memory.

"What did you do? Did you cry?"

"I quit school."

It wasn't long after, he said, that someone showed up in the village telling his parents that he could go to school and learn carpet weaving in his spare time. He would be paid for his work, the man said. He would make good money and have it sent back home.

Munnilal was taken away.

"I was given no money," said Munnilal. "I was hit again and again. I have scars on my back. Children who asked about their parents were burned with cigarettes and beaten up so others wouldn't ask."

I could say nothing, only stare in his eyes at the awful memories.

"I cried for my mother. And when I cried, the master beat me."

"It must have been very hard for you," I said.

"I would not have the master make me cry. After that, I would only cry in my heart. It was very bad. I saw my mother in my dreams."

"Soon you will see your mother for real," I said, hoping to comfort him. "You will be together again."

From time to time, the Jeep stopped and everyone burst out to stretch their legs. The children raced about like frisky colts, stopping occasionally to soak up the wide open spaces. They picked up rocks and hurled them as far they could. Boys again, like boys anywhere.

I asked Munnilal what he wanted to do when he grew up.

"Be a policeman," he said. "I will go back and beat up the carpet masters like they beat me up."

Eventually we came to a river. By this time it was getting dark. The river was so wide and with such a strong flow of water that I wondered how we were ever going to cross it. A big fuel truck had attempted just that, and was now stuck in the river.

Everyone piled out of the Jeep. "We'll never get across here," I said to Alam as we stood on the bank and surveyed the scene. "There's too much current. Maybe there's a bridge farther down river."

The words weren't out of my mouth when the Jeep shot past us and ploughed into the river. Water flew in all directions.

"What is he doing?" I exclaimed. "He'll sink!"

Nobody seemed as concerned as I was. I guess I hadn't realized the rough and ready ways of travel in rural India.

The Jeep caught hold of the riverbed and began grinding its way slowly forward. At one point it was practically submerged, though still inching along. The boys on shore were all shouting, urging it on.

"Keep going! Keep going! A little more, a little more!"

But the Jeep came to a stop and moved no farther. Now what do we do? I thought.

Everyone else, it seemed, knew exactly what to do. They all rushed into the water and headed for the stranded vehicle, the current nearly toppling many of them. The slighter children grabbed hold of the older ones to keep their balance.

Then Alam took the plunge, and I was left alone on shore. But not for long. Soon I, too, was chest-deep in water. Coming from Canada, I had expected the water, even in a mild winter, to be cold. To my amazement, it was almost lukewarm. I might have swum to the Jeep except for the videocamera and tapes I was holding in a bag high over my head.

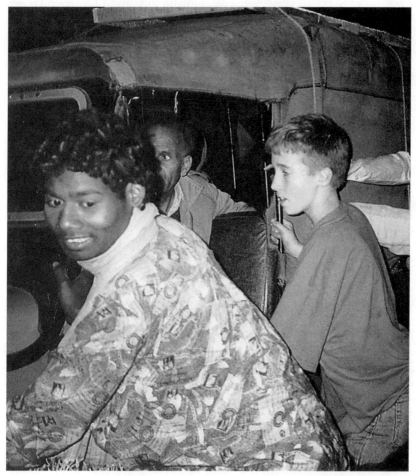

Dripping wet, dead tired, but all smiles, we pushed our stalled Jeep out of a river en route to the children's village. After congratulating one another on our feat, we watched as the second Jeep also got stuck.

Soon everyone had gathered around the Jeep and I had found a dry spot for the camera bag on the roof.

"Now," someone shouted in Hindi. "Everyone ready?"

We all grabbed hold of the metal frame. "Yes!" came a chorus of voices.

"Here we go."

We dug our feet into the river bottom.

"One! Two! Threeee!"

We gave an almighty push. The Jeep didn't budge.

Digging our shoulders into it even more, we tried again. Nothing. We took a breather before attempting yet again.

"We'll do it this time. Ready? One! Two! Threeee!"

On the third try, it did move, ever so slowly. Inch by inch, farther and farther. Out of the water we pushed, and up the hill on the other side.

Everyone collapsed on the riverbank, exhausted.

That wasn't the end of it, of course. The second Jeep proceeded to get stuck in the very same way. We rushed back into the water, but in the commotion we all lost our balance and toppled into the river. We righted ourselves and, with a new spurt of energy, out came the second Jeep. We dragged ourselves out behind it.

The riverbank was a riot of laughter and excited chatter. We cheered in celebration.

"Let's try the truck," someone shouted, laughing the loudest of us all.

The truck would have to wait for a strong towline and something more than human power. We stood on the bank and wrung out our clothes. Then we were off again – wet, but too excited to care.

Except for Munnilal. He looked at me and saw that I was soaked from head to foot. I was no wetter than he was, of course.

One of the SACCS workers had given him a blanket. He held it out to me. "Take it," he said. "You will catch a cold."

"No, no." I shook my head, smiling. "Thank you very much, but you must have it."

His kindness struck my heart. His needs were greater than mine, yet he was so quickly willing to give up even his small bit of comfort. I looked at his thin, undernourished body and heard his congested lungs. Yet his first thoughts had been for someone else. I smiled, but my smile of thanks was no match for his generosity.

Perhaps that was how the children had all survived their years in the carpet factory – looking out for each other in the face of brutality, finding comfort in sharing what little they had. I imagined how, at night, when they were finally allowed to sleep, the children whispered encouragement to each other, told each other that a day would surely come when they would be free.

As we came ever closer to their village, the singing started up again. It rang out through the black stillness of the night. The only light was the beams of the headlights quavering over the rough dirt roads. Occasionally it caught a late-night traveller on foot or bicycle. Our noise must have been more frightful than that of any wild animal.

Wet and tired and cramped together, the children still had the energy to sing out their joy at returning home. The crowd in the Jeep behind heard us and joined in. Soon it became a competition, each vehicle trying to outdo the other. In the end, we all bellowed the words as loudly as we could, our voices and clapping booming through the night.

All the boys were from the same village. When we finally reached its outskirts, it was two o'clock in the morning.

"This way, this way," the kids called out in Hindi, their fingers pointing.

Not one of us had slept. We were wide awake and wildly excited in anticipation of what was to come.

"A little farther," said one boy. The headlights fell on a mud hut. He paused and craned his neck for a better view. "Yes, this is it! This is where I live!"

An unearthly quiet descended on us all when the vehicles finally came to a stop. It felt as if I had gone back in time. The village was so remote it had no electricity. Telephones, Kailash told me, were unheard of. There was only the murky light of the moon, cast over a village of mud huts sound asleep. The dwelling where we had stopped stood in pitch-black silence.

One of the boys jumped to the ground, looked around, and shuffled his feet, almost as if he wanted to be certain of his footing. He looked back at us all in the Jeep, then slowly walked towards his home.

He looked back again as he knocked on the door.

The door creaked open, just a crack. The boy said his name. "I am freed from the carpet factory. I am back."

The door flew open to reveal a woman. For a second she stood there, absolutely still, as though trying to make sense of the sight before her.

Trembling, she reached for him and pulled him tightly to her chest. "Is it possible? Is it possible?"

"We raided the carpet factory," one of the men called to her. "We freed all the boys from the village."

"Can it be true? We were all so worried. I thought we would never see him again." She turned to her boy. "So thin," she said, "so thin."

Kailash walked over and explained to the mother how it all happened. She had heard that some parents had been trying to get the boys free.

"I am a widow," she said. "I had no way to get him back. Thank you, thank you."

The boy looked at us again in the Jeep. He was smiling. He raised his hand to his friends and waved goodbye before stepping through the doorway. He was waving still, and hugging his mother, as the door closed behind them.

The same scene was repeated many times. We made our way through the village, following the directions of each boy in turn. "A little this way. To the right a few metres. There, I can see it. I know the place. There's a new roof, but that's it."

And out each rescued child would climb and run to the door of his home. Sometimes it was another child who answered, a brother or sister. Sometimes an old man. But often it was a mother or father who threw open the door at the sight of their lost son and hugged him long and hard.

Kailash would accompany each boy to the door and tell the parents what had happened, why we were showing up in the middle of the night. He must have seemed like a messenger from heaven.

Munnilal was one of the last to leave the Jeep. He had gone from a few shy monosyllables to relating the pain of his bondage. He had offered me his blanket, laughed at my singing, and taken my video-camera in hand and playfully zoomed in on the collection of faces all around us. We had become good friends.

I hated to see him go, but, like him, I could hardly contain my excitement at the thought of him being home.

"That is my house," he said to me. "The one through those fields." It was at the far end of the village. The Jeep stopped and let us out, and we took a shortcut through the fields.

Munnilal knocked on the door.

We could hear stirrings inside. And the mumble of voices.

Finally, the door opened, again just a crack. It was an old man. He looked at Munnilal. His smile and excited words lit the night. He embraced the boy, shouting back into the house, "Everyone, wake up! Quick! Come quick! It's Munnilal!"

One after another, the whole family emerged from the house – his father, his grandmother, his younger sister, and, finally, his mother.

His mother came with tears in her eyes. "Munnilal, can it really be you?" In her arms she carried Munnilal's brother, a year and a half old. A brother he had never seen before.

His mother looked at him, in shock at seeing the thin boy before her. Her hand touched his face, ran down to the boniness of his shoulder. She put her arm around him and pulled him tightly to her. There was a long moment when they both stood motionless, as if all the world had stopped. Neither said a word.

The silence was broken by Munnilal's name being called through the darkness of the night. "Munnilal, where are you?"

"Mikindre!" Munnilal shouted. It was his best friend, the boy who walked to school with him.

The boy came rushing in, completely out of breath. The two stood staring at each other. An awkward smile broke the silent look between them. They flung their arms around each other and hugged.

We all went inside the house. Munnilal's parents wanted to share with us what food they had, a token of their gratitude.

We had some tea and plain biscuits and talked together of the ordeal the boy had suffered and the rescue to set him free. Kailash, sitting next to the parents, asked them how they ever came to let him be taken away.

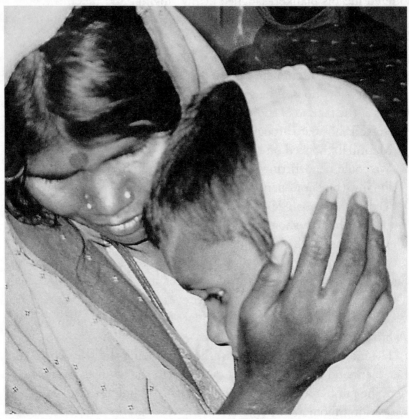

One of the most emotional moments of my trip was when I saw Munnilal in his mother's embrace. I will never forget the moment when Munnilal looked at his mother and said, "When I hurt the most, I saw you in my dreams." She responded, "Munnilal, I saw you in *my* dreams!"

"I was cheated," said the boy's father. "I was told that Munnilal would learn carpet weaving and earn good money. I never received one rupee!"

"Would you ever send him again?"

"Impossible!" said his mother. "Damned impossible! Look at him. Look how thin he has become!" Her face revealed the immeasurable pain she was feeling for her son. "He was never like that in the past." Tears filled her eyes.

Munnilal quietly held his mother's hand. "When I hurt the most," he said, "I saw you in my dreams."

His mother held his hand tighter. She wiped her eyes. "Munnilal, I saw you in *my* dreams."

That moment between them is one I will never forget. It was an emotional reunion, and, I think, a reconciliation. For I wondered if Munnilal ever resented his parents for sending him away, when other boys, like his friend Mikindre, stayed in the village. And if his mother and father ever felt guilty for letting him go. As I looked around me I could see their extreme poverty. I could see how it could lead to what had happened, parents led astray in a futile search for a better life for themselves and their son.

Everyone present was enormously touched by the reunion we had witnessed, and by what followed. Munnilal took his brother in his arms, the boy he had never known before, and hoisted him to his shoulders. He put an arm around his young sister, who hadn't recognized him. The boyhood that had been lost, seemingly forever, was returning.

I could not leave without a last word to my new friend. I put my arm around his shoulder.

"Goodbye."

"*Alvita*," he said in Hindi. "Goodbye."

"I wish you lots of happiness," I said.

Kailash translated. Munnilal nodded and gave me a smile. I hoped he would remember me, the boy from Canada who had heard him shout, "I am free!" Who had witnessed his pain beginning to heal. I would always remember him.

As we walked back over the grassland to the Jeep, I knew that Munnilal was the reason I had come to South Asia. He was the reason

I believed so strongly in the cause of ending child labour. To know that change was possible, to know that a smile could again return to the face of a child who had been forced to work endless hours in hard labour – that was all the inspiration anyone could ever need. The children who laboured were the ones to teach the world a lesson in courage, not the brand-name sports stars, not the businessmen and their millions. These children are the real heroes.

After the last child was returned to his home, we were left to find a place to spend the night. At first we thought of sleeping in the Jeeps, but decided against it. We knocked on a stranger's door in the village and asked if we could use his barn. "Yes," he said. "You are welcome to it."

It was all we wanted, a place to stretch out and get a few hours' rest before heading back. He came to the barn with us and spread some hay on the floor. I couldn't imagine what would have happened in North America if we had knocked on a stranger's door at such an ungodly hour.

We woke early the next morning and dug ourselves out of the hay. The village that had been so eerily quiet was suddenly a flourish of people and animals. Chickens scurried about noisily. Young children hung around doorways and ran through the fields. Men with walking-sticks lead mules loaded down with great swaths of hay.

We thanked the owner of the barn, and though he asked for nothing, we gave him a little money in payment for our accommodation. We boarded the Jeeps and were gone, heading back to the main road. I learned later that the children who had been freed on the raid would eventually go to rehabilitation centres, and some SACCS people would return to the village to instruct the families in how to avoid scams like the one that had taken away their children.

The return journey was a rather sad one in comparison to that of the day before. We longed for the noise, and the singing, and even the crush of so many bodies. We missed the uncontrollable excitement that had soared higher and higher with every kilometre that brought us closer to the children's village.

I wondered what the boys were doing now. Had they lingered in bed, something they hadn't been able to do for so long? Were they up and walking the village, looking for old friends? Were they laughing and singing still, "We are free, we are free"?

They were free of their master's cruelty, but what did their futures hold?

I thought about Munnilal. Was he playing with his baby brother and chasing his sister around the house? Was he telling Mikindre about the beatings he'd had to endure?

Had the tears in his heart stopped for good?

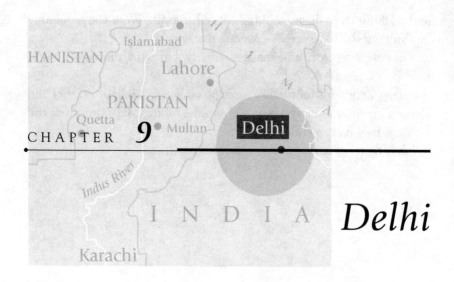

CHAPTER 9

Delhi

IF I WERE ASKED TO SUM UP the time I spent in India in one word, I would have to say, *amazing*. It's an overused word, I know. But it was just that. Amazing.

I went from sleeping on straw on a barn floor in a village without electricity or telephones to holding a press conference in a hotel with marble floors and chandeliers. I went from scribbling a few misspelled words in my diary to writing "A Joint Declaration Between the Youth of India and Canada." I went from splashing chest-deep in muddy water behind a Jeep to having my face splashed across the front page of newspapers across Canada.

On the same day that we arrived back in Varanasi, we boarded a train for Delhi. We were extremely tired and certainly weren't looking forward to sitting up all night. We mentioned to the conductor we were willing to pay a little extra if he could do something for us, and a couple of sleeping berths suddenly became available. We had discovered that in India lots of people expect that "little extra" for their services. It's the way things work.

A good sleep that night revived me. Unfortunately, the same couldn't be said of breakfast next morning. Every guidebook, every traveller I talked to, said the food on trains was safe. The pre-

158

packaged, tasteless clump of vegetables I had for breakfast certainly wasn't. It contained something that sent my temperature soaring within a few hours.

All through the trip we had been careful about what we ate. Any time we bought food straight from the market, we made sure it was well cooked. Nothing had happened. I never thought for a second it would be train food that would do me in.

By the time we reached Kailash Satyarthi's house in Delhi, all I wanted to do was lie down. My stomach felt as though it had been tied in a knot. I winced with cramps, and rummaged though the syringes and blood-transfer kit in my medical supplies, all in vain. Nothing for an upset stomach. Something for every possible ailment known to humanity except for an upset stomach. My only relief came when I vomited. It was back to bed with two Tylenol and a vow never to eat train food again.

The next day, I felt a little better. At least I could carry on a decent conversation and was reasonably mobile. I was able to spend time with Kailash's family, getting to know them better and hearing more stories of the past raids carried out by SACCS.

And getting to know "Tiger." Kailash's famed guard dog was a Great Dane, covered around its middle with a woollen sweater. He was the biggest dog I had ever seen, and gave new meaning to the word *canine*. He ate grains, vegetables, and milk. This canine was a vegetarian! Except when a stranger entered the house. When we first met, I came very close to having the imprint of his teeth in my hand.

The rest of the family were vegetarians as well. And Alam, of course. In fact, I was surrounded by vegetarians. Meat was not mentioned in the house. My stomach couldn't have handled it anyway.

Later that day, I felt well enough to visit a rehabilitation centre for freed child labourers called Mukti Ashram. Some of the children we had carried home a few days before would soon be finding their way there, while the others would be going to a government rehabilitation centre. Children usually came for three to six months. It was a time for physical and psychological rehabilitation, to build up their self-confidence. During their life of slavery, they had been taught that they were only valued for their labour, that otherwise they were worthless.

But the centre also taught the children basic reading and writing, to give them greater control over their lives, and vocational skills such as carpentry, metal work, and weaving to help them eventually find a job.

Mukti Ashram was a high-walled compound with wrought-iron entrance gates, heavily monitored by security guards, all of whom carried rifles. Every precaution was taken to protect the centre from factory owners seeking revenge on the children for the raids carried out by SACCS.

The compound was large, but not elaborate. The children had space to roam freely, something they hadn't experienced for years. They often ate in the open air and, of course, played games. While we were there, I had a chance to join them in two of my favourite sports: badminton and volleyball. One end of the volleyball net was tied to a huge tree. It was great fun to be playing outdoors under the brilliant Indian sunshine.

We had arrived at the centre on the day of a farewell party for a group of the young people who had completed their program of rehabilitation, and were about to go home to their families. One of the SACCS workers had brought along an electric keyboard; someone else, a set of Indian drums. Other instruments appeared, ones I had never seen before. Together they set a wild and throbbing beat. The boys joined in, clapping an infectious rhythm. A spontaneous dance broke out, the moves a combination of old and new – traditional Indian, a little Michael Jackson, a lot of improvisation. They revelled in it – hands in the air, hips swaying, feet shuffling over the floor.

Afterwards, a special ceremony was held to commemorate their weeks at Mukti Ashram. Each boy stood up in turn and spoke about being forced into bonded labour and the abuse he had suffered. Everyone ended with the words, "Now I am free."

Kailash presented each of them with a certificate. For kids who had been belittled and degraded, it was a proud moment they could remember with pride in the years ahead. Loud clapping followed every one of them back to his place.

I talked to one boy, Nagashir, who was staying on at the rehabilitation centre, not yet ready to return to his family. His story was particularly horrific.

Nagashir had literally been branded for trying to help his younger brother escape from the carpet factory where the two of them had

Mukti Ashram is a transition step between a life of slavery and one of freedom. At the centre, the children undergo psychological and physical rehabilitation, and learn basic literacy skills and a trade. Taking part in the children's daily exercise routine was a lot of fun.

Nagashir had been branded with red hot irons for helping his young brother escape from a carpet factory. His story of abuse and torture was gut wrenching, but his determination to overcome the trauma he had endured gave hope for his future.

been enslaved. Both of them had been caught and punished. He showed me where they had marked him with the hot iron, on his legs and arms, and against his throat. It was hard to believe such barbarism exists. But the scars were there for everyone to see, and for Nagashir to live with for the rest of his life. And those were only the physical scars. The boy's soul had been ravaged, his humanity violated in a way that should make the world cringe.

I asked him how old he was when he started to work in the carpet factory.

Nagashir spoke very little. The trauma he had suffered had impaired his speech. He set his hand at the height of a young boy, and said something to the translator in a raspy whisper.

"He does not remember exactly," the translator told me. "But we have been able to discover that he was only seven."

"And how old are you now?" I asked Nagashir.

"Fourteen."

"The day he was freed," I was told, "when he was taken by the magistrate and the police, it was impossible for him to give a statement. He was not speaking a single word. He had forgotten everything. He looked at the people, not crying, not smiling; no emotions, no feelings."

The staff at the centre worked many hours with him. But only after three weeks did he begin to respond. One day he was sitting by himself in the garden and he quietly began to sing. It was a faint whisper.

Nagashir was willing to sing his song again for us. The staff member translated it line by line.

If you want to live, live with a smile,
live with love, don't cry.
Don't shed your tears.
There are storms, there are disasters;
in life there are ups and downs.
But don't shed your tears.

Smile – pain is part of life,
but finally you get joy.
If you want to live, live with new hopes,
live with new aspirations.

Live with love.
Live with a smile.

I don't know where he learned the song. Maybe it was one he had heard as a small boy. The important thing was that Nagashir had found the spirit to sing.

I saw Nagashir many times that day. Each time, he was a little more talkative. Behind his words, though, there was always pain. His master's cruelty had marked him so deeply he could never fully heal.

Nagashir's story was what forced me to gather my courage and hold a press conference in Delhi. His experience struck me so forcibly, I felt as many people as possible had to know about it. I believed that telling this one story would create such outrage people would immediately demand an end to child labour.

As our trip had moved along from city to city, the idea of holding a press conference to bring attention to the issue of child labour began to stir about in our heads. Now, in Delhi, with loads of Canadian newspaper, radio, and TV reporters on the tail of the prime minister, we thought this might be just the time to put it together.

Of course, my experience at the press conference in Calcutta only made me more nervous this time. What if the press didn't like what I had to say and turned on me? Perhaps more likely, what if we held a press conference and nobody came? We'd end up looking plain silly.

But that press conference in Calcutta had made me realize just how powerful a tool the media can be in bringing about change. If we were going to attack the issue head on, to get moving on it, then we would need the support of ordinary people everywhere. And only through the media can you get the word out quickly and to millions of people at a time. I was convinced that if ordinary people knew the story of Nagashir, they would have to be moved. No question about it.

No one on "Team Canada," as they called themselves – not the prime minister, the eight provincial premiers, or the 250 businesspeople – had addressed any issue of human rights while on their trip. I had given the FTC office the go-ahead to contact the Prime Minister's

Office requesting a meeting with him while we were in India. His office had refused us. Twice.

I know what some people were thinking: Who the heck does this thirteen-year-old kid think he is? Doesn't he realize the prime minister has a thousand and one things to do on his trip?

But I wanted the prime minister to at least think about child labour at the same time as he was going around signing business deals. That was all. Maybe that was something I could raise at a press conference.

With the decision made to hold one, the question then became who would speak at it. I was adamant that the speakers all be children. It went against the basic principles of Free the Children to have adults speaking for kids. Our old maxim – Who can better understand and sympathize with children than children themselves? – never sounded more logical.

I thought I could speak as a representative of Canada and that we could then ask someone to speak as a representative of India. I immediately thought of Kailash's daughter, Asmita. She was ten years old, fluent in both English and Hindi, and very knowledgeable about child-labour issues. She had taken part in several protest marches with her father.

And, of course, the heart of the press conference would be child labourers speaking for themselves. We asked the staff at Mukti Ashram if two children would be able to tell their stories directly to the media. And if so, we wondered, would Nagashir be willing to be one of them?

We were told that rescued children had gone before the media in the past, and there were a number of children who, after months of rehabilitation, were strong enough to deal with such a situation. They asked Nagashir, and he was willing to do it. A second boy, Mohan, also agreed to take part. I had met Mohan at the compound and remembered him as an outgoing, talkative boy.

Now for a place to hold the press conference. For a brief moment we thought of holding it in the street, where there were working kids, but decided it would be too impractical for the media. We had no money to rent a hall.

While we were giving it more thought, we went to the Intercontinental Hotel in Delhi to talk with a Canadian press attaché about how we would go about distributing a press release to all the reporters. Could we have a list of room numbers so we could slip it under their doors?

The guy chuckled. "I think we can do it a bit more professionally than that," he said. "Where is the press conference being held?"

"Well, we haven't quite decided yet. It's proving to be a bit of a problem...."

"Are any of your group Canadian? We have a room set aside specifically for press conferences. If you're Canadian, you're entitled to use it."

"I'm Canadian!"

"I'm Canadian!"

We must have sounded like a pair of eager beavers.

"Then I see no reason why you can't use it."

We booked it on the spot for ten-thirty the following morning.

"It's used primarily for companies signing business agreements, to announce contracts," he said as we were about to leave. "Handshake photos. That kind of thing."

While all the big businesspeople from Canada were here signing deals with Indian companies, Asmita and I decided to sign one of our own – "A Joint Declaration Between the Youth of India and Canada" – an agreement on behalf of the youth of the two countries to work together and call upon their respective governments to help eliminate child labour.

That night, Alam and I ate and slept at the SACCS office. Their fax machine had been spewing out a steady stream of messages for me that day, including one from my school friends in Canada. Every student in the school had signed the fax! It ran to twenty pages, and was certainly the longest and nicest fax I received during my whole trip. It was great encouragement.

Late into the night I worked on the wording of the press release and the declaration. It had become my style to do everything at the last minute. For food we had an old standby: samosas, accompanied by water, both of which Alam had purchased from a street vendor's stall. Hot spices were not good for a stomach on the mend, but that was all there was to eat and I was hungry.

"Oh, for a jar of peanut butter," I moaned.

Asmita and I had spent an hour and a half the next morning finalizing the wording of the declaration. We were pleased with it, and now, with copies in hand, and our press release already distributed by the friendly press attaché, all we had to do was wait for the two boys from Mukti Ashram to arrive so we could all leave together.

We started to get worried. Had something happened to them? Finally, just a few minutes before the press conference was due to start, Nagashir and Mohan showed up. We jumped into the SACCS van straightaway and we drove off to the hotel.

We dashed through the lobby to where the press conference was being held. The door to the room was closed and two journalists were standing outside. I was relieved. At least someone came. Two was a lot better than none.

One of the journalists rapped on the door before opening it.

"That's to let people know you're here."

"What people?"

"We were all scheduled to leave for another event, but we've delayed the press bus to attend your conference."

The doors swung wide open, and there before us were two dozen journalists. Lights glared our way and cameras started rolling as we headed inside.

I honestly thought I had walked into the wrong room.

The microphones and cameras all had stickers on them – CTV, RDI, CBC – all the big Canadian networks. The national *Globe and Mail* newspaper was there, and even some of the business journals. I was just about to turn around.

"This is the real thing," Alam whispered to me. "You got them all."

I was too nervous to reply. I took a deep breath and walked on. We had agreed that we wouldn't use a podium or a conference table. Asmita, Mohan, and I sat on a long couch, and Nagashir sat on an adjoining chair. The media gathered in a semicircle, their microphones on a coffee table in front of us.

We all seemed so out of place. The ornate couch was covered in rich red plush. The legs of the coffee table curved elegantly to the luxurious rug on the floor. The chandeliers and fancy light fixtures on the walls... it all seemed such a strange place for four kids, especially with me in my trusty blue T-shirt, which had definitely seen better days, and Mohan in his red Teenage Mutant Ninja Turtles sweatshirt. I'm sure I smelled, and my hair probably looked like it hadn't experienced a comb in a week. Under normal circumstances, we would never have made it past the security guard in the hotel lobby.

But we were the reason all these people had gathered (some of whom I recognized from TV news shows at home), and now we had to give them what we had promised.

"Sorry we're a little late," I said. "I had trouble finding any clean clothes." It seemed to break the ice. The tension in the room dissipated. Some of the reporters settled into chairs and others sat on the rug, all with notebooks and pens in hand. They looked the part of journalists – equipment weighing them down, ties loosened, cigarettes wedged between their fingers. The cameramen and the sound technicians stood nearby, their equipment ready to roll.

"Thanks very much for coming. I have to be honest – we didn't expect quite so many people." I introduced the three other participants, then informed the media that each of us would be making a statement, after which they would be free to ask questions.

Then I turned it over to Asmita. She spoke in clear and precise English, telling the reporters of the long marches across India in which she had participated to protest child servitude. She called for a serious look at the products that Canada and other countries import, to ensure they are not made by child labourers. "I also urge the prime minister of India to use his good offices for the total elimination of child labour, and for free and compulsory education of children."

They seemed impressed by her self-assurance and fluency in English. I hoped they were taking equal note of the content of her message.

I spoke next. "It is estimated that there are 250 million children working in child servitude around the world. These children don't have a chance for education, to live a normal life, even a chance to play."

I hit them with statistics and with specific examples of child-labour practices. I told them about Free the Children and what I hoped to accomplish by taking this trip to Asia. I told them the story of Iqbal. But I kept it brief and to the point, for I knew the biggest impact would come from the statements of the two freed children. I could only tell about what I had seen and heard. Nagashir and Mohan had actually lived it.

Nagashir told his story as best he could, through a translator. I knew it was difficult for him, to be facing this barrage of reporters, none of

With Asmita and Mohan, a freed child labourer, I faced the horde of reporters. We were nervous, but we knew we had to tell as many people as possible about abusive child labour.

whom spoke his language or had ever been near a carpet factory. It was his scars that spoke when he couldn't find the words. The reporters were noticeably moved when he held out his arms and legs to show the marks left by the hot iron. He turned his neck to point out more. Perhaps the most poignant moment of the whole press conference was when he quietly sang the song, his first words after his many days of silence, and Asmita translated each verse.

Mohan was next. I had not heard his story before. Mohan would say a sentence or two in his clear and confident voice, then wait until the SACCS worker had translated them.

"I was working in a carpet factory. I was supposed to be given chapattis. We did not get them, even on a holy day.

"We didn't even get money for our work. We used to work every day for twelve hours. When we felt sleepy, they didn't even allow us to sleep. When I was sleeping, the master hit me.

"If we wanted to go to the toilet, they would go along with us with the stick. I worked with my elder brother, and when he ran away the loom owner beat me."

Mohan told them about two young children in his factory who had tried to escape. "One of the owners saw them and they were caught, and they killed them. The owner put the bodies into this car and threw them in the river. When the father of those two children came, the loom owner said, 'Your children ran away, we don't know where they are.' "

I could see the reporters writing as fast as they could, making sure they had every word.

When Mohan had finished, the first questions from the reporters, simple though they were, helped make it all the more real for them.

"How old are you now?"

"I am now nine years old," Mohan answered.

"How old were you when you started working?"

"I started working when I was five years old."

Many of the people in the room must have had children of their own. I think it was the thought of a five- or six-year-old child working at a carpet loom all day, every day, in return for nothing but punishment, that struck at the heart of these people.

The reporters had other questions. They wanted to know if I had been in touch with the prime minister.

"I have faxed and written to the prime minister requesting to meet with him and to discuss the issue of child labour and the exploitation of children. I did not get a response until yesterday. Unfortunately, he said his schedule is too booked and that he doesn't have time to meet with me. But I hope at least he will find the time to speak with working children.

"Just a few minutes would give a glimpse into their lives. I would ask him to walk down the street and stop a child who is selling fruit and say to him, 'Would you like to go to school? Do you have time to play?' Speak to an ex-bonded labourer and ask him, 'How was your life in the factory? Did you enjoy it?' "

I pointed to Nagashir and Mohan. "These children certainly didn't."

One reporter asked me, "Are you certain that you are not being exploited by adults in any way that might have some other political motive?"

"We are doing this totally on our own. There are no adults with political agendas behind us. Adults have to understand that youth do want to take action on various issues and that youth do want to become involved. Young people helping young people is what Free the Children is all about."

I answered several other questions and then brought out our "Joint Declaration Between the Youth of India and Canada."

I said to the reporters, "Here is an example of what the youth of Canada and the youth of India are doing about the issue of child labour. As a thirteen-year-old child from Canada, and as a ten-year-old child from India, we have prepared the following declaration. I will read the first part and Asmita will read the second."

A JOINT DECLARATION BETWEEN THE YOUTH OF INDIA AND CANADA

We, the children of India and Canada, would like to say that we are glad that our two countries are coming together to trade. We see this as an opportunity for growth and the building of a greater friendship between Canada and India. We think that trading will greatly benefit both countries, but there are other issues that need equal attention.

We ask our government leaders, Prime Minister P. V. Narasimha Rao and Prime Minister Jean Chrétien, and the business leaders of both

Canada and India involved in the trading negotiations this week, to remember the children. We ask that our governments live up to the promises made at the 1990 World Summit on Children, by making education and the protection of children a priority.

We ask that both countries help in the elimination of child labour and the exploitation of children:
by refusing to deal or negotiate with businesspeople that exploit children and letting them know that consumers do not want to buy products made by the exploitation of children;
by giving a clear message that both governments oppose child labour and the exploitation of children;
by looking at their trading policies and seeing what effect they have on human rights and especially child and bonded labour.

We ask that companies and corporations coming to India for trade be willing to pay their workers a fair and just wage, with rights regarding working conditions, so that children are not forced to work to supplement their families' income. That they include a clause in their trading agreements that if child labour and especially bonded labour is found then strict penalties will be enforced, and they have the right to cancel the contract. That they take every step possible to ensure that child labour and especially bonded labour is not involved in the production or distribution of their products.

We ask that free compulsory education for all children be an immediate government goal to help in the elimination of child labour. We ask that corporations taking large profits from these trade deals be willing to donate towards a fund which will help make the education of all children a reality.

The United Nations Declaration on the Rights of the Child in 1989 declared that children have the right to an education (Article 28) and the right "to be protected from economic exploitation and from performing any work that is likely to be hazardous or to interfere with the child's education or to be harmful to the child's health or physical, mental, spiritual, moral, or social development."

We, the children of India and the children of Canada, promise to work together and to support one another as we strive to promote the rights of children in our respective countries, as outlined by the United Nations Declaration on the Rights of the Child. Children all over the world have the same rights whether they live in Asia or North America, Canada or India.

We hope that this is only the beginning. Together we can achieve much on the issue of human rights. We sign this statement in the spirit of friendship and solidarity.

I had forgotten to bring a pen and had to borrow one from a reporter. Several copies of the declaration were placed on the coffee table in front of us. As I signed each one, I passed it along to Asmita for her to do the same.

I announced, "I want to give the first copies of this declaration to the two children with us who were rescued from bondage."

I presented one each to Mohan and Nagashir. I wanted this to be a symbol of hope for children. It was a commitment that we would do our best for the millions of children who were suffering as these two boys had suffered.

And with that, the news conference was over.

It was an immense relief. The media seemed pleased with what we had done. We certainly were pleased, but I had no idea how much of it would translate into actual news items. With luck, it would be a side story to all the events surrounding the prime minister. If it appeared in a newspaper or two and maybe on a TV broadcast, then we would consider it a great success.

There had been a couple of people in the room who were not media personnel, who had come in partway through the press conference. One of the reporters leaned over after the press conference and told me they were members of the prime minister's staff.

"I suspect," he said, "the PM will be getting a full report."

Newspaper reporters cornered me with further questions. It seemed no one was interested in taking the press bus to their next engagement.

We had a couple more things to do before we could call it a day. The first was to try to get a copy of the declaration we had just signed into the hands of the two prime ministers. I didn't want to leave Delhi without them being aware of what we had done.

But just how would we go about that? I had been told that the prime minister of India was hosting a state dinner for the Canadian prime minister that evening at his official residence. Why not just show up at the gates and find someone who would pass a copy of the declaration along to them? It seemed perfectly sensible to me.

The security officials at the gates had other ideas. "No, no, no. You must leave," said the fourth guard we encountered, the first one that spoke English. All the guards stood tall and straight, a wall of immaculate blue uniforms.

"But can we possibly give the declaration to a Canadian official so that he can hand it to the prime minister?"

"This is not possible. For this you must go to the Canadian embassy."

"Is there anyone from the Canadian embassy here?"

"No."

Right, I thought, it's only an official state dinner! But I could see that the security guards were rapidly running out of patience. One took a copy of the declaration and refused to give it back.

"You must leave immediately. If you do not, we will have to remove you forcibly."

"I see," I said.

"I think we should get out of here," Alam whispered between his teeth. Asmita, Nagashir, and Mohan had already decided to make a quick trip back to the van.

The guards were much bigger than we were. They had guns. They looked like they meant business. Alam and I decided it was definitely in our own best interests to move.

We retreated across the street and started filming, with the gates of the official residence in the background. "Here we are, in front of the official residence of the prime..."

The same guard showed up and made us stop the videocamera.

Our only option was to get out of his sight altogether, before we found ourselves on the wrong side of the Delhi lock-up.

We resumed the filming...in the parking lot. "Here we are *near* the official residence of the prime minister. We were stopped by security from giving our declaration to him. Asmita, myself, and Alam had all tried to explain what we were doing and the cause that it was for. Unfortunately, they gave us no sympathy."

We'd gotten nowhere. Should we give up? Should we just leave Delhi, knowing that we had failed in our mission?

"Yes!" Alam declared. "Now, let's get out of here."

"Have you no spirit of adventure?"

"You're determined to get us arrested, aren't you?" I rarely heard such a serious tone of voice from Alam.

I gave in. Still, it had been worth it. It's not every day I can say I was stopped by armed guards for trying to pass a piece of paper to my prime minister.

I don't think Mohan and Nagashir had much idea of why I had been so persistent. But by the time we dropped them off that night, we were all laughing together at our encounter with the guards.

We all shook hands at the gates of Mukti Ashram.

"Thank you both very much," I said. "The press conference would never have worked without you."

They both smiled. "You are welcome," Nagashir said.

"Maybe one day we will see each other again," Mohan added.

"I hope so."

They left us, still smiling. I think they were taking with them stories about a couple of crazy Canadians trying to get past guards with guns.

Our episode outside the prime minister's residence seemed to have set the tone for the evening. It stayed with us as we headed off to dinner in celebration of the success of the press conference.

It was also Kailash's birthday. Secretly, Alam and I ordered ice cream for him. We knew he *loved* ice cream. At our table arrived a gigantic plate of it, with nuts, fudge sauce, and sparkles. There were even candles. It was enough to feed an army.

Little did we know, but back at the prime minister's residence there was also a birthday being celebrated. The honoured guest was presented with a cake (his was chocolate, with a cream filling), and those gathered sang "Happy Birthday." January 11 was the birthday of Jean Chrétien.

I thought of him that night as I lay awake in bed, going over the events of the day. I wondered if he had any thoughts about me.

Our time in Delhi was drawing to an end. It had been a very busy few days, and I hadn't had much chance to take in the city. Most of what I saw was from inside a taxi or the SACCS van.

The massive amount of traffic and the resulting air pollution are big problems in Delhi. In fact, the city ranks second only to Mexico City as the most polluted in the world. The government is making some attempt to clean it up, and to beautify the city with freshly planted trees. "You know why this city is always planting trees," a newspaper vendor said to me. "It's because the trees don't live more than a week with this pollution!"

However, if you are able to see beyond the pollution, there is a captivating side to Delhi. The capital of India is actually two cities in one. There's Old Delhi, whose forts and monuments speak of its place as the centuries-old capital of Muslim India. Its imposing mosques include Jama Masjid, India's largest, with room for twenty-five thousand people in its courtyard.

New Delhi was built as the capital when the country was a colony of Britain. Its wide avenues and neo-classical buildings proclaim the grandeur of the old British Empire. I was more interested, however, in seeking out a monument not to the colonial past, but to one of this century's greatest leaders, the man who led India through its turbulent years leading to independence in 1947.

Mahatma Gandhi is one of my heroes. His belief that non-violent resistance could overcome suppression was a principle I had read much about. It had certainly influenced my own view of how the world must go about solving its political problems. I knew I could not leave Delhi without visiting Raj Ghat, the memorial to him built on the site of his cremation.

I was greatly disappointed by the entrance to the memorial. Vendors selling everything from peanuts to shoeshines crowded the area around the gates. Hindi music blared from a gift shop, whose bold sign advertised "Gandhi video cassettes. Gandhi's favourite devotional songs. Gandhi's diary. Gandhi photos."

Once past the gates and inside the high stone walls, however, it was as if the outside world had dropped away. The tranquillity drew me into the mind of the man and the tremendous influence he had on his country and the world. Carved into a marble wall are his words:

Recall the face of the poorest and the most helpless man whom you may have seen and ask yourself if the step you contemplate is going to be of any use to him. Will he be able to gain anything by it? Will it restore him to a control over his own life and destiny? In other words, will it lead to swaraj or self-rule for the hungry and also spiritually starved millions of our countrymen? Then you will find your doubts and yourself melting away.

With these words alone, he had said so much. If the leaders of the world would only listen.

I walked slowly along one of the stone paths leading to the eternal flame that marked his cremation site. The black marble base of the monument was strewn with richly coloured flowers, small tokens of the affection in which he is held. A true affection, like that for Mother Teresa, also lay in the hearts of people who could not afford the flowers, but who knew that the greatest leaders never forgot them – the poor and the helpless.

I remembered the flame later that day when at Kailash's house the family gathered round to offer their prayers, as part of their religion.

Kailash had put wood shavings and a scattering of herbs into a small metal bowl. "It is not fire we worship," he explained. "Fire is a symbol. All of us have a fire within us, but there is a need to ignite it. That fire will help to purify the mind, the heart, the soul."

He sprinkled water around the bowl. "Water is life; the earth is life. We must not waste water; we must not destroy earth. The whole universe is one, and the creator of the universe is the one god who is almighty, who is merciful. We pray for wisdom and strength so that the entire world is like a family.

"And whatever we work through our hands should be sacred and good."

Then he struck a match to the contents of the bowl. The fire lit the darkness.

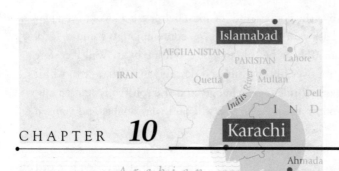

CHAPTER **10**

Karachi and Islamabad

We had mixed feelings about going to Pakistan. I had no doubt I wanted to go; visiting the place where Iqbal had lived and seeing his grave were one of the first things I wrote down when I drew up my itinerary.

But I was told that Pakistan is not always a safe country. A number of human-rights workers I had met advised me against a visit. Pakistanis who had spoken out on child-labour issues had been beaten, imprisoned, or had disappeared altogether. And after all, they pointed out, it was the place where Iqbal was murdered.

I didn't tell my parents all of this. They had known before I left that I would have to take extra precautions while in the country. They also knew how much I wanted to go to Iqbal's village.

When we arrived in the port city of Karachi, it was night. Darkness only added to our concerns, so we decided it was best to get in touch with our contact straightaway. We went in search of a pay phone, but discovered that the lines were all dead. We were told that because of the flourishing drug trade, the city had shut down all public phones, since the police had no way to tap them.

We did find a phone that we could use in a store.

"You've arrived at the worst possible time," we were told by our contact, a Canadian journalist who was visiting her parents in Karachi.

"Because of the elections, there's been a lot of ethnic unrest. Several protestors have been murdered. Be very careful." She suggested a hotel in the centre of the city, one that was safe and reasonably priced.

We grabbed a taxi and headed for the Metropole Hotel. As we inched along in the "donkey-to-bumper" traffic, our driver warned us not to roll down our windows and to be sure to keep the car doors locked at all times.

Our hotel room was a little classier than we had been used to (it actually came with its own bathroom), and the price a little steeper. But for that extra measure of security, it was definitely worth it.

In the daylight, Karachi looked like a city under siege. Because of the ethnic unrest, there were police officers on every street corner. We learned that the head of one of the Muslim groups had been assassinated. Rallies and demonstrations were breaking out across the city, and the police suspected there would be killings in retaliation, leading to even greater violence.

Often the officers stood inside sandbag bunkers, and we sometimes saw only their helmets bobbing up and down as they paced around inside. A few of the shelters had their domestic touches – in one case the occupant had tied a blanket overhead, supported by a dead tree, to protect him from the rain and hot sun.

We headed across the city to the offices of the Pakistani Institute for Labour and Education Research (PILER). There had been unseasonably heavy rain overnight, and many of the streets were under a foot or more of water. Our drive was delayed several times, but it was worth the effort. The well-informed staff at PILER had strong opinions on the problem of child labour in their country. They told us that UNICEF and the ILO put the estimate at eight million labouring children in Pakistan.

According to some organizations, they added, 80 per cent of the workers in the carpet industry are below the age of fifteen. By Pakistani law, child labour was absolutely forbidden in these factories, but in practice the employers were never punished.

"Punishment is not the only solution," we were told. "If you punish them, they will simply throw the children out. Then what will there be for these children to do? What we need are alternatives, alternatives which at the moment are not there."

I had heard this opinion expressed in other countries, of course. There had to be a movement to employ adults, and, equally important, a movement to provide more educational opportunities for children.

"What percentage of the government's budget is spent on education?" I asked.

"Education and health together, they are not spending more than 4 per cent. That is education *and* health, mind you. And not just for children. That is the entire population: men, women, children."

"And on the military?"

"Thirty-eight to 40 per cent."

The gap between the two was astounding. I knew that relations between Pakistan and its neighbours were not good, but I had never realized so much money was spent just to defend Pakistan's borders. It is not only in war that children suffer; the mere threat of war is enough.

The staff at PILER were equally disturbed by the actions of the World Bank and the International Monetary Fund (IMF).

"They create conditions that must be met if we are to get loans. They dictate the policies of our country. They only want us to devalue our currency, to cut down on our import duties. Then, if we follow these conditions, we become poorer and we need to get more loans. That is what they want, they want to lend us more money. And then take the interest. And the poorer we get, the more indebted we become."

"Why don't the rich countries and the World Bank and the IMF give us relief and write off some of the loans?" they asked. "The fact is, we've already paid them many times over because of the high interest rates."

I was no economist, and didn't feel I had enough information to understand the problem fully. But I could see their point. Was it a case of the rich wanting to maintain their wealth, and not caring what went on in the Third World? Was this bonded labour on an international scale, with high interest rates keeping countries poor, with no hope of ever repaying their loans? Perhaps it was the officials of the World Bank and the IMF who needed to visit the carpet factories.

"What guarantee is there that any money saved from reducing the military budget or writing off loans would go to benefit children?" Alam asked. It was a concern we had both discussed.

"We must have a proper national policy in place. There have to be international agreements. Let the World Bank and the IMF say to the government, You must change, you must bring about land reform so that 5 per cent of the population does not control 95 per cent of the resources of this country. A feudal system is running this country. These ruling classes don't want change; they want everything for themselves. They wield all the political power, the economic power."

I could see the frustration in their faces. I could see the years of hard work and so little change in a country that desperately needed it. I tried to bring the discussion back to child labour.

"But you can't just separate the issues," came the reply. "No one problem can be solved right away. Child labour can't be isolated from the solution of other problems."

Clearly, the cause of child labour was not to be found solely in the country where it was taking place. Were we not all to blame, the people of the rich countries as well as the poor? Didn't it come down to a matter of greed? That we all wanted as big a piece of the pie as possible, no matter how little was left for others?

"Change can come only when people unite and fight for it."

These words, spoken near the conclusion of our meeting, were the ones that stayed with me longest. I was left to wonder how many people in Pakistan were viewing things the same way.

Unfortunately, we were not able to meet with other groups in Karachi. Due to the political strife, our attempts to set up further meetings were unsuccessful. So we decided it was probably best to see if we could catch a flight that evening to Islamabad.

Late that afternoon, my mother and I were finally able to get in touch with one another. She called the home of our contact, where we had arrived for dinner.

These calls always filled Alam with anxiety, because my mother invariably had me call him to the phone so she could remind him, yet again, to be sure I was eating well and getting plenty of sleep.

Alam would roll his eyes and I would have to struggle to keep from laughing out loud. It was only maternal instinct, I explained after each call. "It's a mother's job to worry about these things. Would *your* mother have let *you* travel through South Asia when you were thirteen?"

After Alam, it would be my turn to speak to her again. She'd need confirmation directly from the horse's mouth. What exactly are you eating? Are you sure you're safe? How sick were you? Are you okay now? Was there nothing in the medical kit that might have helped?

That afternoon, though, she quickly moved on to something else.

"Your story is all over the papers! The press conference was the lead story on all the TV news shows! It was even on CNN! And at an official dinner, Chrétien said Canada would be open to looking at new ways to combat child labour."

"Really?" I could hardly believe it. "That's fantastic!"

"The press people have been phoning here all day. Everyone in Delhi is looking for you," she said.

"What do you mean? Who's everyone?"

"The press, the Prime Minister's Office, everyone."

"Why?"

"Don't you know? The newspapers are all saying the prime minister agreed to meet with you."

"That's impossible! No one told us anything about a meeting!"

Of course, we *had* left very early the morning after the press conference.

"Well, apparently the media cornered him on the issue and he changed his mind. Now they are saying he wanted to set up the meeting when you were in Delhi, but then you left."

"You're joking! They could easily have found out where we were staying. Or contacted you."

We talked for a while longer, but Alam could hardly wait for me to hang up. I told him all the details.

"How were we supposed to know?" he groaned.

But I had saved the best part for last. "I'll give you three guesses where the prime minister is stopping next on his trip."

Alam looked at me and laughed. "Don't tell me Islamabad."

I paused for a moment. "Islamabad."

Once again the hand of fate had pointed us in the right direction.

We sat down to dinner, still shaking our heads at how things had worked out.

The next morning we arrived in Islamabad, a thousand kilometres to the north. As the capital of Pakistan, the city is home to all the major aid agencies. And one of my reasons for coming to Islamabad was to meet with UNICEF.

Islamabad is not your typical Pakistani city. It was built specifically as the capital. Careful planning and a location at the foot of the Margalla mountain range had made it an attractive seat of government.

Even after driving past the numerous modern buildings on the city's broad, tree-lined avenues, I was surprised by the sight of the office tower where the UNICEF offices are located. As the home of an aid agency, it seemed extravagant, with marble floors and elaborate architectural details – more like the home of a rich multinational corporation than the branch of an organization whose mandate is to help the undernourished and destitute kids of the world.

We stepped off the elevator onto the third floor and walked over more marble and under a chandelier. As the stone floor gave way to plush carpeting, we were led down a hallway to the office of the director.

It was the biggest office I had ever seen. One whole side was glass, with a spectacular view of the city. There was a huge desk, and several pieces of fine furniture were scattered around the room, including a richly upholstered sofa and chairs arranged to form a separate meeting area. The director shook our hands and greeted us warmly.

I knew that UNICEF was doing some good work around the world, and that it was crucial to have a global children's organization supported by national governments. And nobody would suggest the employees of aid agencies should not work in comfort and safety. Yet I was greatly bothered by what surrounded me at the headquarters of UNICEF Pakistan. It was all I could think of as we sat there, sipping tea with the director. It seemed to be yet another case of a human-rights organization working out of fancy offices far removed from the people they are set up to help.

It was a relief to be going out into the streets. Before long we had met a nine-year-old boy working as an electrician, another boy sweeping the streets, and a group of street children.

A little later we heard a banging sound, metal against metal. It appeared to be coming from the back of an automobile repair shop. As

This boy works as an electrician in Pakistan. Many children begin work as apprentices at a very young age. When work becomes abusive, or is exploitative, or prevents a child from going to school, then the world must speak up in defence of the child.

we walked to the back of the dimly lit shop we came upon two boys. One looked to be about eight, the other ten. The older boy was holding a screwdriver in his hand and leaning under the hood of a car.

He had come from a remote, tribal region of Pakistan, and had been working as a shepherd in his village. "His relatives decided to send him here so he could learn something better than just being a shepherd," we were told.

"Are you well treated?" I asked the boy.

He looked up at his boss, then back at me. "Yes," he said.

"He is learning a trade here," the boss told us.

When I asked the boy how much he made, he only smiled. He wasn't willing to tell.

"Would you like to go to school?"

"I want to learn the training, but I would like to learn other things, too, like reading and math."

"In another five or six years he will be an actual worker," his boss said. "Then he will get a full wage."

The boy was smiling; he seemed reasonably happy. It was certainly not the abusive work of places such as fireworks factories. And if he had to work to help support his family, it was good that he was at least learning a trade. Yet here was an example of how little value was being put on education. It seemed to be an accepted practice that children of an age for primary schooling were instead in the workplace "training" for a job. The Pakistani government's lack of commitment to education had created a situation where children were being denied a basic right, and everyone accepted it as normal.

When I looked up and down the wide avenues of Islamabad, when I glimpsed the lavish interiors of its office buildings and the homes of the rich inside their high-walled compounds, I couldn't help but conclude that this was a "showcase" city. Like many capital cities of the world, it didn't reflect the realities of everyday life throughout the country. You only had to go a few streets away from the fancy buildings and towering monuments to find children born into a life of poverty and neglect.

A reporter from Reuters told me where we would find Prime Minister Chrétien. The press reports had said that the PM was willing to meet with me, but no invitation had ever been sent our way. So, how do you arrange a meeting with the head of your country? In this case, you go to the hotel where the PM is staying and look for something called the PMO: the Prime Minister's Office. Actually, in this case, a makeshift PMO.

We arrived at the predictably ritzy hotel and were directed to a hallway, where we found a door with a sign saying, "The Canadian Office."

Alam knocked at the door, twice. A woman opened it, then walked back to her desk without looking at us.

"Excuse me, is this the PMO?" I was getting used to the lingo.

She was busy with some files, and was still not looking our way. "Yes. Can I help you?"

"We are trying to arrange a meeting with the prime minister...," I began.

She glanced up, with a look that said, I really don't need this bother. Who are these people, anyway?

"Really? A meeting with the prime minister?"

At that moment, Alam (who by this point on the trip was pulling out his camera anywhere and everywhere) stood back and snapped a picture of the woman.

"Would you tell your Asian friend that I do not appreciate having my picture taken!"

"I apologize," Alam said. "By the way, you can tell me yourself. I'm Canadian."

"And so am I," I chimed in.

"I'm afraid I don't have time for this." Her level of irritation had taken a sudden jump. "I will find someone else to speak with you."

She walked into another room. We waited, and when she didn't return, we ventured to the door to the next room and found her reading a file, half sitting on a desk. Near her was a young man, reading another file.

"Excuse me, but we do need to talk to someone about meeting with the prime minister."

The woman pointed to the man next to her without saying a word.

I continued, "We had tried to schedule a meeting some time ago with the prime minister, but were unable to do so."

The woman smiled to herself.

"But the Canadian media reported that the PM had agreed to the meeting after all, and wanted to schedule it in Delhi. The problem was that we were not informed of the new meeting and we left the country. Is it now possible to reschedule the meeting for Islamabad?"

"You have to understand that the prime minister is a very busy person, and he doesn't have the time to meet with everyone," the fellow said. "His schedule is completely full. I am sorry, but it's not possible."

I am sure they were both hoping we would just go away and leave them alone, that I was just some kid making a nuisance of himself. They hadn't taken seriously one word I'd said. The man had already gone back to his reading.

"Could we at least leave a note for someone to look over?"

"Just leave it in that box." He pointed to an overflowing box of memos, faxes, and thick documents.

Alam found me a pen and a piece of paper.

Dear Mr. Chrétien:

My name is Craig Kielburger and I am thirteen years old, from Toronto. I recently held a press conference in New Delhi on the issue of child labour. The press reported that you had agreed to a meeting with me in that city. I am very sorry but I was not able to attend the meeting because nobody told me it was taking place. I would still love to meet you if you can find the time.

I then listed all the ways that I could be contacted. I looked at the overflowing box and asked if I could possibly deliver this to one of the prime minister's aides personally.

By this time, the man and woman could barely keep a straight face. "Anywhere on the fourth floor you should be able to find someone who can help you." She pointed to the door and waved her hand to the left.

We turned around and quietly left the room. I was tempted to wait outside to hear if there was an eruption of laughter, but we pushed on.

What they had failed to tell us was that the entire fourth floor was reserved for the prime minister and his entourage, and was therefore entirely off limits. Within seconds of stepping out of the elevator we were in the hands of two members of the Royal Canadian Mounted Police.

When we tried to explain about the meeting, they rolled their eyes and led us down the hallway.

"The Mounties always get their man," I whispered to Alam.

"And their boy," he countered.

They weren't mean or trying to intimidate us; they thought we were pulling a prank. But what we couldn't figure out was how we had been able to make it to the fourth floor in the first place if it was such a high-security zone.

We were brought to the head RCMP officer.

"We found these two wandering the halls," said one of our escorts.

"They tell us they're trying to schedule a meeting with the prime minister," added the other.

"Reschedule," I corrected him.

We started to explain the situation to the officer in charge. He looked at us and shook his head. "Leave them with me."

He took us to his room, which was also being used as an office. I could see the famous scarlet Mountie uniform hanging in his open closet, and the trademark hat on the top shelf. We sat on the edge of the bed and started to explain the story.

The officer peered at us rather sceptically. But our story was so unbelievable, how could he possibly think we were making it up?

The officer opened a small case and removed a two-way radio. He began to speak in French. We sat quietly and listened. He had no idea that both Alam and I understood French.

"Yeah, I found these two guys wandering the halls of the fourth floor," he said. "What should I do with them?"

"Get an officer to escort them out of the building," came the gruff reply from the other end, also in French.

Alam looked at me and said, "It doesn't look good."

"Well, it's not that simple. They say they missed a meeting with the prime minister in Delhi and they want to reschedule it."

There was a long silence at the other end.

"Describe them to me." There was a noticeable irritation in his voice.

"One's about twelve or thirteen, white, and the other's around twenty-six or twenty-seven maybe, and he's Asian. They both speak English."

Et français, I was tempted to say, but thought it wiser to keep my mouth shut.

The voice on the other end returned. "Did they say anything about a press conference?"

"Yeah."

There was a long pause. Alam looked at me and smiled.

"Get their phone number and tell them we might be in touch."

The officer put the radio back in the case and turned to us. "I need your..."

Alam was already holding out the note I had written downstairs. "The phone numbers where we can be reached in Islamabad and at home in Canada are all here," he said.

The officer looked at us and frowned.

"Can we have a phone number where we can call to see if there is going to be a meeting?" I asked.

"No, we call you. There is no other way."

He summoned the same two officers who had first discovered us, and asked them to escort us down to the lobby. He was smiling. It was obvious that he, too, found the situation all very amusing.

We thanked him. And as I was leaving I added, "*Au revoir. À bientôt.*"

The following day a call came from the PMO. A man introduced himself as a member of the prime minister's staff. He said Mr. Chrétien would be pleased to meet with me on January 16. It would have to be a short meeting, about fifteen minutes. Could he confirm my intention to attend?

"Yes, of course. When exactly on the sixteenth?"

"I'm afraid I'll have to call you later with the details."

The next day a second call came through from the same man. The time had been set for eight-thirty in the morning.

"I'll be there."

The room where the meeting would take place would remain a secret until we arrived at the hotel.

With less than two days to go, I had a lot of preparation to do. Alam and I began by going through what, over the course of our trip, had come to be known as "the box." It was a duct-taped, warped, and water-stained arrangement of cardboard, containing the many documents we had accumulated since the start of our travels.

It was a daunting task. We quickly realized that there was no way I was going to absorb all that material. I put away the documents and took out a blank sheet of paper and began to list, in order of importance, what I should discuss with the prime minister.

In the meantime, Alam continued to read through the contents of "the box." But soon he put it all aside and said, "Trust me, you're ready."

Alam and I talked about the meeting at great length, and I had discussions with the director of UNICEF in order to get more background on several of the issues I wanted to raise. UNICEF had recently instituted a policy that the organization would not purchase products from any company that did not respect the rights of children as outlined in the UN Convention on the Rights of the Child. This was the same policy I wanted Canada to adopt.

It wasn't until the morning of the meeting that I began to feel nervous. Yet I knew the prime minister was really just another person. I had read somewhere that he was the eighteenth child in his family. I knew he couldn't help but understand children and would not disagree that they all had basic rights, whether they lived in Canada or Asia. It was as simple as that: if I could just convey to him the seriousness of the situation, how so many children were suffering needlessly, then there was no way he would not do something about it. Unless he had a heart of stone, he couldn't just ignore the issue of child labour.

We arrived in the lobby of the hotel twenty minutes early. I was immediately set upon by reporters. A "scrum," they call it. I remembered my brother, Marc, using the term when he talked about rugby. This was a scrum of a different sort, though I did notice a similarity between journalists and rugby players. They swarmed around me with their microphones and cameras and notepads, all vying for a good position, and bombarded me with questions.

What issues are you planning to raise with the prime minister? What action would you like him to take? Where are you travelling next? What do you plan to do when you get back to Canada?

They came from all sides. I hardly knew where to turn. "Look into the camera," one of them kept saying.

I felt out of place standing in the opulent hotel lobby, with its elegant furniture and beautiful paintings, as I waited for my meeting with Jean Chrétien, the Canadian prime minister. The TV reporters were constantly telling me to "Look directly into the camera! Speak clearly into the microphone! Step to your right! Tilt your head ... now smile!"

As quickly as they attacked, they were gone again, this time swarming around a woman who had appeared in the lobby. Her husband had been detained as a suspect in a bombing and she wanted Chrétien to intervene on his behalf. As I viewed them from a distance, the journalists reminded me not of rugby players, but of lions attacking their prey.

Actually, most of the journalists were very pleasant to me. They went out of their way to chat when there was a little free time. We talked about jet lag and getting sick from the food. What I appreciated most was the fact that they took me seriously, that they didn't treat what I was doing as some human-interest story. They knew I was concerned about an important issue and they dealt with it in that way.

"When you're finished, make sure you come back out here so we can talk to you," one of them said as it drew near to the time for the meeting. "A quarter to nine. No joking. We need to talk to you."

Alam and I waited in the hotel lobby – amid the potted plants, the brass and marble – for the word to proceed upstairs. I took off my sweatshirt. I would be chatting to the prime minister in blue pants and running shoes and a T-shirt with a small maple-leaf crest joined to the Olympic rings.

A member of the prime minister's staff came looking for us and led the way up to the fourth floor. We passed the same two guards we had met before. They smiled and we did the same, only more broadly. We were each given the once-over by Security and a offered a glass of orange juice.

"No bags. And no cameras or recording devices. Mr. Chrétien will be ready to meet you in about five minutes. Remember, the meeting will be for fifteen minutes, no longer. When I come and knock on the door, that means the meeting will have to wrap up."

"I feel like I'm in school," I whispered to Alam.

"The ultimate learning experience," he said, chuckling.

Alam and I had joked a lot about meeting the prime minister, but suddenly I was within a couple of minutes of doing it, and it dawned on me that this was something extraordinary. I was about to come face-to-face with the political leader of my country, the most influential man in all of Canada. I looked at Alam and managed a weak smile.

The staff member returned. The moment had come. Alam and I stood up.

"Just you," he said, pointing to me. "Your friend will have to wait here."

This is not what we had planned. I wanted Alam for moral support. "Excuse me, but Alam is more than a friend. He is my chaperone, and it was my understanding that he would be able to sit in the room while the meeting is taking place."

"I'm sorry, but there is to be no third party."

"Alam will not be speaking, but I'm afraid he must be present. We are a team."

After a little pleading from me and reassurance from Alam that he would not be taking part in the discussions, the fellow gave in. He nodded to two RCMP officers, who then walked with us down a hallway to a closed door. The little dispute to include Alam had eased the tension. Suddenly, I wasn't feeling so nervous.

I closed my eyes and took a deep breath as one of the officers raised his hand to knock on the door. I opened my eyes again and all of a sudden I found myself inside.

The prime minister reached for my hand and shook it vigorously, and in the next instant we were posing for an official photograph. He had greeted me like a long-lost friend.

We took our places at a long table – Mr. Chrétien at the head, me to his right, and an adviser to his left. The photographer and Alam quietly took seats at the other end, some distance away.

I sat close to the edge of my chair so my feet would touch the floor. I cleared my throat. "Mr. Chrétien, thank you very much for finding the time to..."

I had hardly started to speak when Mr. Chrétien, leaning back in his chair to get comfortable, almost fell backwards. At the last second, one hand flew to the side of the table, the other to the arm of the chair. He had recovered just in time.

I didn't know what to do. Should I smile? Should I say something about the faulty chair?

The prime minister smiled weakly. He chuckled a little. It seemed to break the ice.

"Mr. Chrétien, I realize that you are an extremely busy person, and I want to thank you for the opportunity to meet with you."

He congratulated me on the work of Free the Children, and made a point of mentioning some specific things we had done. He had been well briefed.

I had only fifteen minutes, and I wanted to make sure we didn't waste it on casual conversation. I thanked him for his compliments and moved on. "Mr. Chrétien, as you know, Canada has been a leader on human-rights issues in the past. However, there is a new issue that Canada must take the lead on, and that is the rights of the child. I feel that your trip is a wonderful opportunity for our country to really show we are concerned about this issue."

At this point, Alam, who had been sitting to one side, slipped a compact camera out of his pants pocket and stood up to take a picture. He flipped up the flash and moved in to get a close-up of Mr. Chrétien. Hadn't he been told just minutes before that cameras were forbidden? My friend, the renegade in track pants.

What could the prime minister do? He seemed surprised, maybe a little shocked. His adviser winced.

Eventually Mr. Chrétien just smiled and let Alam have his picture. I think he even found it amusing.

I was determined to keep the meeting on track. "Mr. Chrétien, in a letter your office sent to me a couple of months ago, you stated that whenever possible you would raise the issue of human rights and, specifically, child labour. It would seem to me that this trip is the perfect opportunity."

"Of course, we try to raise the issue when we can," he responded. "However, you have to understand that we are guests in this country. When this trip is over we will have strengthened our relations. That is when the issue of human rights can be better addressed."

He was avoiding the question. I decided I had to push the issue. "I'm suggesting Canada could adopt the policy that UNICEF has put in place. It is based on the UN Convention on the Rights of the Child, which, as you know, Canada has signed. UNICEF's policy forbids the purchase of goods from companies that violate their country's child-labour laws. Would Canada not consider adopting this same policy?"

"We are slowly making progress on this issue, Craig. But things are not always as simple as they seem. Take P.E.I. potatoes, for example. P.E.I. potatoes are the best in the world. Have you tried them?"

"I'm not sure...," I said, resisting the urge to scratch my head.

"Well, some countries have banned this great Canadian potato, or imposed large tariffs. Why? They will tell you lots of reasons, but what they really want to do is protect their own markets. It's the same thing with Spanish shoes. The Spanish make wonderful shoes."

I didn't doubt it. But what did they have to do with child labour?

"But the countries of the European Union are banning them because they say Spain is not protecting its environment. But what are they really out to do...? Protect their own market. So we have to be very careful. If we boycott, or we impose fines on products that are made with child labour, other countries will accuse us of discriminating against them."

Potatoes from Prince Edward Island? Spanish shoes? Why put them in the same class with the violation of human rights?

"But if you had a blanket policy that linked all trade to human rights," I said, "you couldn't be accused of discriminating against any one country or product."

He seemed to listen to what I was saying. He nodded politely, but avoided making any direct comment.

"It's a very complicated issue," he said. "Things like this take time. Of course, Canada is addressing this issue by giving money to the World Trade Organization..."

I looked at him, confused. His adviser made a quick note on a scrap of paper and handed it to him.

"...Of course I meant the ILO, the International Labour Organization."

I realized that the prime minister was confronted with hundreds of issues each day, and I certainly didn't expect him to be an expert on each one.

I almost felt sorry for him. Sometimes his eyes were half closed and he looked weary. I knew he hadn't wanted to meet with me, that he had been pressured into it by the press attention. He had been travelling from country to country, attending dozens of meetings without a break.

He came to life when, for a few minutes, he got caught up in singing the praises of Canada. How we do have problems, but they are nothing compared to what developing countries such as Pakistan have to face. And how he had been visiting a Canadian-funded project and had seen all these mud huts, and the people living in poverty, and how when he returns to Canada he will remember these things and remember what a great country we live in.

I really wanted to interrupt him to say that because we are so fortunate, then we have a responsibility to those suffering human-rights abuses. But by that time, the fifteen minutes were nearly up. I was determined to get a firm answer on one question, a distinct yes or no.

"But, Mr. Chrétien, will you bring up the issue of child labour with the South Asian governments?"

I waited for his answer, not holding out much hope. I thought he'd just say he would take my point under serious consideration, or something equally noncommittal. He, too, realized the meeting was coming to an end. In a minute he would be free of me.

And then, for a few seconds, it seemed he was suddenly tired of playing the politician. He shrugged off any doubts about what he should say.

"Yes. Yes, I will bring up the issue. And yes, child labour will be on the agenda."

I was a little stunned. It was almost as if he had said, To heck with my advisers, let the kid have his way. Or, You know what? You're right. Child labour *is* a horrible thing. No child should have to go through that.

I felt I was seeing the real Mr. Chrétien, the fellow who grew up with so many children in his family, the fighter on the streets of Shawinigan, Quebec.

The knock came on the door. Alam checked his watch...right on time. The meeting had come to an end.

The prime minister stood up for another photo with me. Alam stood next to the photographer and took another one for our records. I thanked the prime minister for his time and wished him good luck on the remainder of his trip. He wished me luck in return.

Alam and I were escorted back to the elevators. When the door opened into the lobby, we were met by an avalanche of reporters. So many, in fact, that for a minute it looked as if I wouldn't be able to get out.

They all wanted to know how the meeting had gone, what we had discussed, whether Mr. Chrétien had made any promises.

I will never forget the surprised expression on the PM's face as I stepped into his path. With the cameras flashing, I extended my hand, which he took with a strong grip. He then introduced me to his wife, Aline, and we spoke briefly.

"He said he would be bringing up the issue of child labour with the South Asian governments," I told them. "And he did say that Canada is looking seriously at adopting the system of labelling carpets that guarantees they are made without child labour. I was, however, disappointed that Mr. Chrétien wouldn't agree to making any long-term commitment."

People from the PMO had emerged from the elevator behind us to say that the prime minister would be leaving the hotel in less than one minute. Suddenly all of the reporters were asking me if I would stand in a certain spot so I could greet the prime minister as he went by. They wanted a photograph of the two of us together.

The elevator doors opened. The entourage emerged, led by three members of the RCMP. A few paces back walked Mr. Chrétien, his elegantly dressed wife, Aline, at his side.

"Hello, Mr. Prime Minister," I said, stepping his way. "It's nice to see you again."

He looked pleased to see me. He stopped, bringing the entourage to a halt. He introduced me to his wife. Every camera was flashing.

The entourage moved on quickly, the reporters trailing behind. Alam and I were abandoned in its wake, left to contemplate for a moment all that had happened.

"How do you feel the meeting went overall?" Alam asked.

"This is a chance for Canada to lead the way on this issue. But it didn't sound to me like our government is willing to do that."

Alam nodded as we made our way out of the hotel.

We were just in time to see a stream of limos disappear down the street. I hoped the prime minister was taking time to look out his window. Perhaps he would glimpse a working child.

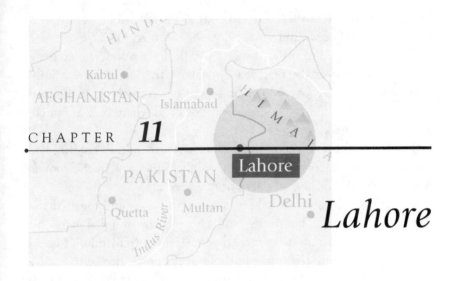

CHAPTER **11**

Lahore

Lahore

LATER THAT DAY, WE BOARDED a bus for Lahore. The ride would save a few hundred dollars in plane fare. With still two weeks to the end of my trip, I had to make a little money go a long way.

There was only one stop for food and a trip to the washroom. Partway to Lahore, the driver announced our arrival at a small restaurant. Alam and I went inside. I ordered a curried soup, while Alam decided on a lighter snack and some jasmine tea.

Before we had a chance to taste our food, we caught sight of the bus pulling away from the restaurant, heading towards the main road! We tossed our money on the table and made a mad dash out the door.

Jumping aboard the bus, a few more passengers scurrying on behind us, we stared at the driver in astonishment. He ignored us, shifted the bus into higher gear, and drove on.

Only later did we discover the reason for his crazy behaviour. Apparently, bus drivers expect a little money from a restaurant owner for bringing their passengers by. In this case the owner refused to pay, so the driver just up and left.

The bus ride gave me plenty of time to reflect on my meeting with Prime Minister Chrétien. I thought that, generally, it had gone well.

How successful it really was depended on just what action Mr. Chrétien would be willing to take once he returned to Canada.

My mind turned to other things. Specifically, I wondered what we would discover over the next few days about the life of Iqbal Masih. Lahore was the city where Iqbal had spent much of his short life, and the town of Muridke, where Iqbal was born and where he was buried, was only fifty-six kilometres away.

I had thought much about Iqbal since our arrival in Pakistan. I had begun to hear rumours that the story of Iqbal I had read in the *Toronto Star* that April morning was not entirely accurate.

As we rode the bus to Lahore, I closed my eyes and recalled the newspaper article. The words, and the picture of Iqbal with his clenched fist in the air, were etched permanently in my mind. I could hardly bear to think that some of those words might not be true.

But that's exactly what the director of UNICEF had told me in Islamabad. "The true story of Iqbal is much different than what was reported in the international press," he said. "Here, you should read it for yourself." He handed me the report of an inquiry into Iqbal's death written by the Human Rights Commission of Pakistan.

The contents of that report left me reeling.

Iqbal Masih – my hero, the boy who had motivated me to become involved in the issue of child labour and whose story I told in each and every one of my speeches – was a fraud?

I couldn't digest the news; it was like a heavy rock in the pit of my stomach. As I knew that I couldn't leave Pakistan without trying to discover who Iqbal Masih really was and how he was killed.

While in Islamabad, we were given access to all the UNICEF files on Iqbal. We scoured them for details. Gradually, we began to piece together a story.

Iqbal Masih had become an international spokesperson for children's rights through his contact with the Bonded Labour Liberation Front (BLLF), an organization that for years had led the fight to free Pakistani workers from slave labour.

The roots of the organization went back thirty years. It was in 1967 that a student, Ehsan Ullah Khan, first began to organize workers to fight against their enslaved labour in brick kilns. Khan had discovered that entire families worked twelve to fifteen hours a day in the torrid heat to repay small loans from the brick-kiln owners that had been taken out years, and sometimes generations, earlier. These debts, called *peshgi*, increased with each passing day. Workers were charged for mistakes they made, no matter how small. They were charged for their food, often at rates many times its actual cost. They were paid nothing for days they could not work, such as during the rainy season. Original loans of fifteen hundred rupees often rose to thirteen thousand rupees and more. Families had no recourse; they were trapped. They were treated like property that could be bought and sold. Many were physically and sexually abused, or, when they fell ill, were denied medical care.

In 1987, workers in one of the brick kilns spoke out against their owner, who, it was said, often tortured the labourers and raped the women and children. When the master decided to sell the wife of one of the labourers to another brick-kiln owner, the workers rebelled. In retaliation, it was reported, the owner chained the children, whipped many of the men, and tied a pregnant woman to a wagon and then dragged her across the site.

Khan moved in to help the workers organize, and to bring the case to the Supreme Court as a violation against the constitution of Pakistan. Teaming up with Asthma Jahangir, a young female lawyer and general secretary with the Human Rights Commission of Pakistan, Khan convinced one of the workers, Darshan Masih, to testify against the brick-kiln owner. In September 1988, the verdict was declared in favour of the workers and a new law was passed that declared the *peshgi* illegal.

It was a great victory. Immediately, Khan and his group, the Bonded Labour Liberation Front, began to reproduce and distribute copies of the new law.

Public demonstrations and pressure by Khan and the BLLF led to another Supreme Court decision on March 11, 1992. It proclaimed: "The bonded labour system shall stand abolished and every bonded labourer shall stand free and discharged from any obligation to render any bonded labour."

But in spite of the new law, bonded labour continued. Khan and his people renewed their efforts. They travelled throughout the villages of Pakistan to spread the news among the workers, especially the children.

Stories differ as to how Khan first met Iqbal. It is said that in September 1992, a demonstration was organized in Shekhupura, a city west of Lahore, in the state of Punjab. Khan's people visited the brick kilns and the carpet factories to invite the workers to attend.

Munnawar Virk, a lawyer with the BLLF, walked up and down the streets of Haddoquay, a village not far from the planned demonstration. In one of the carpet factories, he stopped to speak to the person who ran it, a man named Arshad.

Two of the children working as bonded labourers in the factory, Iqbal Masih and his brother Patras Masih, decided to skip work and attend the demonstration.

Iqbal had been working as a bonded labourer for Arshad since 1986. His mother had sold Iqbal into bondage to help pay for the wedding of an older son, Aslam. This was not unusual in Pakistan, where a type of feudal system existed. Poor families often had no alternative but to pledge their children's labour to raise funds for marriages or to pay for medical bills. Middlemen would travel from village to village, searching for children to work in the carpet factories and the brick kilns. They would lend parents a small sum, with the promise of more money in the future or the chance for the child to learn a skill. But, just as in the brick kilns, the child and the family became entrapped for years with little hope of escape, and a debt that continued to soar.

Although Iqbal and the other children were the ones who made the carpets, it was a long list of people who actually benefited from their labours: the middlemen who had found the children and indebted their families with the *peshgi*, the local factory boss who directed the making of the carpets; a representative of the carpet merchants who oversaw a number of factories; and the powerful carpet merchant himself. In addition, good money was to be made by the many people involved in the transport and the selling of the carpets to the European and North American markets. It made everyone rich, except the children who actually made the carpets.

At the demonstration in Shekhupura, Iqbal, a very small child just over four feet tall, was led to the front row along with the other children to listen to Khan speak about the new freedom law. Following his speech, Khan asked if any of the children wanted to come up and talk about their work. Iqbal walked to the front of the crowd and took the microphone in hand.

"My name is Iqbal Masih...," he began in a soft but clear voice. Iqbal spoke about his family's debt, which had continued to grow despite his many years of labour. He told how his fingers hurt from tying the knots hour after hour, and how his legs pained him every day from crouching as long as fifteen hours at the carpet loom.

Khan was immediately impressed with Iqbal. He was so small and yet so articulate. Khan must have seen how Iqbal, with his gift for speaking, could help move the struggle of liberation for the children of Pakistan to a new level.

Khan quickly negotiated Iqbal's release by promising to repay the original loan. He went to Iqbal's mother, and asked her to allow her son to go to Lahore to live and study in one of their freedom schools. Iqbal, aware of the new freedom law, refused to return to the carpet factory. His mother agreed to send her son to Lahore.

Over the next two years Iqbal learned to read and write. He advanced quickly, completing four levels of school in two years. He spoke at rallies and led demonstrations, openly criticizing the bosses of the carpet factories and the brick kilns. He became one of BLLF's most important spokespersons in the campaign against child and bonded labour in Pakistan.

In November 1994, Iqbal travelled to Sweden with Khan to speak to students, the media, and human-rights groups. He appeared on television and told consumers not to buy carpets from Pakistan because they were made with "the blood of children." He participated in a documentary film by Magnus Bergmar called *The Carpet*, in which Iqbal told the world about the abuse of children in the carpet industry.

One of the most powerful moments of the trip came with his words: "I am no longer scared of the factory owner. He is scared of me."

A trip to the United States followed a short while later. There Iqbal received the Reebok Youth in Action Award for his work in helping to free children. He told the American press, "Don't buy carpets made by child labour."

Sales of carpets from Pakistan began to drop.

When Iqbal returned to Pakistan, a controversy surfaced. It was reported in the United States that Iqbal was eleven years old when he received the Reebok award, but many people who knew the family contended that Iqbal was, in fact, much older. Travelling throughout Asia, I learned that it was sometimes difficult to determine the age of children who worked long hours indoors, rarely exposed to sunlight, and with little to eat. Crouched in front of carpet looms, with dust in the air and little circulation in their legs, they develop many health problems. Malnourished, their growth is stunted, and often they appear much younger than their actual age. But it was said Iqbal looked like a small child not only because of the number of years he spent in the carpet factories, but also because of a genetic disease he had inherited. They pointed to his paternal uncle, Sadar, who was a dwarf. Iqbal, they said, was also a dwarf. He was, they said, nineteen years old, not twelve, as I had read in the *Toronto Star*.

On Easter Sunday, April 16, 1995, only five months after his return from the United States, Iqbal, a Roman Catholic, travelled to Muridke to spend the day with his mother and his younger sister, Sobia. His mother asked him to stay the night with them, but Iqbal said that he had to return to Lahore for his growth-hormone pills, which had to be taken daily.

Iqbal left Muridke with his two cousins, Faryad and Liaqat, who lived in the direction of Lahore. For some reason, Iqbal got off the bus at his cousins' stop. He visited one uncle, and then he accompanied his two cousins to the fields to bring dinner to Amanat Masih, Liaqat's father.

It is said that all three boys were riding the same bike – Iqbal on the front handlebars, Faryad in the middle, pedalling, and Liaqat on the back. On an abandoned stretch of road leading to the fields, Iqbal was shot dead.

Our bus pulled into the station. Alam and I left, carrying all our luggage, late at night, and without a clue where we were going. We just knew what we were looking for: a cheap hotel. We would walk in one direction for a while, then backtrack and try another street, then go back the way we had come.

From my travels in developing countries, I have learned that it is difficult to guess the age of children with any accuracy. Years of hard labour, poor nutrition, lack of sunlight can all affect their growth. In many cases, because of illiteracy, parents do not know the ages of their own children. Frequently, when I ask a child to tell me when it was that he began to work, he simply raises his hand to indicate the height he was at that time.

We might as well have had a sign on our backs saying, ROB ME. Every hotel we came across was either full or too expensive. After a half-hour of this wandering about, I was getting very nervous. We could hear in the distance what sounded like firecrackers. When we asked a street vendor if he knew what they were celebrating, he told us that what we were hearing was gunshots.

Alam stopped to buy some roasted nuts from him. We had passed his cart so many times that the vendor had begun shaking his head and giving us strange looks. Finally, he pointed down a dark, narrow street behind him. We ignored his gesture. He was adamant.

It could be a set-up, I thought. We could get mugged.

The vendor was not about to give up. He insisted we follow his direction. Finally, we gave in and cautiously moved down the street, poised to defend ourselves against any attack.

We came to a building with a small sign in English that read, "Hotel." We went inside and, sure enough, their rooms came at a price we could afford. Needless to say, the street vendor's cart was a regular stop when we left the hotel each morning and when we returned at night.

Our room was simple: two beds, a night stand, a small table, and a broken radio. Its one luxury was a built-in washroom, for which we had paid extra. We were not willing to take a chance on meeting someone in the middle of the night in a dark hallway. We even decided to keep our one window locked, with the blinds closed at all times. We avoided going too close to the window, and I always ensured that the room door was locked and bolted. I thought I was maybe getting a little paranoid, until I discovered Alam doing exactly the same thing.

Early the next morning, we headed to the office of the Human Rights Commission of Pakistan. I carried with me the report they had written on Iqbal's death.

We were led into the most disorganized office I have ever encountered. There was a mountain of documents, books, and loose paper piled on a desk. Some looked like they hadn't been touched in years. Bits of uneaten food and dirty teacups were scattered among it all.

I cleared a pile of papers off a chair. But once I was seated I had to sometimes crane my neck just to see the man behind. His thick glasses and wild bush of grey hair made the meeting all the more unreal.

I was sceptical at first, thinking he might not have anything useful to add to any discussion of child labour. But, before long, I realized I had underestimated him.

"Children do not have votes, and anything that benefits children does not bring immediate political benefits," he said, running his fingers through his forest of hair. "So the government is not terribly keen on the idea of children being removed from their places of work."

And I was especially grateful to hear him emphasize one particular point – that child labour is everyone's concern. So often had I heard it said that child labour is a cultural issue, that outsiders should not be getting involved in the internal problems of a country. Yet here was a representative of the Human Rights Commission of Pakistan saying the opposite.

"Human rights is no longer divisible according to national boundaries," he asserted. "Governments should place it on the agenda of every bilateral meeting. In that way, each country would be forced to defend its human-rights record. It should feel obliged to answer to the international community."

It was refreshing to hear someone take such a stand.

But not long after, our discussions turned to Iqbal. Specifically, to the report the commission had released.

"You must have heard about the murder of Iqbal Masih," I began.

"Yes, but it was an unfortunate *accident.* From our findings, it was not because of his stand against child labour."

"I read your report," I said, as I fingered the document on my lap. "It says that Iqbal and his two cousins were riding their bike to the fields when they saw Ashraf Hero, a farm worker, in an indecent act with a donkey. It says the boys made fun of him, and that Ashraf picked up a gun and fired at them, accidentally killing Iqbal. This is really how Iqbal was killed?"

"That is right," answered our host. "According to the police report, this story was also given by Faryat and Liaqat, Iqbal's two cousins, when they were brought to the police station immediately after the shooting. Liaqat's father said the same thing, and Ashraf Hero admitted to killing Iqbal accidentally."

"But can you be sure this is true? The newspapers and the BLLF said he was killed by the 'carpet mafia.' "

"Everyone we talked to gave the same version – his family, his relatives, the people in the area all said the same thing."

"Why didn't you interview Iqbal's cousins who were with him the night he was murdered?" I asked. "They're not part of your report. Weren't they the most important witnesses?"

"The relatives we spoke to said that the two cousins are staying with the BLLF," he said. "There is no access to them."

"What about Iqbal's mother?" I responded. "What does she say about the killing?"

"She first gave the same version that all the others gave – that her son was accidentally killed. Then the BLLF got to her, and then she changed her version. She said that it was the carpet mafia. In any case, the last that one heard about her was at the official inquiry. And that court of inquiry also ruled it was not a conspiracy, that the shooting was accidental."

He seemed to be dismissing the theory of the carpet mafia out of hand. I was not willing to let it go by so easily.

"But why do you think Khan continues to say the carpet mafia was involved?"

He shrugged. "One reason could be that he initially suspected that's what happened."

"But he still says it now."

"Since he has taken that position, and since it has become controversial, there would be a loss of face if he retracted. The government has been angry with him and there is a case against him, so it serves his purpose, apparently. There is no question that Ullah Khan in the past did a great deal for bonded-labour children."

From all that I had read, I couldn't help but think that Khan was a great man. I wondered why so many people in Pakistan seemed quick to turn against him. He had dedicated most of his life to freeing children and entire families from bonded and slave labour. He had been instrumental in bringing in laws against these practices. Surely his opinions deserved more credit.

The court of inquiry the official had referred to had been held on April 28, 1995. All witnesses were recalled to testify. At the hearing, the two cousins who had been with Iqbal the night of his murder stated that their testimony as reported by the police was false. Like

Iqbal's mother, they had changed their story. They did not see Ashraf, the farm worker. There was no donkey. A shot in the dark killed Iqbal.

In August, the case was opened again, this time in the High Court of Lahore. The two cousins stated that because they were illiterate they had agreed to place their thumbprints, by way of signatures, on blank sheets of paper. They swore under oath that they gave no report, and that what the police had written was not their story. Liaqat's father now dismissed his previous story about Ashraf and the donkey as being untrue. Ashraf in turn changed his testimony and denied killing Iqbal, or even being in the field that evening. With no witnesses, he was set free.

As I sat listening to this official from the Human Rights Commission of Pakistan try to deal with all the conflicting reports, I couldn't help thinking we were no closer to the truth.

I had heard that Khan had not returned to Pakistan after Iqbal's funeral because he knew that he would be thrown in prison. During the month of May alone, following Iqbal's murder, there had been a ten-million-dollar loss in carpet orders. Khan had been accused of high treason against Pakistan, a crime punishable by death.

It was painful listening to it all: the conflict between the Human Rights Commission of Pakistan and Khan; the carpet manufacturers leading a campaign against human-rights groups to regain their image; the government accusing human-rights activists of treason.

Somehow the life and death of Iqbal seemed to be lost in the bickering and the rivalry of adults. It was time to pay a visit to Iqbal's village to see his gravesite and talk with his friends.

We left for Muridke the following day. Through the Human Rights Commission of Pakistan, we had made contact with a group called the Bonded Labour *Freedom* Front, and it was this group that offered to escort us there. We discovered that these people, too, were strong critics of Khan's BLLF. In fact, they claimed that the BLLF was a sham, and that the group had embezzled money from foreign donors and governments.

We were four hours late getting under way, and it was after dark before we arrived in Muridke. We were told there were no relations of

Iqbal's to be found and that it was too late to go see his father. We wondered if our hosts had figured that would be a convenient way of avoiding such encounters.

We were taken, instead, to see the parish priest at the church where Iqbal had worshipped that Easter Sunday of his death. As we neared it, a solitary neon cross, red in colour, seemed to float mysteriously in the night sky. Only when we were close enough that our vehicle's lights outlined the church, did we see that the cross was attached to the very top of the church steeple.

Iqbal's ancestors had converted to Christianity long before India and Pakistan became separate nations, in order to escape the lowest levels of the Hindu caste system. In a country where Islam is the dominant religion, Christians are a small minority. Some people had even suggested that religious tension was a factor in Iqbal's murder.

We spoke to the parish priest in a small side room of the church. He was a heavyset, middle-aged man with glasses.

One of our hosts translated for us. I was never certain, of course, that the English given back to me was an honest translation of what the priest had said. I suspected that there may have been some "adjustment" taking place, but I had no way of knowing for sure.

"How long had Iqbal been going to this church?" I asked.

"Maybe since he was four or five years old," the priest told me. "For about ten years."

"How old do you think he was, then?"

"The baptism certificate in Lahore would put him at nineteen years of age when he died."

"But if he was coming to this church when he was about five years old and he came here for about ten years..."

"I have only spent six years in this parish. Iqbal was here before I came."

"Is there a priest who has been here longer?"

"No."

We were getting nowhere and saw no point in continuing the line of questions. By this time, Alam and I had decided that what we really must do was go to the church in Lahore where Iqbal had been baptized and see for ourselves what evidence there was of the date of his birth.

That evening held a quieter, more personal moment for me. I went to visit the site of Iqbal's grave.

Since I had first read about Iqbal's death, just nine months before, my life had undergone an incredible transformation. I had travelled thousands of miles, but more importantly, I had travelled an equal distance in my understanding of the world and the complexities of its people.

One such complex life had ended abruptly, with the firing of a shotgun. With that shot another life had intensified and grown.

I came upon the burial site with the help of the priest and some friends of Iqbal. They led us through the dark, silent streets of Muridke to the graveyard. An occasional light through a window was our only guide. The graveyard was enclosed by a brick wall, about five feet in height. The entrance was a high, simple archway, etched in places with Urdu letters and simple drawings. We walked through, our way lit by the light attached to our videocamera. The light swept the graves. Some had headstones, but many were mere knolls of clay. It was difficult to avoid stepping on some, to find space between the brownish red mounds where we could walk.

"This is Iqbal's," the boys said, stopping before one of the unmarked mounds. The only thing to distinguish the grave was a low wall of red bricks around its perimeter. No marker, not even a simple wooden cross or plaque. Nothing to say: Here lies Iqbal, child labourer, fighter for the rights of other children.

I knelt before the grave and ran my hands over the clay and wondered at the life that had been Iqbal's. My favourite image of him had always been the one before an audience, in his scarlet vest, a carpet tool in one hand, a pencil in the other. "We are free!" he would shout. "We are free!"

Another image came to me, that of his body being carried through the main street of this village as the church bell tolled, the very same street I had just walked. I could see the stream of mourners, mainly children, holding hands as they surrounded the body of a boy, the red of his burial clothes as red as the blood that had soaked his clothes the night he was shot.

In death, the struggle continued. If there was any consolation, it was in the knowledge that around the world he was remembered, that

Iqbal's grave has no marker or tombstone. There is nothing to distinguish it, just a pile of dirt surrounded by red bricks.

others had taken up the cause that had perhaps cost him his life. In places he had never heard of, they knew his name. They knew what he had championed and vowed to continue his struggle.

I stood silently for a long time. I wanted him to know that I was one of those people. "We are free!" Almost an echo from the grave. There are those who will continue shouting his message wherever it needs to be heard.

After a few moments I walked away. I didn't look back.

We made our way to the road and back to the church. We thanked the priest and the boys who had guided us to the gravesite. As we drove away, I turned around. In the sky, as if suspended, was the simple red cross.

The following day we went to St. Francis Church in Lahore, where, it was said, Iqbal had been baptized. I didn't know what to expect. At the Human Rights Commission of Pakistan, we had been shown a photocopy of a baptismal certificate, which showed Iqbal's date of birth. I wanted to see the original.

The priest knew exactly where it was. "There have been many people here looking for it – reporters and many organizations," he said in English.

He took us into a room where several large books were stacked in a cupboard. The one for 1976 was buried under a pile of others. It was dog-eared and the pages had yellowed. But I had to admit it looked very official.

He opened the book on a table. "Page one fifty-three," he said. He turned the pages carefully. Each of them was divided into columns and each column filled with writing. The weeks went by, until April was reached. The priest ran his finger down the column and stopped at the name of Iqbal.

" 'Navidus,' " he read. "This means birth."

He pointed to the figure across from his name: 4.4.76.

"According to this, he was born on the fourth of April, 1976," I said.

"Correct."

"What does it mean, 'Iqbal Alphonse'? Wasn't his name Iqbal Masih?"

The priest explained that in Pakistan *Masih* means "the Christian";

that most Christians in Pakistan would use Masih as their last name. But that Iqbal's real last name was Alphonse.

The priest's finger continued along the line. "And the date of his baptism – the fifth of December, also 1976."

And there it was written. As were the names of his older brother Patras, and Iqbal's father, Saif Masih, and his mother, Inayat Bibi.

Alam had a question. "Do you know of any evidence that Iqbal was a dwarf?"

"He was a very stunted boy," the priest said. "He looked as though he was a boy, not like nineteen years old. He was quite a grown-up gentleman. But he still looked like a child."

In the report presented to the High Court of Lahore, Bert Thrybom, a leading pediatrician in Sweden, stated that while Iqbal was in that country he had examined him. A series of X-rays were taken of Iqbal's arms, legs, and vertebrae to determine the cause of the great pain he continued to experience in his legs and the reason why he was not growing. On that date, November 18, 1994, the doctor prescribed a series of growth hormones. On that same day he determined that Iqbal's bone age, and thus his chronological age, was eleven years.

We thanked the priest for his time.

What conclusion could I reach? Was the medical expert wrong; was Iqbal really nineteen years old? Were the baptismal records authentic? They certainly appeared to be. The yellowed pages, the faded ink and handwriting, the record-keeping in chronological order in the large bound book were hard to deny.

Early the next morning Alam and I went in search of the office of Khan's group, the Bonded Labour Liberation Front (BLLF). We had been told earlier that they no longer existed, that the office was boarded up. We decided we had to go look for ourselves.

As we walked along the streets, I said to Alam, "Even if we do find them, do you think it will bring us any closer to the truth?"

He shrugged. "We've come this far. There's no point in giving up now."

We had an address for the organization, but there were very few street signs to lead us there. We were walking around the general area when I spotted a sticker of a clenched fist in a window.

"Isn't that their logo?"

Indeed it was. We wandered inside and followed a small imprint of the logo, then another, until we came to a door. We knocked quietly. The door was opened by one of several men we had obviously woken up with our knock. They were as surprised to see us as we were to see them. One of them spoke some English, so we were able to explain who we were.

He invited us into an office. The place was in a shambles. The man sat behind a desk, his bare feet up on his chair, his hair still showing the signs of a long sleep.

"We expected this place to be boarded up," I said. The fellow was not surprised. At one time, he told us, there had been only one group, the Bonded Labour *Liberation* Front. Following Iqbal's death, there was a power struggle, a fight for the leadership. It ended with a split in the membership and the formation of the Bonded Labour *Freedom* Front, the organization that had escorted us to Muridke. It was these rivals, he said, who were the source of much misinformation about the BLLF.

It was hard to believe that after all the years the BLLF had fought for the rights of workers, the two hundred schools it was said to have opened, and the massive demonstrations it organized across Pakistan, that this was all that remained: a handful of loyal followers hanging out in the shell of an office.

We were told that on June 8, 1995, the police arrested Iqbal's mother and sixteen others from the BLLF office. Though they were later released, the police raided the BLLF office.

"They confiscated all our files and computer equipment and photographs. Everything. They froze all our bank accounts. They later arrested Ahmed Zafaryab, a journalist working for BLLF, and threw him in prison."

One could understand why these people would have such strong enemies. Had Khan not accused the prime minister, Benazir Bhutto, of using child labour, and Asthma Jahangir, of the Human Rights

How old was Iqbal? It was hard to deny the authenticity of his birth date as recorded in an official-looking book at the church where he was baptized. The yellowed pages, the faded ink, the entries in strict chronological order, all suggested that the date was authentic.

Commission of Pakistan, of siding with the exploiters of children? Had they not caused a huge drop in the sale of Pakistani carpets to a world community that did not want to buy carpets made from "the blood of children"?

Khan and the BLLF had never been afraid to speak out and to use any means they could to liberate their people from bonded labour. When Khan saw the power of Iqbal to move people to support this struggle, it is easy to understand why he chose him to further the cause, and perhaps allowed people to think Iqbal was younger than he really was.

Our encounter that morning came with an unexpected offer. Would we like to be taken to the BLLF compound where Iqbal's mother and his two cousins were in hiding? Would we like to put our questions about Iqbal directly to them?

I could barely believe our good fortune. Certainly we would. Even after we found out they were not living in their village, I had still held out hope that it would be possible to meet them.

Finally, after all the conflicting information we had been fed, there was a chance to find out the truth about Iqbal.

We met Iqbal's mother, Inayat Bibi, and his sister, Sobia, in a heavily guarded compound in Lahore. Inayat Bibi's accommodation was sparse, no more than a converted storage room, with a few scraps of furniture. I sat on a bench on one side, opposite Iqbal's mother and a translator from the BLLF.

About her head she wore a multicoloured cotton shawl. She stared ahead much of the time, speaking only when the BLLF official asked her a question. Sometimes she raised the shawl to her eyes to wipe away tears.

The translator was neatly dressed, in traditional Pakistani clothing, but with a Western-style jacket and grey scarf. He seemed to constantly have a cigarette between his fingers. Behind him stood another person from the BLLF. He videotaped our entire meeting.

I looked across at Iqbal's mother and smiled, hoping to ease her discomfort. I realized it would probably be the only opportunity I would ever have to speak with her.

"Why do you think that your son was killed?" I asked.

She spoke quietly.

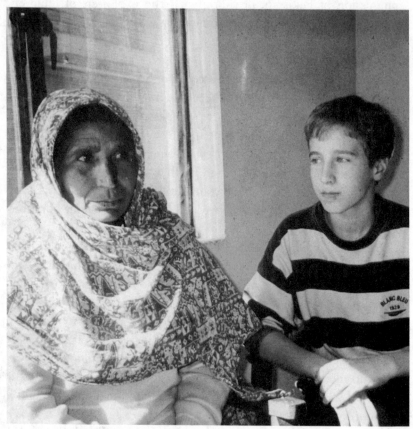

After the many conflicting stories about Iqbal's death, I hoped that Iqbal's mother would hold the key to solving the mystery of what really happened to her son.

"She is telling that Iqbal had some enemy by carpet owner," the translator said. "And she thinks that carpet owner and her husband are involved in this."

I had heard how Iqbal's father was now living with his stepdaughter in another village. I had also been told that he was a drug addict. The Bonded Labour Liberation Front and Iqbal's mother maintained that Iqbal's father was paid off to publicly support the police story and to denounce Khan and the BLLF.

Iqbal's mother looked away. It seemed to me that she did not want to talk about it further.

I thought I would try to pinpoint Iqbal's age, but like so many others I had met who had never learned to read or write, she wasn't certain of anyone's age, not even that of her own children. Many times during my trip I had asked children how old they were and at what age they had started to work, and they would hold up a hand to indicate a certain height, unaware of the actual age.

I decided to try a different tack. "How old was Iqbal when he was sold into bondage?"

"Six years."

I did a quick mental calculation. Everyone seemed to agree that Iqbal had started working for his last boss, Arshad, in 1986. If he was six years old at the time, that would place his age at the time of his death at fourteen or fifteen years old. According to the report of the Human Rights Commission of Pakistan, Iqbal's mother had said that he was fifteen or sixteen when he died. I was beginning to realize that when Iqbal was murdered he had to be older than twelve, the age Khan had given the international press. How much older was still a mystery.

I wondered about other things that had been reported by the international press. "Was he literally locked up with chains?"

"No, without chains."

"So he could come home? Every night?" I asked.

His mother nodded. "Yes, every night he can come," the translator said, "because the factory was situated near her home."

It was said Iqbal sometimes worked from four o'clock in the morning until seven o'clock at night – fifteen hours a day. I thought of how exhausted he must have been at night, even if he were allowed to come home.

I asked Iqbal's mother some more questions. Then, for a moment, I looked at her sad eyes. They seemed to be so distant, so filled with pain.

It was time to talk about happier days, I thought. "Can you tell about some of your fonder memories of Iqbal's life?"

"Iqbal was very fond of cooking," the translator related. "And spending time with his sister, Sobia."

I nodded. "If Iqbal were alive today, what do you think he would say to young people in Canada and around the world?"

"She is telling," the translator said, "that Iqbal released about three hundred children from bondage, and his message was that child labour should be finished all over the world. Many times he told about the importance of education of the children – for all young people, all over the world."

If there was one message to take back with me to Canada from Pakistan, it was this.

When Iqbal's mother had finished, she stood up. The two cousins, Faryad and Liaqat, who rode with Iqbal on the night of his murder, came into the room. They were big, much taller and broader than I was, especially Faryad, who had the beginning of a beard. The two of them sat down where Iqbal's mother had been. She moved to the bench beside me.

I said to the translator, "Can they tell me a little about the story, about how they were with Iqbal?"

The boys answered. "They were taking food for the uncle. They were riding their bicycle and singing, and suddenly someone fired at them," the translator said. "When the gun fired, Faryad was also wounded, and he fainted at that point. And when he came to his senses he saw many people around him, like the landowner and the police inspector."

Perhaps, I thought, Liaqat would be able to provide some insight into just what happened, since he was the only one not hit.

"Can he explain a little of what happened after the shot was fired?"

Liaqat's answer caused the translator to raise his voice slightly at him. Iqbal's mother broke in briefly, and she, too, raised her voice at Liaqat. It was as if he had not given the answer they wanted to hear.

"He was crying and he was confused," said the translator.

I knew it could not have been all that Liaqat had said, but we had no way of probing further.

"Then what happened?" I asked.

"They were taken to the police station. They put their thumbs on a blank sheet of paper and were told to leave."

Alam asked if he could videotape the wounds that Faryad had received from the gunshot.

Faryad raised his sleeve to show the inside of his left arm. I looked at scars from six pellet wounds, running from above his elbow to his hand.

My heart sank. It seemed he really had been shot, but now something else just didn't make sense.

"On what side was Iqbal hit?" I asked the translator.

"On his right side, in the back," he replied, running his hand up the back of his right leg to his shoulder.

The autopsy report given at the judicial commission of the High Court of Lahore had said the same thing, but if Faryad was sitting on the bicycle behind Iqbal while they were riding, how could it be that Faryad had pellets in his *left* arm, and not on his right side, like Iqbal. And how it could be that Iqbal was shot in the back at all if he was indeed sitting on the front of the bike with his two cousins behind him. Would his cousins not have been a shield and taken the brunt of the pellets, especially since they were so much bigger than Iqbal?

And what had happened to the bicycle, which might have shed some light on the shooting? The police had never collected this vital piece of evidence.

It seemed that for every answer I received, two more questions were raised.

I wondered how many people had been paid off. I thought how easy it was to control desperately poor people who had few alternatives for survival. So many people had their own agendas, their own reasons for lying about Iqbal Masih.

Alam and I packed our luggage and took a flight that night to Delhi, en route to Madras.

In the end, there were only two things I knew for certain. That Iqbal Masih died on the evening of April 16, 1995, as a result of gunshot wounds. And that Iqbal had been able to lift himself out of the cycle of bondage and bring a voice to the silenced.

I realized something else. It didn't matter if Iqbal was nineteen or if he was twelve when he was murdered. It didn't matter whether he was killed by local carpet manufacturers whose factories he was forcing to close, or by local jealousy because he was a Christian child travelling and getting an education, or by the man known as Ashraf. All that mattered was that his work was still not over and that we were challenged to continue it. In his life and in his death he moved the hearts of those who heard his story. That will never be in doubt.

As the plane continued towards Delhi, I looked over at Alam in the seat next to me. He had fallen asleep, exhausted.

So was I. Keeping me awake were images of Pakistan: the graveyard, Iqbal's mother, the cluttered offices...a brick kiln. I wondered what Iqbal would have said about the brick kiln.

On our second day in Lahore, we had travelled a couple of hours outside the city to visit a brick kiln. I was uncertain what to expect. A place for making bricks, obviously, with hot ovens perhaps.

What we came upon was a world unto itself. A landscape of reddish brown clay moulded into a small town, a huge smokestack at its centre, sucking in oxygen and spewing out thick smoke. Its people worked the clay from dawn to dusk, preparing it to be shipped away in heavy trucks, their only contact with the outside world. The people lived entirely in labour.

They started young. Eight years old, and even younger sometimes. It was natural to be helping, since they had played in the clay since they were old enough to crawl. The help turned to work, like that of their brothers and sisters, and their parents, and grandparents.

They would spend a lifetime at the same endless tasks – chopping clay from the open pit, shovelling it onto wheelbarrows, dumping it into a pile, mixing it with water, slapping it into moulds, turning out bricks, stacking them in wheelbarrows, pushing them to the kiln, lowering them inside, stoking the fires, loading the cooled bricks aboard the trucks.

Day after day, for a lifetime.

I tried my hand at moulding one. "At the rate you work," the boy had said to me, laughing, "you will not eat tonight."

"School," I had asked him, "would you like to go to school?"

"What is school? What is it like? What do people do there?"

The debts of people working in the brick kilns can be passed down from generation to generation. In this boy's case, his grandmother took out the loan that forced his family into bondage and continues to enslave them. He told me that he had never been outside the area of the brick kiln and did not know what a school was.

"What do you hope for the future?" I said.

"I will do the same job. I will work to pay the debt. I will work to eat. One day I will take a loan from the owner. My children will have to pay."

He had never been off the site of the brick kiln. One day, perhaps, he would get to ride on the truck, to go to Lahore to help unload the bricks. What freedom that would be.

As I thought back to the brick kiln, my mind wandered from the boy to Iqbal, then back again to the boy. Perhaps the bricks that outlined Iqbal's grave had been made by that boy.

Iqbal knew what freedom was. He had showed it to others. "We are free!" And one day that boy, like Iqbal, must shout it, too.

That was the real power of Iqbal.

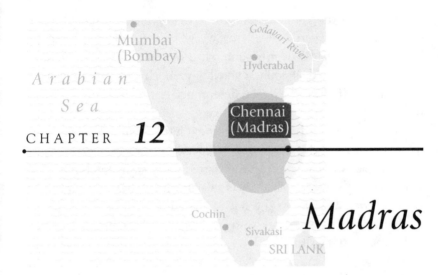

CHAPTER *12*

Madras

Mumbai (Bombay)
Arabian
Sea
Godavari River
Hyderabad
Chennai (Madras)
Cochin
Sivakasi
SRI LANK

MY FINAL MEMORY OF LAHORE was of a monument on one of its traffic islands – a full-sized fighter jet with the flag of Pakistan painted on its tail. One of my lasting memories of Madras would be of an old, bare-chested man, his hair as white as the plodding pair of oxen he was leading through the heavy traffic of the city centre. I knew I had come to a different part of Asia. The port city of Madras is the gateway to southern India, and a zealous protector of Tamil culture. Its weather is hotter and its pace a little slower. The city is full of narrow and overcrowded streets, bazaars and restaurants, and, as we were to find out, a lot more than first meets the eye.

Throughout our trip we had been carrying the Lonely Planet guide to India. As we left each city, Alam would tear out the corresponding pages in the book and promptly dispose of them. The man was fanatical about not carrying any extra weight. When we arrived at the airport in Madras, we took out our trusty book and fingered through what was left of it until we found "Madras: Places to Stay – Bottom End."

Alam decided on a place with the charming name of "Green Sea." It was not far from the ocean, rated safe and clean, and, most importantly, reasonably priced. The driver of the airport bus was even willing to drop us off near the hotel. What more could we ask for?

225

The clerk at the front desk broke it to us as gently as he could. "The rooms have all been booked for weeks. It's a religious holiday." The Green Sea had suddenly gone down the drain. "And, to be honest," the clerk added, "I doubt if you'll have much luck anywhere else."

Alam set off down the street, determined to find us a room, while I waited in the hotel lobby with our bags.

He reappeared with a long face. "We'll just have to take a rickshaw to another part of the city and try our luck there."

We lugged our bags outside and started walking in search of a rickshaw. Suddenly, down a side street, a sign caught Alam's attention, a small wooden one against the side of a building.

"I'm sure that's the Tamil word for 'lodge.' Wait here, Don't move."

He returned, this time with a smile on his face. "Twenty-five cents each a night," he announced. "They want two nights in advance."

"Sounds like it's just our style."

Twenty-five cents was fair exchange for two small beds, a window with only iron lattice covering it, a broken mirror, a stool, a small table in one corner, and our own personal padlock. And millions of mosquitoes.

The little bloodsuckers invaded the premises at night, ate the best meal they would ever get in their entire lives, and left us awake and scratching. After the first night, Alam counted forty-two bites from his fingertips to his elbow.

"Too bad the geckos didn't stay," I moaned, scratching my own collection of bites. When we had taken over the room, there were two of the little lizards climbing the walls. They are harmless creatures that feed off spiders, small cockroaches, and mosquitoes. At the sight of us they had made a quick exit out the glassless window.

"We both look like we have chicken pox," Alam observed. "Anything in your medical kit for insect bites?"

"Not unless they've taken so much blood you require a transfusion!"

If it wasn't the mosquitoes keeping us awake at night, it was the incessant music blaring from the tea shops and restaurants up and down the street outside. When the music finally died out, the carousing drunks took up the lyrics. I tossed and turned over in my sleeping bag and tried to conjure up pictures of the silent Canadian wilderness. It didn't quite work.

Much of our travel in Madras was in a vehicle common in the south of India known affectionately as a "baby taxi." They were a rough-and-ready three-wheeled contraption, cheap and manoeuvrable, but not big on shock absorption. They didn't have anything that might interfere with the view, such as glass in the windows. The baby taxi was in keeping with our routine while in Madras – free and open.

We decided our time in the city could be best spent in trying to better understand the lives of working children. It led us to places we could never have predicted. In Madras, our encounters with working children were more diverse than in any other city we visited.

We quickly saw in the children the one thing they had in common – they were almost all from the lowest ranks of society. And in India that meant being at the bottom of a very pronounced social order: the caste system.

Yogesh Vaharde, a contact we had in Canada, had explained to members of FTC how the Hindu religion divides people according to the tasks they perform. In its most basic pattern, at the top are the literate Brahmins, meaning "priests," who perform the intellectual and ritual tasks; followed by the Kshatriyas, the soldiers and administrators; then the Vaishyas, the artisans and commercial class. At the lowest official level are the Sudras, the peasants and farmers. But outside of the class structure entirely are those who literally have no class, the "untouchables." It is believed that the untouchables were actually the indigenous inhabitants of India. Many centuries ago, the conquering peoples had reduced them to slavery and assigned them a separate class in society. Yogesh himself had been born an untouchable in India.

I had wondered if a parallel could be drawn to the treatment of our own native people in Canada by its conquerors. Like the poor untouchables of India, they had not been allowed to own land, and were relegated to a life of poverty.

At one time (and apparently still, in some rural communities), if a high-caste Hindu came in contact with an untouchable, used the same temple, or even if the untouchable's shadow fell on him, that person would have to go through an elaborate series of rituals in order to be cleansed.

When I first heard about the caste system, it was a very strange notion to my Western mind, and I had trouble believing such a system could be so entrenched in everyday life. There are changes taking place – the government has formally outlawed the concept of the untouchables and initiated programs to help them – but in many rural communities life is little better for this group than it was a hundred years ago.

Four months before our arrival, a young untouchable from a community on the outskirts of Madras had been severely beaten for drinking from a water fountain that was reserved for the higher castes. The girl was made to stand in front of her class at school and was beaten so badly that when it was over she lay unconscious and bleeding and had to be hospitalized for several days.

It was quickly obvious to us that the Sudras and the untouchables performed the most menial jobs, and that almost all child labourers come from these groups. Their parents are often landless peasants and are, in just about every case, illiterate, because until recently untouchables were rarely given the opportunity to go to school. We did see some signs that change was coming. We visited two projects set up to encourage street kids to attend school. In one, students were provided with uniforms and school supplies, as well as money for extra help if they needed it. During an interview with a group of these ten- to fifteen-year-olds, we learned some of the boys were from a previously segregated caste.

"This is a true breakthrough," the local human-rights representative said to me as I talked with the boys. "Most children like them end up as manual labourers and have to resign themselves to a life of poverty."

Many of the children in the school we visited had worked as "rag pickers." To make money, they rummaged through garbage for anything they could sell – not only bits of cloth, but metal, glass, plastic, whatever they could find that had value. They saw education as a means of getting away from such work and were very proud that they were going to school.

Life on the streets had hardened many of them, and their outward appearance was bold and tough. But after a few minutes talking to them, I could see that outer shell weaken. Though it never entirely dissolved, now and then their smiles and laughter shone through. They loved being kids again.

The translator and I, and Alam with the videocamera, took to the street outside the school.

We weren't walking long when we came upon a group of schoolboys more than willing to answer our questions. I asked them how they felt about children of their age having to work and not being able to go to school. They were adamant that ways must be found for more kids like themselves to get an education. And then they turned the tables, and wanted to ask me some questions.

"Where do you live? America?" They all had seen American TV programs. "Everyone in America has lots of money."

"No, I live in Canada." They were a bit puzzled. "North of the United States," I added.

I dug out a Canada lapel pin from my knapsack. "This is our flag. The maple leaf."

They eyed it intently. "What games do you play?"

"Hockey."

They knew field hockey. India was very good at field hockey.

"Field hockey on ice."

It was too funny to think about. "Do you play cricket?"

"No," I had to admit.

"You don't play cricket? Everyone plays cricket!"

"Not in Canada."

"Football?"

"Yes, yes, I play football. We call it soccer."

And then they had an idea. How about they all come along with us? They would show us where to go if we wanted to find children working. They would be our tour guides.

The idea was hardly out of their mouths before two of them each grabbed an arm and started dragging me along the street. I couldn't help but smile. Before I came to Asia, when I was planning the trip, this was exactly what I pictured myself doing: being led around the streets by other kids my age.

It was all Alam and the translator could do to keep up with us. Since there were no sidewalks, we made our way along the side of the street, often having to dodge rickshaws and baby taxis to make our way through. The sight of a white kid being paraded through town by a half-dozen local boys was quick to turn heads.

We were not long on this march when we heard a loud, grinding noise. As we continued, the sound grew even louder.

"Metal factory," one of the boys informed me, pointing to a partially open doorway.

We peered inside. It looked more like a workshop. A fan revolved overhead, and a couple of naked light bulbs gave the only light except for what came through the door. There were no windows, and I was suddenly hit with an incredible heat.

We asked one of the boys if it was okay to come in and talk with him for a few moments.

"Yes, yes. Okay."

His name was Khasia. He was thirteen, and he knew a few words of English. He was wearing sandals, shorts, and an oversized yellow shirt that hung to his knees. He broke into a broad smile several times while we were there. He seemed to enjoy the attention.

This small factory employed Khasia and a second, younger, boy, as well as three adults. Their job was making and packaging the small metal cups used by hotels and restaurants for condiments, such as the chutneys served with curried dishes.

Much of the machinery was ancient, its naked wiring a very visible threat to safety. The machinery was overworked, and ran hot much of the time, its constant clatter making conversation next to impossible. The children showed us the various stages in the process of making these cups. One at a time, flat metal discs were inserted into a slot, where a metal press automatically shaped them into cups. A second machine curved their rough edges. The cups fell into a pail beside the machine and, once the pail was filled, it was carried to a side room by one of the boys. There he crouched and quickly inspected the cups for flaws. They were stacked and taken off to another room and put within reach of a man sitting before another machine, even noisier than the others. He put each cup in place, where it was forced against a grinder to polish it. As I watched him, a circle of sparks jumped from the machine, sending me scrambling backwards. The man wore no protection for his eyes.

Khasia threw me over one of the cups as it dropped away from the machine. It was scorching, and I tossed it from hand to hand like a hot potato. It was also incredibly shiny. In a few days it would be making its way to a dinner table.

Back near the entrance, the second boy was kneeling on the floor, quickly counting the stacked cups, five at a time. He counted them by

This boy drops a metal disc into place with a quick movement of his hand. The machine presses the metal into the shape of a little bowl. If not for his practised split-second timing, he could easily lose a finger or a hand.

touch alone, running his thumbnail along the edges, looking up at us as he worked.

Khasia took a turn at the machine that pressed more discs into shape. I was amazed at his dexterity. Each pressing required a quick spin of a metal wheel and split-second timing to drop the disc into the slot. I could see that one false move would easily cost him a finger.

"What do you do with the money you earn?" I shouted.

I could hear only two words from the translator over the noise: "family" and "chocolate." I found out later that almost all his wages went to his family. What remained was only enough to buy himself a very small treat now and then.

We left the boys to their labour. They were obviously skilled at their jobs, and worked quickly. I bet they also would have made very good students.

"Thanks," I said to the boys as I left.

"Thanks," Khasia replied in his thick accent. "Goodbye. Thanks." Back on the street again, my convoy of newfound friends and I continued on our way.

"Tell us what snow is like," one of them said.

"It is white and it is cold, like flakes of ice, only not so hard." They seemed to have trouble with my explanation.

"Can you eat it?"

"It will turn to water in your mouth."

"Clean water?"

"Most of the time."

"All the water you can *eat*. That is wonderful."

"You can make snowballs from it," I announced.

They stared at me, thoroughly confused. "To play football?"

"No, no," I laughed. "To throw at your friends, for fun."

They all found such an idea uproariously funny.

"Or make snowmen." I tried to describe the process of making a snowman. I think I completely lost them when I came to the part about a carrot for a nose.

Farther on, one of the boys suddenly tugged at my arm and drew me back to a open doorway. We looked inside and discovered three people gathered around a heap of small brown balls in the centre of the floor.

"Sweets," the translator told me. "Candy."

One of the three was a young girl. She looked to be about eleven. She was crouched on the floor, and beside her were empty plastic bags. As she held one open, with the other hand she counted out sweets and deposited them into the bag.

She counted ninety to a bag and stacked each of them to one side. She was amazingly fast, grabbing a small handful each time, adding them to her total, and whipping them into the bag. At times her hand was almost a blur.

She was extremely shy, and would often turn her face away when I spoke to her. I noticed she wore a nose stud in the shape of a flower, and an ankle bracelet made of many strands of silver chain woven intricately together. Her feet were bare. Her black hair, in a ponytail, fell forward over her shoulder. She wore a dress patterned in blue and purple, with a scattering of red leaves.

"Do you go to school?" I wanted to know.

She hid her face and mumbled a few words to our translator. "I stayed until the second level, but I left a few years ago."

"Why?"

"I wasn't doing well. My family needed me here to help."

Whenever she showed her face, I noticed the touch of a smile. She was puzzled by our attention, but secretly, I think she was enjoying it.

The bags of candy were eventually handed to her father crouching nearby. He would take each bag and slip a small label inside, before folding it closed and sealing it along a heated metal bar. The plastic sizzled as the hot metal touched it, discharging a foul smell that hung in the air. There was no ventilation except for the door to the outside.

In the meantime, a small crowd had gathered in the doorway, anxious to find out what we were up to. Most were children, but our group drew several adults, even some who stopped their bicycles to poke their heads inside.

"How much are you paid?" I asked the girl.

"Fifteen rupees a day."

She worked from seven in the morning to six at night – eleven hours a day. Her pay amounted to less than four cents per hour.

How long would she be doing this? I wondered. Her mother was sitting across from her, doing the same job. Would the girl be bagging sweets all her life?

In a tiny room filled with the smell of burning plastic, this girl spends the day counting out sweets before dropping them into a plastic bag. She would like to be a teacher, but without an education the cycle of poverty will continue, and her own children will be forced into labour.

"What would you like to do when you are older? As a job?"

"I don't know. Maybe a teacher, like the teachers in my old school."

Of course, without an education there was no chance of her ever becoming a teacher. Maybe one day she would end up having to take her *own* children out of school and put them to work to help support a family.

This family was, in fact, better off than many we had encountered in India. In their attempt to rise above the lowest levels of poverty, they worked long and hard for some middleman. Yet did the hopes of the girl have to end there? Was there no way that society could help her to fulfil her dream of being a teacher? Perhaps it was, in part, another case of education for a girl not being valued, of her childhood being viewed only as a waiting period until she was married.

A young girl we met later in the day seemed to confirm this notion. She was a domestic servant, one of the countless number of young girls we knew were hidden behind the doors of homes in South Asia. Many human-rights organizations had told us that physical, sexual, and psychological abuse of these domestic servants is commonplace.

Most children working as domestic servants were not working for rich families. Those families could afford to hire adults. It was the middle class who hired children, looking for a cheap form of labour to do their household chores.

This girl was in open view. Barefoot and in a tattered dress, she was crouched down a few feet outside the main door to the house. In front of her was some bread dough on a board, and a rolling pin. As we approached her, she stopped her work and looked up, curious as to what we wanted. We told her who we were and asked if she would mind answering a few of our questions. She didn't mind, she said.

Her name was Vedavalli. She was eight years old and worked in the house with her older sister. They shared the household work and in return were given a place to sleep and food to eat.

"You are making chapattis?" I said quietly.

She nodded.

"And do you do this each day?"

"Yes," she said.

"Would you tell us how many hours you work?"

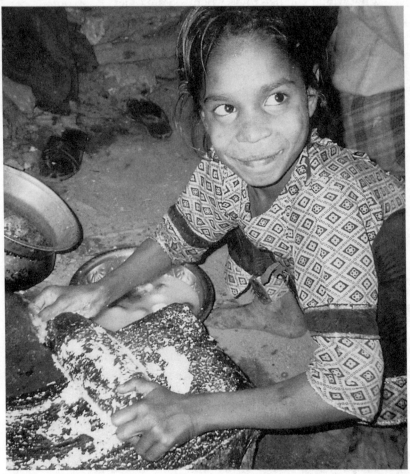

The millions of child domestic servants around the world are often excluded from the statistics on child labour. Many of them face extreme forms of physical, psychological, and sexual abuse.

"I get up at eight and go to bed at ten."

As she looked up to answer our questions, her tiny hands continued to knead the bread dough.

I asked why she and her sister were not at home with their own family.

"They do not have the money to look after us," she said.

"Do your parents work?"

"My father has tuberculosis. My mother works as a beedi roller."

Our translator explained that a beedi is a type of cigarette smoked by poorer people in India.

At that point, a man and woman suddenly appeared in the doorway, wondering what was going on. We stepped back a bit from the girl, worried that she would be in trouble for talking to us. Once we explained what we were doing, I expected the couple to send us away at once.

But on the contrary, they invited us inside. The family was more than happy to talk with us, they said.

We all sat around a living room. It was getting dark outside, and they had no electricity, so the man lit two oil lamps and placed them on a table in the centre of the room.

"We treat the girls as if they were our own children," the woman said.

We found that hard to believe. The couple had two daughters of their own, sitting with us in the same room. They were well dressed, with their hair neatly combed, and had just changed out of their school uniforms because they were going out with their parents for dinner.

We knew that a child domestic's life included cooking, sweeping, polishing, washing clothes, grinding spices, cleaning the toilets, and much more. It did not include school. It did not include going out with the family to dinner. They always ate separately from the rest of the family and were often given just the leftovers.

The couple did not view it that way. I think they saw it as a rescue mission. They had saved the girls from desperate poverty and were giving them shelter and food. They saw it as a fair exchange. They were being Good Samaritans, and getting their housework done at the same time.

After we left the house, Alam looked at me and declared, "They talked as if they were doing the girls a favour!"

"I think it goes back to the caste system," I added. "You are born into a slot in life and it is very hard to move out of it."

Our "tour guides" had been waiting patiently for us to return. From time to time, as we made our way through the streets, boys would have to drop out of the group and head for home. But as quickly as we lost some, we picked up others. There were never less than a half-dozen boys in our group, all eager to point out everything they thought might be of interest – their schools, where they went to play games, where their parents bought food for them.

We passed through a produce market and watched as the vendors closed up their stalls for the night. Women and children had gathered to help them load their wagons.

"For their work, the vendors give them the food that has gone bad," one of the boys told us.

We would have bought some fruit and shared it with the boys, but we were in the Muslim holy month of Ramadan. During that time, no food or drink is consumed from shortly before sunrise until shortly after sunset. As Alam pointed out to me, the fast is meant not only to cleanse the body, but also to teach self-discipline, and help the person become more spiritually aware.

It was now late-afternoon, and we were all starting to feel the effects of the hot sun and lack of fluids.

"You are thirsty," one of the boys said. "You are Muslim?"

"No," I told him.

"Then you drink all you want. You want tea?"

I explained that Alam was Muslim, and I had decided to join him in his observance of Ramadan.

"Then you sleep all day, and eat all night, like my uncle," one boy blurted out.

The others laughed.

"Tell us some Canadian food."

"The best Canadian fruit is apples."

"Apples?... Like mangoes?"

"Not quite," I said. I decided to have some fun with them. "In Canada, we put a tube in trees and drink the juice from it. We call it maple syrup."

"Canada is a crazy place," one boy declared. "Very crazy."

"Sometimes we put the maple syrup on pancakes."

"What are pancakes?" another boy asked, staring at me suspiciously.

"Like chapattis, but not so flat."

"All this talk of food is making us hungry!"

Another of the boys had to head home, so we followed him for part of his route, a shortcut between several buildings. Only one of them had a window, high up, with its glass shattered. Alam was tall enough to peer inside.

"There's a young girl," he said to us. "She's crouched next to a pile of things. I can't tell what they are. She seems to be sorting them."

We were intrigued. The translator asked the boys to wait at the end of the alley. The door was slightly ajar, so we opened it a little further and looked inside. The young girl was alone. We asked if we could come in and talk with her. She nodded.

We approached her, only to draw back slightly in astonishment. Before her lay a heap of used syringes.

Even though I was seeing it with my own eyes, it was difficult to believe. The girl, no older than eight, was pulling apart the syringes and depositing the parts into three separate bins. She wore nothing on her feet, and no protection of any kind on her hands.

"The outer plastic part goes there," she said, pointing to one bin, "the inner plunger here, and the needle tip in that one."

Her name was Muniannal. Her little hands picked up the syringes one at a time and went about the job of separating them, as if it were the most natural thing in the world to be doing. She wore a pretty yellow-and-purple dress and bangles about her wrists; her black hair was tied back with colourful ribbon. She looked as if she should have been going to a birthday party.

"Where did these come from?" I asked.

"From hospitals, the streets, garbage," the translator told me. "The parts are resold."

Using a pen, I pushed some of the syringes around and saw that many still had their metal tips in place. They were all dirty, many with dried blood caked to the insides.

Yet the girl was handling them so mechanically that sometimes she didn't even look at the syringes as she pulled them apart. As I raised

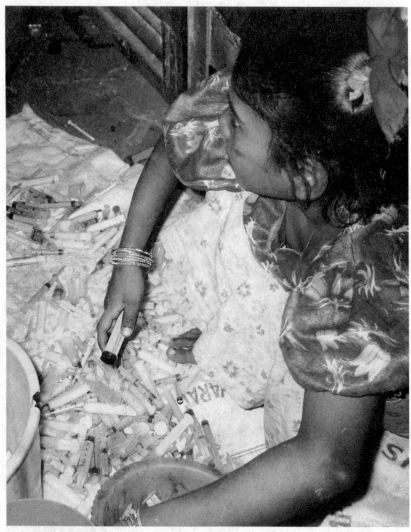

This eight-year-old girl with a pretty ribbon in her hair spends her days squatting in the middle of a pile of used syringes. With no protection for her hands or feet, she dismantles the syringes to recycle the plastic.

one of my feet, I realized that the floor felt tacky. It was covered with a build-up of medical waste from the hundreds, more likely thousands, of syringes the girl had separated there.

Once the bins were full, she stood up and carried them to the other side of the room and dumped them in larger bins, then returned to her spot. She paid little heed to where she walked. I cringed to see her step on syringes with her bare feet.

"This is very dangerous," I said to her, almost pleading with her to stop what she was doing. "Are you careful not to cut yourself with the needles?"

She was shy and slow to answer, perhaps still wondering why this group of people, one with a camera, was so interested in her.

"Sometimes I cut myself," she said, her voice a bare whisper.

She did not know her exact age. She had attended school, but stopped going because of the poverty in her family. She worked eleven hours a day and was paid less than two cents per hour.

At that moment another worker, a woman, entered the room. On seeing us there, she gathered up something from the floor, then spoke an urgent few words to us before leaving again.

"Quick, we must go now," the translator said. "She says if the girl's boss sees us, he will beat her."

I had already noticed a purple bruise near the girl's eye. I wanted to ask her more questions, but all I could do was give her a final glance as we hurried to the door.

"Isn't she worried about diseases? Those needles could have been used by people who were sick, maybe drug addicts," I said to the trans-lator as we stood in the street.

"She has no concept of protecting herself against a virus. If she pricks herself with a needle, she will wash it with water and try to stop the bleeding, but she will receive no other treatment."

Of all the cases I had seen of children being exploited and working in horrible conditions, this is one that affected me most. It had been drilled into me from a very early age never even to *touch* a syringe if I came across one. The image of the soles of her bare feet coated with medical waste, her small fingers being pricked by dirty needles... they would haunt my sleep that night. But even more heart-wrenching was the smile she had given us when we first entered the room where she was working.

Muniannal was no different from any child living on my street or going to my school in Canada. I could have been born in her city and she in mine. Fate was the only thing separating my life of privilege from her life of abuse and neglect.

As after many of my encounters with children during this trip, I was left with a feeling of guilt. I could not suddenly lift any of those children out of poverty and bring them back to Canada. I could not promise any of them a better life. The only thing I could do was to take the story of Muniannal and the many others back home with me and tell them to everyone, wherever in the world I travelled. This I swore to do.

Our day ended on a more heartening note. I led those who remained in our group of "tour guides" into a kite shop. It was a small place, a single room, with an elderly white-haired gentleman settled onto a stool in one corner. The shop was a multicoloured sea of kites, of every possible shape and size that would fly. The owner told us he worked the entire year making kites and sold them all within two weeks of the annual kite-flying festival. People had already begun placing orders for special colours or designs for the next year.

I asked the boys to help me pick out a kite. They inspected every one – lifting it, feeling the weight of it, making pronouncements on its strength and its design. Their choice was a diamond-shaped kite in various shades of red. We negotiated a price with the owner and took to the streets outside to give it a try.

It was incredible the way they were able to manoeuvre the kite through the overhead wires, around clotheslines and past the roofs into the open sky. They each took turns flying the kite and argued continuously about who could fly it the highest. Our afternoon with them ended as boisterously as it had begun.

"It is time for us to be getting back to the hotel," Alam informed them.

I jotted my address on scraps of paper and gave one to each of the boys, telling them if they ever wanted to practise their English, they should write and I would certainly respond. We gave each of them

Canadian pins and helped them to put them on their shirts. One boy wanted his on his hat.

"Goodbye," I said, shaking their hands, one after the other. "Thanks for showing us around. It sure was a lot of fun. If I come again, you'll have to teach me how to play cricket."

Alam and I climbed into a baby taxi to return to our hotel.

One of them yelled something as we were leaving. I looked at the translator, who was about to head off to his home.

"He said, 'Have fun with your snowballs!'"

I looked back and waved. They were clustered together, waving crazily and laughing.

Our thoughts turned to food. Soon we could break our fast, and my stomach was anticipating something substantial to make up for the last thirteen hours. At a restaurant we ordered *masala dosa*. It arrived on a banana leaf – a flat bread accompanied by more than a dozen side dishes, called sambal, and chutneys in separate bowls. What a fantastic way to end a day of fasting.

We retired to our room and collapsed on our beds, completely stuffed. My mind drifted back to Canada for a moment. I didn't really want to think about returning. I thought of the boys and smiled. I would long remember them. And no matter if I tried, I could not forget the girl with the syringes.

"It's been a long day," I said to Alam. "We should get some sleep."

Alam wasn't ready to call it a night. "So, I didn't see *you* fly the kite."

"All the boys wanted a chance, and we were in a hurry."

"Do you have an unnatural fear of kites?" he asked. "A kite phobia, perhaps?"

He was definitely up to something.

"Wait right here," Alam said, leaving the room

A couple of minutes later he returned. "Take the kite, and come with me."

"Whatever you say, Dr. Rahman."

I followed him down the hallway and up three flights of stairs. At the top we came to a door. Alam opened it and we stepped onto the roof of the building. The roof was vast, and provided a dazzling view of the city at night. The Hindi top ten was blaring from an adjacent apartment building, in competition with the traffic below. Our friends, the singing drunks, added their personal touch to the scene.

"I feel like I could fly." I shouted into the night.

"I suggest you take this string and concentrate on the kite."

High above the sparkling lights of Madras, Alam showed me how to fly a kite. At first I had trouble getting it to stay in the air for more than a few seconds, but after a while it caught the breeze and almost flew out of my hand. At one point the wind was so strong we both had to hold the string to keep it under control.

"I'm cured," I called out.

We laughed so much we lost control, and in a moment the kite took a sudden nosedive to the ground below us. Someone came along the street, promptly broke its string, and ran off with it.

We lay on our backs and let the warm Indian night flood our senses. The noise of the city below, the stars above, the two of us laughing at the thought of a mosquito-bitten boy who first learned to fly a kite on the roof of a cheap hotel in Madras while the world all around prepared for bed.

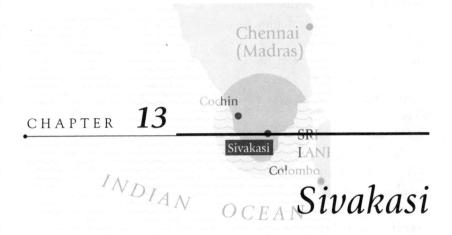

Chennai
(Madras)

Cochin

Sivakasi

SRI
LANI

Colombo

INDIAN OCEAN

CHAPTER **13**

Sivakasi

IN COMING TO SOUTHERN India, we knew we had to visit the Sivakasi region. Its fireworks and match factories are infamous for their dangerous working conditions and their abuse of workers.

It was an explosion here that led to Free the Children's action the year before to have Toronto ban from its city-sponsored events all fireworks manufactured with the use of child labour. Even while I was researching the background material to present to Toronto's City Council, I had imagined getting inside one of those factories to see for myself the conditions under which these children laboured. But as we neared the region that day, I still had no idea how we might accomplish that, for factory owners were always on the lookout for strangers seeking access to their operations, thinking they might be activists out to expose them.

Kailash Satyarthi had given us the name of a contact person in the city of Madurai, near Sivakasi, a ten-hour bus ride from Madras.

It was two o'clock in the morning when the bus pulled in at Madurai. Wearily, we gathered up our bags. It took the sight of an all-night market stall to finally pull Alam out of his drowsiness.

Moments later, a plump watermelon under his arm, he fished out the address of the contact Kailash had given us. We crammed ourselves,

245

with our bags, inside a baby taxi, our knees to our chests, our heads pressed forward by the sloping roof.

Twenty minutes later we knew we had a problem. The driver was lost. Up and down streets he went, with a constant, "I remember, I remember. Over here. This way. Ah, over here."

Another half-hour of this and the taxi finally pulled over in front of a building.

"This is it?" Alam asked.

"Yes," the driver said, his one word slurred.

We stared at the building. Number 37. We checked the address. Number 37.

Out we piled, and stacked our luggage at the doorstep. Alam handed over the fare and thanked the driver. Finally, we had arrived. It seemed like forever since we had left Madras.

We decided not to wake our host at such an ungodly hour. We would sit and wait for the sun to rise before knocking. Alam positioned the watermelon on his knees. My pocket knife in his hand, and his mathematical mind in gear, he cut it into precise slices.

He handed me a piece. I'm the only kid I know who doesn't find much to admire in a watermelon. To me it's like eating water. My biggest thrill is spitting out the seeds. I took one slice of the pulp to quench my thirst, and donated the rest of my share to Alam.

As we sat with our luggage, Alam systematically devouring the watermelon, I began to suspect that something wasn't quite right. I gazed at the house. It seemed rather big to be that of a human-rights worker. I walked to the side and discovered a large, elaborate garden. Was this really the home of our contact?

"Guess what?"

Alam's watermelon feast sputtered to a stop. "What?"

"I think the guy let us off on the wrong street."

"No?"

"Yes! Look around you. This is not how Kailash described it."

Alam scanned the street, reluctantly, then walked to the corner to check the sign.

"You're right," he said when he returned.

"So, what's our next move?"

He shrugged. "No next move. We stay right here until daylight. No point in just wandering the streets."

"What do we do if whoever lives in this place comes out and finds us on his doorstep?"

The question remained unanswered.

Two bicycles turned onto the street. Each had a powerful headlight turned at an angle so its beam scanned the houses along the street. Two more bikes turned the corner and drew up smartly behind the first two. Now there were four headlights, advancing towards us in a menacing formation. I was sure we were about to meet a nasty fate.

They stopped squarely in front of us.

From beyond the blinding headlights came words in Tamil, then Hindi, maybe even a few words of Bengali.

"English, English," we shouted back.

"English? What are you, tourists?"

"Yes! Yes! Can't you tell? Now, please turn off the lights."

They redirected their lights so the beams struck the ground.

They weren't robbers, but police officers on patrol.

We told them our story and showed them our slip of paper with the address. Alam even offered them some watermelon.

They politely refused, but picked up our bags and told us to follow them. "It's one street over. This way."

Off we went, our military pace interrupted only once: the police officer directly in front of us slowed down and jabbed a finger in the direction of a sign bearing the name of our misplaced street.

We arrived at the new Number 37 with great relief and thanked our rescuers for their kindness. "We'll wait here, and when it turns daylight we'll knock."

"No, no."

I thought it might be too much to expect.

One of the police officers pounded his fist on the door, much louder than was civil at four o'clock in the morning on a deserted street in the middle of Madurai.

A man emerged, his eyes barely open. We stood embarrassed, hoping he had a gentle nature, and sound sleepers for children. The police officer spewed out our story.

The man in the doorway looked us up and down. "I'm afraid I don't know these people," he said.

"We're friends of Kailash Satyarthi," Alam exclaimed. "He was in touch with you. Remember...?"

We prayed he'd remember, or we'd be taking a fast trip to a Madurai police station.

"Ah! Kailash's friends! Of course. Come in, come in."

We thanked the police officers again and grabbed our bags, and what was left of the watermelon, and went inside. They readjusted their lights and off they went, in a perfectly straight line.

We stood in the entrance to the man's house, still a little in shock at how openly he had welcomed us. We had barged into his house in the middle of the night, and now his wife was preparing to make us something to eat.

The main part of the house consisted of a general living area, where meals were also served, and which became the sleeping area for part of the family. There was a separate kitchen, a bedroom for the parents, and a washroom outdoors. And a work area for making jujubes. The family had a little candy business set up in their house.

Within a half-hour of our arrival the adults in the family were instructing us in the art of making jujubes. They demonstrated how they pressed the moulds for the candy into trays of powdered sugar. We watched them mix the glucose and cane sugar, then add the colouring and flavouring before pouring it all into the moulds. Alam captured the whole process on videotape. So intent was he on his camera work, in fact, that his foot landed in a box of finished jujubes. Fortunately, our hosts were more than forgiving. They even gave us some of their candy for later on our trip.

Later the same day, we were on a bus with the father of the family, heading for Sivakasi. It is estimated that in this one region of India, in the state of Tamil Nadu, there are forty-five thousand children working in the production of fireworks and matches. It is said that this is the highest concentration of child labour in the entire world.

It wasn't long before we saw just why so many factories had been established here. The land was as near to desert as any place I had seen in South Asia. Trees were few and low-growing, and were constantly being blown about by the hot winds. Definitely not a place for farming. Small household plots and a few chickens were the only signs of agriculture.

I quickly found my mouth dry and my lips starting to crack. I could only imagine how hot it would get at the height of the summer.

At the first village we stopped at, there was hardly a soul to be seen: no children playing, no music, no women washing clothes or old men enjoying a beedi. The entire village looked abandoned.

The place consisted of a few stores and a clump of homes. Some were of wood and looked fairly substantial; others were mud huts with thatched roofs and walls a few feet high. We followed a dirt path that led out of the village. What little grass there was gave way to dried brown stubble, then disappeared altogether. All that remained was a strange-looking type of cactus. It grew like a small bush and was entirely white, even the thorns.

"If you are careful, you can wipe away the white coating and find green underneath," our contact explained to me. "The white reflects the sun, so the plant can hold more water."

"I wish I had worn white," I said, "or brought more than one litre of water."

White seemed a popular colour for buildings, too. We came upon a collection of white brick structures, a staggered line of cubes inside a barbed-wire fence that enclosed an area the size of several football fields.

"This is what you have been waiting to see," our contact said. "And this compound is one of hundreds just like it."

Inside the compound was a fireworks factory, and in one corner several separate buildings that housed some of the workers. I stood as close to the barbed wire as I could without making contact. The fence stretched several feet above me.

"The factory owners sure mean business," I commented. The fence kept out everyone, including strangers like us.

We followed the fence until eventually we came to a gate, manned by a uniformed and well-armed security guard.

He gave us an inquisitive, unsmiling look.

We proceeded to introduce ourselves, as earlier instructed by our contact from Madurai.

The guard stared at us. Not often did he see a white boy in the company of two Asians, one of whom spoke only English and Bengali.

"You have received word that we are expected?" our contact and translator inquired.

"No," came the blunt reply.

"Did your boss not receive our letter? It was mailed three weeks ago."

The guard continued to stare at us, now somewhat confused. "I do not know what you are talking about."

"This is ridiculous. You must know. We have come all the way from Dhaka, and you say you haven't heard about us. Surely there is some mistake. We must talk to the foreman."

"I have strict instructions that no one is allowed to enter." He didn't blink.

"Professor Kielburger sent word to this factory that we would be arriving today. This is his son. And this young man is his student. He's doing his thesis on the chemistry of fireworks production."

"My father teaches at the University of Dhaka," I announced.

"This is very important," Alam added. "This interview is absolutely essential to my thesis."

Our friend translated for the security guard. The man was still not impressed.

"I'm afraid you don't understand the urgency of this matter. He has come all the way from Dhaka, at considerable expense. You must go to the foreman and tell him that we are here."

The fellow was standing his ground.

"Here, I will write our names on a piece of paper and you must bring it to your boss."

As he was writing, he had the guard pronounce our names. Mine proved to be the greatest challenge.

"I'm Craig Kiel-bur-ger."

"Grag Kin-ber-nun."

"Very close," I said. "Craig Kiel-bur-ger."

"Crag Kil-bur-ner."

"Close enough!"

The fellow went off with his piece of paper while we waited. Soon the foreman appeared, and we went through the whole story again – how there must have been some terrible mix-up, or the request was lost in the mail. How it was absolutely essential that Alam get his research done or he might never be awarded his degree. It was all very convincing. The story our contact had concocted during our ride from Madurai was taking shape beautifully.

"Yes, come in. When did you say you arrived from Dhaka?" asked the foreman.

It was music to our ears.

A table was soon brought out and placed under the shade of a tree, followed by chairs for the four of us. We were offered tea and a selection of biscuits. Our discussions began with a series of questions about the mixture and quantities of chemicals used in the fireworks' production. Both Alam and I wrote furiously in our notebooks as the foreman went on and on in great detail about mixtures of sulphur, magnesium, gunpowder, and the other ingredients in fireworks. He ended by lamenting that the cost of chemicals had increased dramatically in recent months and how this had a tremendous effect on production.

Our conversation gradually shifted from the process of mixing the chemicals to the work involved in the production and, ever so slowly and innocently, to whether there might be any children involved in the work.

"There are some children working here," he said, "but only in the simple jobs, those that aren't dangerous." We felt confident we were getting closer to the true picture.

Eventually the foreman called on his son and asked him to give us a tour of the compound. We couldn't believe how well our plan had worked. We knew how strict these factories were about letting people inside; if there had been the least shred of suspicion that any one of us was a human-rights activist, we would never have made it past the gates.

Alam casually inquired if he could take photos. It would add greatly to his thesis. Only of the adult workers, we were told, and only specific parts of the production.

As a result of this tour, and our access to other factories that day, we were able to get a good overall view of the production of fireworks, and document much of it with photographs.

The first step in the process is the creation of the outer shell of the fireworks. This is done by tightly rolling, then gluing, old newspaper. Often this work is contracted out and completed in the homes of the area. The tubes are taken to the factory, where they are cut by hand into lengths appropriate for the type of fireworks being made, and then coated in a red dye.

Once the dye has dried, the tubes are packed together tightly inside metal rings so that many fireworks can be created in one batch. A mudlike compound is caked on both ends and allowed to dry in the sun, after which each of the tubes is punctured at one end to allow the chemicals to be poured in. Tar is used to seal the holes, and a wick quickly added. They are then set out again in the hot sun for several hours. Once dry, the tubes are released from the metal rings, cleaned up, and dried for a final time. Several of the finished fireworks are tied together to form a bundle. The bundles are wrapped, boxed, and stored for shipment.

"Our fireworks all go to the domestic market," the foreman's son told us. "Many of them will get used in the 'Festival of Lights.'" I had read about the ancient Hindu festival of Diwali, as it is called in India. It takes place over five days in November. To welcome the goddess of good fortune, oil lamps are lit and fireworks set off throughout the country. And indeed, almost all fireworks produced in India stay there, to be used in the Festival of Lights celebrations.

As in many factories in India, the production of fireworks is labour intensive. It requires a lot of people, and often those workers are children. As we were being shown around, we noticed that when we entered a room, there would often be a child just leaving.

At other times there was no effort made to hide the underage workers. We were aware that on government inspection day, all children were given a "holiday." But during our visit, we saw plenty of them. Children of ten or eleven were cutting the tubes in one room, while in another they were dipping them in red dye. The fumes from the dye hung in the air, wafting between the rooms. There was very little ventilation, and at times the heat was almost unbearable. The workers, adults and children, dripped with sweat. The children labouring at the huge vats of dye were red with dye themselves – their clothes, their hands, even their faces.

One child showed me how to cut the tubes to the proper length, while another demonstrated how to wedge them together inside the metal rings.

After a hard day of work in the fireworks factory, these boys were eager to play a game of volleyball and asked me to join in the fun. One of them told me that on his first day at work there was an explosion in his factory. He ran home and hid. He was afraid to ask what had happened for fear of being told that someone had been killed.

We saw one adult emerge from a chemical-storage room, covered from head to foot in a fine white powder. Outdoors, he ran his hands through his hair and brushed off his clothes. A white cloud drifted away from him, though it took a cloth and considerable rubbing for his true skin colour to return. We couldn't help but wonder how much of the chemical had made its way into his lungs. Inside the compound, Alam and I walked past endless vats of open chemicals.

In one factory we questioned the foreman about what safety precautions were in place if fire broke out. He pointed to two red buckets hanging just outside the doorway.

"Before a fire can spread," the foreman explained, "the workers pour water onto the chemicals." He seemed perfectly serious.

But with two buckets it would be impossible to pour water on all the chemicals throughout the room. The chemicals were highly flammable; the place would be an inferno in seconds. But most shocking of all, the buckets were empty! The heat had evaporated all the water, and dust had even begun to settle in them.

As we made our way between factories that afternoon, explosion after explosion hurled clouds of smoke into the air, almost as if bombs were being detonated. They were all some distance away, but the blasts unnerved us and left us wondering just what was going on.

"Merely a controlled explosion of excess or badly mixed chemicals," we were told. "It happens all the time."

It was a glaring symbol of the reality of working in these factories. One careless spark and an entire compound would be up in flames in minutes. And it was a graphic reminder of the many explosions that occurred over the years across Sivakasi. "Uncontrolled" explosions had claimed the lives of hundreds of adults and children, and scarred and crippled countless more.

As twilight descended, we made our way back to the village we had walked through when we first arrived. The once-empty paths connecting the village to the many fireworks and match factories around it were now filled with adults and children returning home.

For these children, the end of the work day meant, first of all, a game of volleyball. It was their one bit of recreation after long hours labouring in the factories. A net had been set up in the village (a stake in the ground on one side, a tree on the other), and when we arrived a game

All it takes is a single spark and an entire fireworks factory can go up in flames. The only safety precaution in this compound was the two buckets of water pictured here. My horror mounted when I discovered that the buckets were empty; there was nothing but a layer of sand and dust at the bottom.

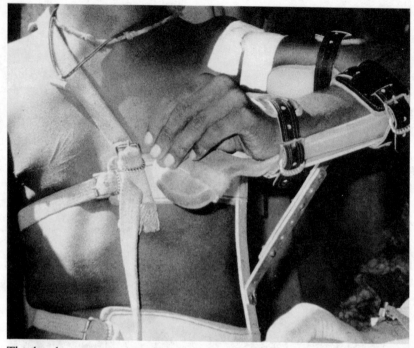

This boy has scars running down his arm and side from an explosion. He considers himself to be lucky because he is still alive. Many of his friends in the factory were killed in the same explosion.

had just started. A line of prime seats were reserved for the elders of the village, and children were cheering for their favourite players. It had all the features of a major community event.

I watched from the sidelines for a while, but before long they wanted me to join them. I love volleyball, and I readily agreed. I made a few good hits, but I was no match for these kids. They were quick to cheer me on, though, even after the ball flew by me at lightning speed.

I had become friendly with some of the children in the village, and when a few of them gathered around later I thought I might be able to find out more about their work in the factories. I knew they had probably been warned not to talk to strangers about their jobs, but I was not so much of a stranger any more. And we had one very important thing in common. I was the same age as many of them. There seemed to be an instant connection between us, the same connection I had experienced with kids throughout my trip. Often what kids are willing to share with each other they would never think about sharing with an adult.

By this time it was dark, so we gathered in the one spot in the village where there was light enough for us all to see each other – under the electric lightbulb in the doorway of a village store. They were fascinated at having a white boy in their midst, and almost as much by the videocamera Alam held in his hand.

One boy, Mariupun, was twelve years old. He had worked in a fireworks factory for two years.

"What is your job?" I asked him.

"Ring puncher. I punch out the holes so the chemicals can be put in."

"Do you like working there?"

"I like the job," Mariupun said. "It helps the family problem, the money problem."

I discovered that all his family worked in the factory – his parents, four older sisters, and one older brother. Two of his sisters and his brother were married.

"How much do they make?"

"Per day, ten rupees each."

The whole family together made about two dollars U.S. per day.

"Have you ever gone to school?"

"I left school at the age of nine."

257

He told me how an explosion had taken place in another part of his factory just weeks after he started work.

"Was anyone injured?" I asked.

The boy shook his head; he did not know. "I was so frightened, I ran home. I hid under the bed."

"You didn't ask your boss if anyone was hurt?"

"No. I didn't want to know. I was too frightened."

"Aren't you worried about another explosion?" I asked.

"No," he said. He didn't sound very convincing.

In fact, most of the children we spoke to that night said they had no fear of a fireworks explosion in their particular factory. Perhaps it took such optimism to go to work each day. But explosions are a reality in this area of India. A reality as stark as the land on which they live. It might only be a matter of time before some of these children had a very different story to tell.

We took a bus back to Madurai that evening.

After thanking our hosts profusely for all their help, and with a supply of jujubes to last the whole trip, we set off to the station at eleven o'clock that night to catch a bus to Cochin. We went to purchase our tickets, only to find out we had missed the bus by two hours. Our spirits sank. The next bus was at seven the following morning.

Our only choice was to go back to our friend's house and stay the night, then return in the morning. We went in search of a taxi. Out in front of the station we looked at each other in disbelief. The only taxi anywhere in sight was the one we had taken the night before.

"This time I know the street," our wandering friend declared, nodding furiously. "I am positive. I know the street."

Alam and I were not so easily convinced. Should we believe him? More to the point, did we have a choice?

We piled our baggage into the baby taxi, jammed ourselves in with it, and off we went.

"This is the house," our driver announced.

"No, this is *not* the house."

"Yes, yes."

"No, no."

It was as if we had looped back in time.

It was twelve o'clock at night. People were few and far between.

The driver did finally spot someone. "Here! Here!" he called. "We need your help."

Four people on bicycles cycled over. One of them took out a flashlight and shone it on the piece of paper with the address on it that we had given the driver. A second later he whipped the light in our faces.

There was an eruption of laughter. They were the same four police officers who had rescued us the night before! And on the exact same street.

They turned on the driver. "How could you do that to these people! How did you get your taxi licence?" Then, still laughing, they hopped on their bikes and led us back to the right house.

Once again they insisted on pounding on the door. And once again our host appeared. He could only laugh and shake his head.

Alam and I sheepishly gathered our bags and thanked the police officers.

"I pick you up tomorrow and take you to your bus," the taxi driver called to us.

We shook our heads. "No, no. You won't find the house."

"I know where it is now! I'll be here in the morning. What time?"

The police officers went off, their laughter echoing down the empty street. We closed the door behind us. We could hear the taxi driver still yelling, "I can find the place! What time do you want me? What time?"

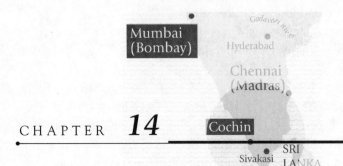

CHAPTER **14**

Mumbai (Bombay)
Hyderabad
Chennai (Madras)
Cochin
Sivakasi
SRI LANKA
Colombo

Cochin and Bombay

Even before I left Canada I felt a connection with the Indian state of Kerala. This part of the country was the birthplace of the parents of Marilyn Davis, my good friend back in Canada. Marilyn and I went to the same school, and she had been a member of Free the Children from its very first day. We spent many hours together working on displays and perfecting speeches. We had both spoken during that first visit to Brebeuf College, and shared our anguish after the question period that followed.

In the speeches she gave, Marilyn often spoke about the Kerala she knew from her visits there, and of the Kerala her parents remembered in the days before they came to Canada. The state had undergone great change. Its government had made the protection and education of children a priority. Kerala now has the highest literacy rate in all of India. Almost every child attends primary school, and an incredible 88 per cent of children go on to high-school level. The rate rivals that of many developed countries. The incidence of child labour is very low, less than 3 per cent, despite the fact that Kerala has one of the lowest GSPs (gross state product) in the country. It is widely praised by human-rights groups as a great success story, evidence of the power of political will in eliminating exploitative child labour. Kerala has shown the world that child labour can be brought to an end.

As we made our way by bus to the town of Cochin, I could already see a tremendous difference from the state we were leaving behind. The road wound past endless tea plantations, and there was not one child to be seen working the fields. I strained my eyes to pick out every person I could, and each time it was an adult tilling the soil, spraying pesticides, harvesting the crops. Even more encouraging was the scene we encountered when the bus stopped at one of the villages to refuel. There were no street children rushing to the bus begging for money. Instead, we saw dozens of children in their school uniforms heading home for the day.

In landscape, too, Kerala was much different from the other parts of India we had seen. After the aridness of Sivakasi, it was a great relief to find stretches of green again, to see, in addition to the tea plantations, coconut palms and mango trees. The fact that the state has a long coastline makes it even more attractive. Historically, Kerala was the centre of the spice trade, a connection point between China and the Western world. In outlook, its people have always been cosmopolitan and open to new ideas. The work of grassroots organizations and a campaign of land reform have opened the way for major education initiatives.

After travelling through other parts of Asia for six weeks, and seeing so much child labour, Kerala seemed like a mirage. As I sat on a bench on the waterfront of Cochin and watched the fishing boats unload their catches, then turned and saw dozens of smiling and laughing children spilling out the front door of a nearby school, I knew it was for real. In fact, it was a loud challenge to all those people I had met who said that child labour was part of the culture and there was no point in ever seeking change. Kerala still had poverty, and it still had economic problems, but had proved the naysayers wrong. Child labour didn't have to exist.

I hurried across the road to talk with students on the steps of the school. English is a mandatory subject in all schools in India, and these kids certainly spoke it well enough that we could understand each other.

I introduced myself and told them why I had come to India, and how good it was to visit Kerala and see so many students going to school. It wasn't long before we were talking directly about the issue of child labour.

Kerala is a success story. It proves wrong the critics who state that child labour cannot be ended. With the state government's commitment to land reform, and compulsory education for all children, child labour has been almost completely eliminated there. Everywhere I looked I saw children well fed and in school. This group of children told me they would like to see all young people enjoy the opportunities they have.

"So what do you think can be done to eliminate child labour in the other states of India?"

"We have to spend money," said one girl, who was nearly fluent in English. "We have to build more schools; and primary education should be made available to all children. Someone should do something."

"I think I know who could introduce the idea in your school," I said. "How about you? You obviously feel strongly about this issue. Why don't you bring it up? You could start a group."

"We need someone behind us who is respected. Maybe the principal."

I looked around me at all the kids who had gathered. "I am from a Canadian organization called Free the Children. It was formed by kids, it's led by kids, and kids run it. You don't necessarily have to wait for your principal. You could start your own group and begin taking action. You could organize a petition to the governments in other states calling on them to make primary education a priority. Or you could start collecting school supplies to send to kids who need them."

"Yes – but still, we need an adult."

"Adults can help, but you don't necessarily need them. Children can run an organization too," I told her. "If you started a core group of committed people, you would be amazed at how many kids will come forward, eager to take on responsibility."

I wasn't sure they would act on my suggestion, but maybe I had planted the seed. Perhaps they would see it wasn't impossible and join together to voice their opinions. And if they did, there was no telling how far they would go.

A short while later, I talked with a second group of students. Our conversation took a similar direction. The children didn't lack ideas or passion, but they did find it hard to believe they could start an effective group. These children had many of the same fears we did in Canada when we started Free the Children. Would adults take us seriously? Would other young people be interested in joining? They questioned their own abilities, just as we did.

Our time in Cochin was spent walking the streets and talking to people. Often it was children we spoke to, and of course, when we were seen talking with one kid, it wasn't long before others joined us. On one occasion, at a construction site, a group of children who knew some English acted as translators so we could talk to the workers, who only spoke the local dialect.

It was great to be able to visit a busy construction site and not find children labouring there. If it had been anywhere else in India, I had no doubt we would have found children among the adults we encountered shovelling gravel into wheelbarrows. Child labour in construction has been long outlawed by the International Labour Organization, but around the world there are countless children still involved in the industry.

I approached some of the labourers as they battled the heat, their sweat-streaked clothing evidence of many hours of hard work. I said to the men how good it was to see that there were no children among them. One man paused and leaned on his shovel to tell us that he had just come from the state of Tamil Nadu, seeking a better job and a better life for his family. Some of his children went to school, he said, but others worked in a mill. This did not surprise me, for I knew that the small percentage of children who did work in Kerala were most often the children of immigrant workers, people who had come from other places in India where education was less valued. But I knew, too, that the government of Kerala had undertaken an awareness campaign to help these people see that education was an important tool for their children.

As I left the construction site, the children who had accompanied me were very curious about why I had come to India. They wanted to know if what I was doing was my job.

"Not my job," I told them. "I am a student like all of you."

And I was very curious about what they thought of Canada. Some of them had seen American movies and TV.

"What do you think life is like in Canada and the United States?" I asked them.

"Lots of money. The streets are clean, it is safe, and everyone has jobs. They all make lots of money."

I don't think they believed me when I said that developed countries have poor people too. "There are people in these countries who go hungry and do not have a place to sleep at night. But there is not nearly so much poverty as I have seen in India."

"Your people are lucky, very lucky," one boy said.

When I thought about all I had seen over the past several weeks, I knew just how true that was.

Even by the end of our stay in Kerala, as we headed to the Cochin airport, I still found it hard to believe I had not been transported to another country. We had not once seen a working child.

Hours later, as we stepped outside the airport in Bombay, the very first sight to meet my eyes was a barefoot boy of eight or nine dashing up to us, asking if we wanted a taxi.

When our bus stopped on its way to downtown Bombay, we were confronted by young girls begging for money. There were a half-dozen of them, none more than ten years old. They wore nothing on their feet, and their tattered clothing was too big for their undernourished bodies. Their hair was matted and wild. They split into two groups and dodged the traffic to get to the windows of the bus, each girl holding out one hand while cupping the other and drawing it to her mouth in the same "I need food" gesture we had seen so often before.

The minute they were given a little money, they rushed back across the street. From behind a pillar emerged a man, his shirt unbuttoned to halfway down his chest and his pants sporting a bright-yellow belt. His shoes were black and shiny. The girls circled him like stray cats around a garbage can. He gathered up the coins they had collected, then quickly turned and sent them off through the traffic again. When he saw the videocamera that Alam had trained on him, he gathered his band and slinked away.

Bombay – city of wealth, city of the homeless. More movies are made here than are made in Hollywood. It's the financial capital of India, the industrial heart of the nation. International fashion boutiques share the city with unbelievable squalor. Walk a few blocks from the Rolls-Royces and Jaguars and you see animal-drawn carts and rickshaws.

It was January 26. Originally, I was due to fly back to Canada the following day – something I had not been looking forward to. Since Madras, I had been desperately thinking of ways to convince my parents to let me stay longer. There was still so much I wanted to do, and so many places I wanted to visit. I just couldn't go home yet.

In Cochin, I called my parents from the hotel's front desk to ask if I could please change my plane ticket and stay another week. I thought I would try a relatively low-key approach first, to see how far that would get me.

"But you've already been gone for almost seven weeks!" was my mother's response.

Even though my parents had allowed me to go to South Asia, they hadn't stopped worrying about me from the moment I left Toronto. My mother told me later that she hadn't slept one minute during the whole time I was in Pakistan. I realized, too, that I was very lucky even to be here. Most of my friends' parents would never have considered it, period.

But I had to have a bit more time, even a few days, *anything.*

"I just can't come home now."

"What about all the school that you've already missed? Have you been able to finish all your math homework on the trip?" my father asked.

"I finished some," I said, hoping he wouldn't dwell on the subject. I had done a total of three pages the entire time I'd been gone and had started to use some of the hundred or so photocopied worksheets as scrap paper for writing notes.

"Just one more week!" I begged.

My parents wouldn't budge. They were definite. I would have to return home as planned.

It was the worst day of the entire trip. I couldn't imagine going home. "Back to Canada" was even worse than "Back to Dhaka."

"Besides," my mother said, "you have a load of media interviews starting on the twenty-ninth. That gives you just two days to rest up and recover from your trip."

My mother was not looking forward to the media intruding into our lives. She wanted time for me to hide out, to recover from jet lag.

Her plan gave me other ideas.

"I'll change my flight. I don't need those two days. I'll sleep on the plane. I promise."

"Craig, you need your rest." Her voice was firm. No hint of compromise.

"I'll sleep on the plane. I promise I will. I'll knock myself out if I have to...with...with the armrest!"

"Craig..." Then a tentative chuckle. A very slight softening of her position.

"Tell you what," I said quickly. "Alam and I will discuss the idea and we'll call you later. Okay?"

But before I hung up I knew that nothing could possibly change my mind.

Before I left Canada I had spent a lot of time imagining the countries I would be visiting. I pictured exotic food, religious rituals, and cities crowded with people. I started reading about the cultures and reviewing all the information that had been sent to Free the Children by the various human-rights organizations. I watched movies that I thought would help give me a sense of what to expect – *Gandhi* and *City of Joy*.

After travelling through parts of India, one movie I had watched really came back to me as reflecting the reality of children there. It's called *Salaam Bombay!*, based on the true stories of street children, and many of its scenes take place in Bombay's train station. With scenes from that movie in my mind, the first place we headed for was that same train station.

Through its great, lofty halls passed thousands of people each day, getting on and off trains that connected to every part of the country. Our goal was to see firsthand the children who worked on these trains in the hope of receiving payment. We decided we would pick a train and ride it for a few stops, then turn around and return to the station.

We had only just made our decision when two girls about nine years old suddenly appeared in front of us and started begging for money.

Before we had started our trip, Alam and I had discussed how we would respond to all the beggars we were sure to encounter. Alam told me that my skin colour would be an instant attraction to people begging for money, and he had been proved right many times. We knew we couldn't possibly give money to them all, and so we had decided our money was better directed to buying food for the children or using it in Free the Children's efforts to end child labour.

We told the girls, in our broken Hindi, that we weren't giving them any money. They grabbed our arms and legs and began chanting. One girl sank her fingernails into my skin trying to get me to respond.

It really hurt inside to ignore these girls. I didn't know if I was doing the right thing. I felt like digging into my pockets and giving them every rupee I had, yet I knew there was probably a ringleader waiting somewhere, ready to take every coin these young girls brought back. I looked at Alam and he looked at the girls and shook his head.

They finally gave up on us and moved to another person in the line, a businessman reading a newspaper. They chanted their beggar's chant and looked up at the man, pulling at the sleeves of his suit jacket, trying to get his attention away from the paper.

Suddenly the back of his hand flew at them and struck one of the girls across the face. She was so slight that it knocked her to the floor. The girl burst into tears, covering her face with her hands. The second girl clutched her and helped her to her feet. They ran off together, down the stairs, and disappeared into the crowds, the young girl crying as she ran.

I stared at the man with disbelief as he unfolded his paper and continued reading.

Eventually we boarded a commuter train, without any doors, that held about forty passengers per car. People slipped on and off at every stop, including a constant flow of young beggars or kids performing a service and hoping to get a few rupees in return.

One was a young boy of ten or eleven. He was barefoot and wore only brown pants cut off at the knees, revealing the many scars on his legs. In one hand he held a small broom made of reeds, and in the other, an orange plastic cup. He shuffled in a crouch along the length of the train, sweeping the dirt from under the seats as he passed.

At one stop a young girl, no more than six, came aboard the train holding a small tin cup. She wore a dress that was much too big for her; a yellow ribbon held back her long hair. She walked to the front of our car and quietly began to sing. At first, no one paid much attention, but gradually the passengers turned away from their newspapers, stopped their talking, and listened. As the train slowed to the next stop, she walked down the aisle, continuing her song, holding out her cup. No one gave her anything, and when the train stopped she was gone.

I felt as if I should have given her something, even a few rupees. But I realized the way in which I could truly help her was to continue with Free the Children and try to change a system that made the lives of children like hers so miserable.

The poverty that we found in parts of Bombay was overwhelming. Out of a population of fifteen million, it is estimated that a million people live on the streets. Sometimes their shelters are no more than barrels or crates tied together with rope. In some parts of the city, the homeless are so numerous that many are forced to walk the streets at night because the sidewalks are full with sleeping bodies. Those who do have a place are extremely territorial. Often, we were told, the homeless paid off the police and store owners to be allowed to sleep in a certain spot. If they failed to come up with the money, they were literally kicked from their places or had water poured on them to flush them out.

It took Alam to help me put it all in perspective. "Even the poor have their times of joy," he said. "And as depressing as poverty is, you must always remember that everything has a solution. You must live your own life to reflect that solution."

As our time together wound down, we seemed to be trying to put together our thoughts on what the whole trip had meant. We spent hours just walking the streets of Bombay, quietly observing the daily routine, sorting through all we had experienced over the past weeks.

My view of the world had changed dramatically and permanently, and Alam wanted to be sure I would be able to deal with the impact of the trip, to come to terms with what it would mean for my future. He seemed to anticipate great commotion in my life upon my return to Canada, and he wanted to prepare me for that.

"Strive for a balance," he said. "Free the Children will grow. You will want to take it to its full potential, but take time for yourself. Take time to study and to learn."

"I'm good at catching up," I said, thinking about all the schoolwork I would have to do when I got back.

"Not only what you find in a textbook," he said. "Your greatest teacher is the world around you. Take time to look at it. Don't just accept it for what it seems on the surface. Look at all the angles."

I had often seen Alam do that. Just when I thought I understood something, he would twist my thinking around and encourage me to see it from a different perspective. His most important rule was to

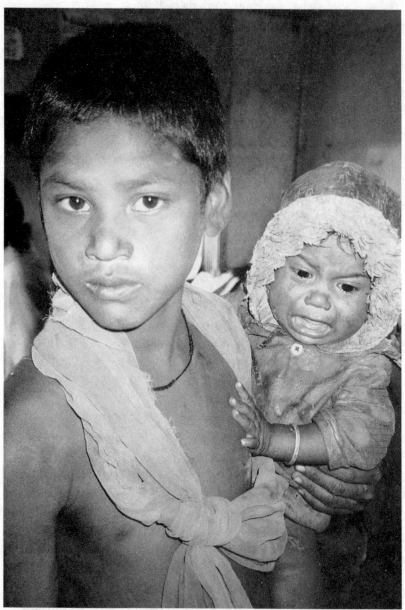

Children as young as seven or eight carry young babies through the streets as they beg for money. Driven by desperate poverty, they will cradle their siblings with one arm and hold out the other, hoping for a few coins. Often children are part of a begging ring controlled by an adult who takes the money.

respect those around you and always try to learn from them. "Put yourself in the other person's shoes for a moment," he would say.

He always stressed the importance of asking questions, and pushing for an answer when I didn't understand something the first time. He often challenged me after the meetings we had with organizations. "You should have been more direct with your question," he would say. Or, "Did you really understand his theory? If not, then you should have told him you didn't understand. And if you think someone is wrong on a point, tell him he's wrong. Be direct. Tell the truth."

Alam was not like anyone else I had ever met. He didn't want much of anything in the way of material possessions. The bare necessities and no more. In fact, he was about to spend many more months travelling through Asia, and everything he needed fit into one small knapsack, no bigger than the kind many kids take to school.

Alam had come to South Asia with no precise plans, except for the seven weeks we were spending together. Little did he realize at the time, but he himself would be so moved by the plight of working children that he would want to commit more of his time and energy to helping them.

He once said to me, "I intend never to own a car. I want you to guess why."

I quickly came up with a list of possible reasons: a car is very expensive, it pollutes the environment, it's made of non-renewable materials, public transportation is better. He shook his head each time.

An hour later I was still digging for answers, going from the reasoned to the ridiculous. Finally, I gave up.

"Because," he said, "I don't *want* one."

Typical Alam. His life is a search for the simple answers and simple joys. His list of pleasures in life include going for a walk, an interesting vegetarian meal, and quiet conversation with a group of friends.

And a *dhabrapani*. On my last evening in Asia, we left behind the traffic and noise. We searched the waterfront until we found a calm and restful spot, the glimmering expanse of the Arabian Sea in front of us. Behind us, the faint strains of Hindi music from a vendor's stall. Alam knew I was feeling sad about leaving.

"Wait here. I'll be right back."

He disappeared, and returned a few minutes later with his hands behind his back.

"Guess what I found?"

"A one-way ticket to Canada leaving in a year?" I answered with a smile.

He took one hand from behind his back and held out a coconut. In the other hand, he presented two straws. We drank our *dhabrapani*, then another, and another, as we talked over our trip.

"What is your favourite memory?" I asked him.

"Walking through the traffic in the dead of night to get to the Indian border. Weaving our way past those thousands of people, all so strangely quiet. Watching the sweep of colours at dawn, just as we reached our destination."

I recounted my true feelings at the moment I first arrived in Bangladesh and ran into the horde of people outside the airport. "I was scared."

"Really?"

"Seriously. I kept thinking, What am I doing here, a kid from a suburb of Toronto? Halfway around the world, and nobody meeting me."

We remembered the funny incidents, such as the reaction of kids in the rural areas who had never seen a white person before. The morning after the children had been freed from the carpet factory and we had returned them to their village, one child came up to me just to touch my face. I stood silently as he ran his hands down my white arms and pulled my hair. He ran off, as if he had touched a ghost, shouting something in a local dialect.

We laughed about how I now had two new notches in my belt because I had lost so much weight on the trip. And how, despite my shrinking waistline, I had grown to love the local food. I had even come to love the desserts. Back in Canada I rarely ate sweets. In India, I often went for second or third helpings. And Indian tea, so strong compared to the kind I had drunk in Canada, was now a drink I thoroughly enjoyed.

"What won't you miss?" Alam asked.

I had to pause and think.

"Those huge pictures of Pakistan's prime minister plastered all over the place – up the side of an entire building, in every subway stop, even in washrooms. Remember them?"

"How could I forget! What else?"

"Train food. Mosquitoes!"

"And the biggest highlight?" Alam asked.

"Meeting the children," I said without hesitation.

I had come to South Asia to meet with children, and that goal had certainly been achieved. My most powerful memories would always be of those children: the look on the face of the young girl separating the syringes; the eyes of the boy in the brick kiln who told me he was working to pay off a loan taken out decades before by his grandfather; the relief on the face of Munnilal when he embraced his mother, the mother he had seen in his dreams.

Now, after seven weeks in South Asia, it was Canada that seemed the strange world I couldn't understand. So much waste, so many possessions. I wondered if I could fit back into my old life. It all seemed so pointless in comparison to the massive problems the children here faced each day.

"Strange how, going back to Canada, I feel even more nervous than when I left for Asia."

"Listen," Alam said suddenly. He held up his hand and stopped me dead in my tracks. "Can you hear it?"

"Hear what?"

"It's getting bigger."

"What's getting bigger?"

"Look, behind you."

He pointed out to sea. I jerked my head around.

"It's growing, it's growing!"

"I don't see anything. I think you've had too many *dhabrapanis*."

"As soon as you land in Canada, it will come crashing down around you."

"Alam, what are you talking about?"

He looked at me and smiled. "The media tidal wave."

When I last talked to my mother on the phone, she had told me my time was booked solid with media interviews for a week. I had told her to accept the interviews; I had learned just how important the media was in creating an awareness of child labour.

Alam stared at me, completely serious. "Will you sink or will you swim? Drown in it, or ride the surf? It's one or the other."

He was right. Even more reason to be reluctant to return to Canada.

We ended the evening with a visit to a market and a last meal out.

The stalls were filled with everything imaginable – from ivory carvings to guns used in Asian wars, from monkey skulls to amulets that were said to emit magic auras. In one stall an older man mixed herbal remedies, something for every sickness ever known. Another stall specialized in animal parts used for religious or medical reasons – bones, eyeballs, shells, testicles, preserved paws and feet. There was a thriving black market in fake designer clothing. Men held open briefcases and hawked "genuine" Rolex watches and, at the sight of police officers, disappeared through the crowds.

My favourite were the stalls that sold spices. They were a palette of rich, earthy colours – dark, intense reds, burnt oranges, bright and tarnished yellows. I watched intently as the vendor weighed the spices carefully on his ancient balance, the powder in one tray, tiny pebbles in the other.

It was getting late. The sun had long set. As we prepared to go, a boy about my age approached us, offering to sell me a drum like the one he had slung by a leather thong around his neck. When I looked at him, I felt as if I were staring into a mirror. Not only did we have similiar facial features, but we were the same height and had the same slim build. As much as I would have liked to have bought something from him, I said I had no need for a drum, and we moved on. I watched as he continued down the street, one hand at each end of the drum, tapping out a beat to attract customers, drifting into a maze of people.

Farther along, Alam suggested we look for a restaurant. My mind was still picturing the boy, and how, by a twist of fate, I had been born into the privilege of the developed world and he into one where he was forced to sell drums in the street to survive.

"Maybe that kid is also hungry," I said to Alam. "Let's invite him along."

We forced our way back through the crowd. It took fifteen minutes before we again heard the sound of his hand tapping the drum. "Would you like to go for a meal with us? We're paying."

I had to repeat it three times before he accepted the offer. It wasn't that he didn't understand, he just couldn't believe my words.

"You want to buy me a meal?"

"Exactly!" I said. "Do you know a good place where we can go?"

The boy led us to a small restaurant with loud Hindi music and a menu written in chalk on the wall. He chose a table near the exit, a sign that he still didn't completely trust us.

"I order anything I want?"

"Anything," Alam told him.

This was my last dinner before returning to Canada. I felt like some-one on death row...the last meal before the execution. Even though the menu was in Hindi, I had no problem deciding what I wanted. I had been thinking about it for several days.

"*Dhal* and *roti*," I said when the waiter came. "That's all."

Alam was surprised. He had been expecting me to try some meat dish I had never eaten before.

Dhal and *roti* were a symbolic choice for me. They are basic, staple foods. I had come to Asia to learn about child labourers. To put myself in their shoes, as Alam would say. I thought it only fitting that the last meal be one a child labourer would eat day after day.

Alam decided to order the same, but our guest wasn't about to waste his opportunity on something so ordinary. He chose an elabo-rate chicken dish, with curried mango and a red sauce.

Between bites we found out a little more about him.

"My name is Shakif," he told us.

"My guess is you are thirteen," I said.

"Right!"

"I'm thirteen too."

He smiled, nodding his head.

"And do you have to work every day?" I asked him.

"From eight in the morning to late at night. No holidays."

275

My final meal in India reminded me why I had come to South Asia. Seated with Shakif, a street vendor my own age, I realized it was only a matter of luck that I had been born into a life of privilege, with all my needs met, while so many children around the world live in hardship.

He told us that the man who made the drums gave him a cut of each sale, though he had not been able to sell one drum in the past week.

Shakif didn't like talking much about himself. He preferred to talk about sports and Hindi music.

When the meal came to an end and I had finished my last cup of Indian tea, we returned to the street. Shakif held out a drum and tried once more to sell us one. We smiled and congratulated him on being such a persistent salesman.

"Sorry, Shakif, we don't really need a drum," I said. "Besides, we've absolutely no room in our luggage for one."

As we were about to leave, he seemed to be looking for a way to thank us for the meal. He broke out into a loud and energetic song.

We stood and listened, charmed by the magic of his playing.

"How about I join you," I said with a laugh.

He passed me another drum and I tried to join in. It was a strange duet. I didn't quite get the hang of the rhythm, and my lack of talent brought laughter from children who had stopped for our impromptu concert.

"Alam, somehow I don't think my years of music lessons have paid off."

But my attempt at drumming was of great value in another way. For a brief moment Shakif shared his life with me, and gave me a lasting memory of my final night in Asia.

The next morning we began the final packing of our bags. I couldn't put it off any longer. The inevitable trip to the airport was drawing near. The dreaded end was in sight.

Alam's packing was a breeze. Besides his two changes of clothing, there was a sweater, a blanket, a small bottle of bleach to purify drinking water, and a couple of personal items. That was it.

"I can't believe you bought so many presents," he said, looking at the few things I had picked up for my family.

"They don't take up much room, actually. It's all that literature on child labour I've collected, and *your* extra clothes." He had given me anything that violated his "bare minimum" rule, so I could take it back to his family in Toronto.

"And what about that Coke bottle?" he was quick to respond.

While in Dhaka, waiting for the bus to arrive to take us to the border, I had spotted an empty glass Coke bottle lying on the floor in the bus terminal. I had picked it up and run my fingers over the Bengali writing on one side and the English on the other. I decided to keep it. I don't even like Coke, but I thought it was a good souvenir. It said a lot about my trip – West meeting East.

I had carefully washed the bottle and slipped it in my bag. In Thailand, Alam caught a glimpse of it and told me to throw it out, that it was extra weight I didn't need. In Nepal, again he spied it, and I told him it would never leave the country. In Lahore, he came across it again and threatened to throw it out himself. And now in Bombay, the Coke bottle came to light once more, having been carried through five countries and more than a dozen cities, by plane, train, bus, car, water taxi, ferry, rickshaw, animal cart, baby taxi, and on foot.

"Should I leave it behind here in Bombay?" I asked, only half in jest.

"Don't even think of it!" Alam reached over and forced it back in the knapsack, out of sight.

Finally, with his help, I managed to close both my bags. Our sense of achievement didn't last long. My eye caught one item lying on the floor, unpacked: the medical kit. I opened it up and gazed at the assortment of unused items – the bottles of pills and liquid medicines, the syringes, the blood-transfusion kit. We both chuckled.

"You're welcome to this, you know. No traveller should be without one. And you have loads of room in that knapsack of yours!"

He shook his head decisively. "I'll pass."

After we had checked my baggage at the airport, Alam and I sat down in the waiting area. We had an hour to kill, and Alam suggested we take a look at some of my math sheets. Sheepishly, I pulled out the three pages I had completed while on the trip and passed them to him.

Alam had won all kinds of awards for math when he was in school. He was amazing with numbers and rarely used a calculator.

He looked my work over and smiled. "I guess we should at least review a few principles so you won't be too far behind when you get back to school."

And so my travelling companion of seven weeks proceeded to explain some basic principles of geometry and algebra, and to pass on a few little math secrets that he said would help me at exam time.

Eventually, looking at his watch, he said, "Well, I guess it's time to go through Security."

I would not hear of it. "We still have a couple of minutes," I said, almost pleading. "Show me a few more things."

He saw through my delaying tactics.

Alam closed the math book and slowly stood up.

I forced the book back in my knapsack. Tears collected in my eyes. I didn't want to go.

As we walked towards Security, neither of us spoke. I didn't want to say the words, because I knew, as soon as they left my lips, the trip would be at an end. Finally and absolutely at an end.

And I just didn't know how to say goodbye. Alam looked down at me and I realized there was no need to worry. After all this time together, through the tough times and the wildly happy ones, he understood my feelings without me having to put them into words.

Alam held out his hand and I shook it. "I hope you're a good surfer, my friend," he said.

Aboard the plane I opened my knapsack to look for my journal. Tucked away inside was a small pouch. I couldn't imagine where it had come from. It was not something I had put there.

I opened it and discovered a yellow mixture of spices. It was a gift from Alam. A little scrap of paper said, "For your next curry. *Extra* hot."

CHAPTER **15**

Thornhill and Beyond

SHORTLY AFTER MY RETURN to Canada, a newspaper quoted me as saying, "I divide my life into pre-Asia and post-Asia." I still do. The trip had a profound affect on me, one that changed me forever. I would spread the word about the suffering of all the children I had met. I would let the world know that we, too, are part of the problem. I would not fail them.

As the airplane lifted off the runway in Bombay, I knew that, after all that had happened over the past seven weeks, my life could never be the same. Just how much my view of the world had changed was as clear as my very next meal.

When the flight attendant announced the choice of meals, I decided on the Western dinner, thinking how good it would be to taste food I hadn't eaten in so long. I uncovered the steaming vegetables and the slices of beef, and eyed the pudding for dessert. This would be a first step back into the culture I had left. I began eating, but then, after just a few moments, I stopped. Something was missing...my taste buds seemed to be waiting for some ingredient to kick in. I finished most of the meal, but I was desperately craving a few spices to liven things up.

On the last couple of pages of my journal were some Asian recipes that Alam had dictated to me while in India. Each dish reminded me of special moments during my trip. *Pad thai* and the markets of

Thailand...*dhal* and *roti* and the night we took the boy selling drums out for a meal...*masala dosa* and the day Alam and I flew the kite on a rooftop in Madras. I flipped to these pages and read through each of the recipes, ingredient by ingredient.

Leaning back in my seat I let the memories of Asia be my dessert.

It was a world so different from what I had expected. When I left Toronto it was with images of children with distended bellies, poor people who needed our help – the images of the Third World that aid agencies depicted on TV.

I had seen poverty, that's true. Unbelievable poverty. But I had also discovered a beautiful world filled with exciting history and culture. A world that also had its rich people. It was a world struggling to develop, but one made up of resourceful people. They were fighters. We had so much to learn from them.

Eventually I fell asleep, and remained so the rest of the way to Amsterdam.

In Amsterdam airport the culture shock hit even harder. As I walked through the airport, I passed store after store with their show-cases of merchandise – jewellery, furs, leather cases, Rolex watches by the dozen. One watch cost more than a rickshaw driver in Bangladesh would make in his entire life.

I had never once felt homesick during the time I was away. But, now, after I changed planes in Amsterdam and was flying over the Atlantic, I felt the moment when I would first catch sight of my family and friends draw ever closer. As it did, the anticipation grew.

When we finally landed, the usual voice came over the intercom: "Please remain seated until the aircraft has come to a complete and final stop." But even before the plane had approached the terminal building, a flight attendant was by my side, telling me that the moment we stopped I was to be in position by the door. She reached into the overhead compartment and pulled out my two carry-on bags and disappeared with them to the front of the plane. It was all a bit strange considering that unaccompanied minors are usually the last to leave an aircraft. The flight attendant reappeared while the seatbelt sign was still lit and led me quickly up the aisle.

As soon as the door opened, off we went, through the terminal, directly to Customs.

"Where did you arrive from?" the Customs official asked as he began looking through my passport.

"We don't have time," the flight attendant told him. "He's with me, and there's no problem."

Confused and a little taken aback, the Customs official stamped my passport and immigration card and handed them back to me.

Something was definitely up.

As I wheeled my luggage cart towards the door that read "Nothing to Declare," another official stopped me and took hold of the cart.

"No, no," he said, shaking his head. "The flight attendant will do that for you. She'll push the cart through the doors, then you wait thirty seconds before leaving."

I did as I was told. As I stepped past the automatic doors, a loud cheer erupted from the other side. Suddenly the bright lights of television cameras were shining in my eyes. A crowd of people was waving, welcoming me home – my family, friends from Free the Children, my entire Boy Scout troop in uniform!

My mother and father and brother wrapped their arms around me. "It's so good to see you! Welcome back!" My mother had tears in her eyes.

Behind my parents was a flurry of waving signs: "Welcome Home Craig!" and "We're Behind You All the Way." Two of the Free the Children members, Ashley and Marilyn, each handed me a red rose.

"What did I miss?" I asked.

"Not much," said my friend Vance, "Just the Super Bowl and a lot of math! Yeah, and we got a new French teacher."

After a final hug from my mother, I walked over to a podium that had been set up for my arrival. The Canadian media were ready to welcome me in their own way. They launched into a barrage of questions.

"What is the first thing you want to do now that you are home?"

"Will you try to meet again with the prime minister here in Canada?"

"How does it feel to see your family and friends?"

"What will Free the Children do next?"

The tidal wave had begun. It was another hour before we could head to the family minivan and complete the last leg of the journey home.

All the kids who met me at the airport followed us home for a party to celebrate my arrival. As soon as I opened the front door, Muffin pounced on me, almost knocking me over.

"Hey, Muffy, calm down, girl!" I dropped my bags and gave her a big hug. She licked my face and barked.

It was great to see my friends again. There must have been a dozen pizzas and a hundred cans of pop. Between games of pool and a quick snowball fight outside, I caught up on all the news. I was exhausted, so we made plans to get together again soon. I slipped away to my room. And, for the first time in almost two months, I slept in my own bed.

I woke very early the next morning, my internal clock still on South Asia time. I wasn't sure if my body was telling me to sleep, to eat, or to wake up. At five-thirty I wandered down into the kitchen. I looked around, taking in all the comforts of my home.

My mother was already up. She was still smiling with the thought that I was finally back home. She poured me a bowl of cereal, barely holding back from giving me yet another hug.

"Are you glad you went, Craig?" It was the first quiet time we'd had together since my return.

"Absolutely. I missed you guys, but I was too busy to think about it much."

That first morning I started telling my mother about the kids I had met. They would always be the most vivid memories.

During our telephone conversations from South Asia, I had kept my parents informed about basic aspects of the trip, but it would take weeks before many of the details finally came out. Even today, some things that I had forgotten will come to mind, and my parents will hear about them for the first time.

My media day began with two interviews for early-morning TV. With the time change, I was wide awake. I was anxious to tell the stories of the children I had met and to challenge people, especially young people, to raise their voices for the rights of children.

After almost a week of interviews, my mother put her foot down. "You need time for yourself. No more media."

It sounded good to me. We all needed a break. That weekend we had a double celebration: my birthday and Christmas. Ours was probably the only house in the city with Christmas lights still lit in February. We had a fabulous turkey dinner, followed by an exchange of gifts. I opened the Christmas and birthday presents that had been saved for me, and the family opened gifts I had brought for them in Bombay. They all sang "Happy Birthday," and I told the full story of the trek to the top of the Golden Mount that Alam and I had made on Christmas Eve.

A couple of days later I returned to school. I handed in my three math sheets, and received a hundred more in return. My catch-up period at school began, although life for me was never quite the same. I finished my homework in record time, and dedicated many of my waking hours to Free the Children. Soon, for every day that I attended class I found myself spending another two days travelling, giving speeches, and meeting with young people.

From the moment I returned from South Asia, our house turned chaotic. Our makeshift office was flooded with telephone calls, letters, e-mails, and faxes, all asking for information. Students across the country, from elementary to university level, were suddenly writing speeches and doing class projects on the issue of child labour. Young people were asking how they could become involved. Teachers wanted us to help inspire their students. Speaking requests from organizations, service clubs, and non-profit groups poured in. Volunteers were given keys to our home to staff the office during the day while FTC members were in class. Young people took over after school. We brought in several desks, and more filing cabinets to handle the paper that began to pile up. We added two telephone lines. Strangers called, asking to come and visit. The telephone and fax lines rang day and night.

One of the first calls I received after arriving home was from the secretary of the new minister of external affairs in Ottawa, Lloyd Axworthy. The minister was inviting me to his office so that we could discuss the issue of child labour.

I immediately accepted the offer. I had been hoping to have a meeting with him to discuss several issues, though there was one in particular I felt required his immediate attention.

One of my most powerful experiences in Asia had been walking through the streets of Patpong in Bangkok and listening as a pimp

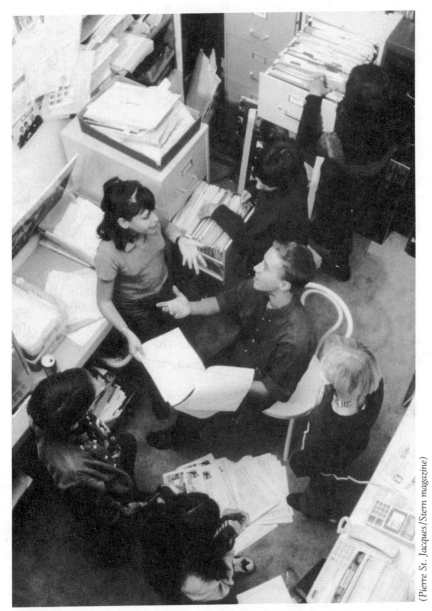

(Pierre St. Jacques/Stern magazine)

Pictured here is a group of Free the Children volunteers in a strategy session in our original home office. In the coming months, our organization would explode into an international movement of young people taking action on the issue of child labour.

promised Mick an eight-year-old boy. I also had vivid recollections of the girls I had met who had been exploited in the sex trade. But what haunted me most was how Mick and the brothel owner had discussed a deal to bring Canadians and Australians to Thailand to sexually exploit young children. I knew Free the Children had to do something to stop Canadians from continuing this abuse. So, after doing some further research, I travelled with another thirteen-year-old member of FTC, Brendan, to meet with Minister Axworthy in Ottawa.

Mr. Axworthy began the meeting by introducing us to his ten-year-old son. "This meeting was the suggestion of my son, and my niece, who is twelve," the minister told us. I shook his son's hand, realizing that we already had an influential ally with us in the minister's office.

The minister was anxious to hear of my trip to South Asia. I began by telling him of the walk I had taken through Patpong, and I handed him three documents. "These are copies of the legislation that has been passed in Australia, Germany, and France, allowing the prosecution of their citizens who go abroad to sexually exploit children. When they return home, they can be prosecuted as if they had committed the crime in their own country. Currently there are eleven countries around the world that have such legislation. We want Canada to be the twelfth."

The minister did not appear to be familiar with this legislation, but he was certainly open to the idea of such a bill being introduced into Parliament. He told us he would speak personally to Allan Rock, the minister of justice, to speed such a bill through Parliament. And, in fact, within months the Criminal Code was amended to include the prosecution of Canadians who sexually exploit children outside our country.

We spoke about several other issues related to children's rights. FTC wanted more development aid from Canada directed to grassroots projects providing educational opportunities for children, especially young girls. We asked that greater support be given to young people who were trying to assume leadership roles in Canada and internationally in defence of children.

I felt that Minister Axworthy had a special concern for children. After our meeting, he was instrumental in setting up a parliamentary subcommittee to examine what action Canada could take on an international level to eliminate child labour. The Canadian government pledged almost three-quarters of a million dollars to the International Program for the Elimination of Child Labour (IPEC), which had been established by the International Labour Organization.

At the news conference following our meeting, the minister stated that the young people from Free the Children had "debunked the notion held by many adults that children have nothing serious to contribute to government policy debates." This statement meant a lot to us. It was a breakthrough, a new way of government seeing children.

There is a growing movement around the world of children and youth seeking a voice and the right to participate in issues that affect them. Unfortunately, they are given few opportunities to be heard.

The World Congress Against the Commercial Exploitation of Children in Stockholm, Sweden, in 1996 brought together over one thousand adult delegates from more than a hundred countries. They met for a week to discuss this abuse of children. Only seventeen young people from seven countries attended the conference. They were cloistered in a room away from the other delegates and the media, and their only direct participation was in the form of a play they performed in front of the general assembly. It was staged on the second-to-last day of the meetings, after all decisions had been made and government representatives had gone home. What kind of youth representation was this, at such important discussions of one of the most serious abuses of children? One of the delegates, fourteen-year-old Ruby Acehedo of the Philippines, told the group, "You who care for us, listen to us." She pleaded for children and young people to be given a voice at all levels of government, including the United Nations, when decisions that affected their lives were being made.

Recently, in Oslo, Norway, an international conference on child labour brought together approximately four hundred adults from around the world. Only at the insistence of young people were three children allowed to attend the meetings. Other children, who were denied participation, met separately and discussed what they could do to protest this lack of involvement. One girl chose to stand outside the formal meetings with a piece of tape over her mouth, to show just what the organizers of the conference had done to the voices of children.

All over the world children are asking to be heard. Strangely, in many cases it is those organizations and groups working "for" children that seem to have the most difficulty listening to them.

Free the Children's work to empower youth to be community leaders led me to a meeting with the executive director of UNICEF in December 1996. UNICEF has a yearly budget of approximately one billion dollars, and regularly brings together staff from around the world to discuss the projects it supports.

We talked in the director's New York office, high above the city. I explained my concern that, even though UNICEF was the world's largest children's organization, it did not have a single child involved in any decision-making process or taking part in any of its board meetings. I asked if UNICEF would be willing to fund an international conference to bring youth leaders together to share their experiences and ideas, and offer UNICEF suggestions on how to involve young people in their decision-making processes.

She dismissed the idea immediately, not even taking time to consult the UNICEF adviser who was participating in the meeting with us. Her response was that UNICEF had no interest in funding more conferences.

I offered another suggestion. "Would UNICEF consider creating a youth committee within each country to offer advice to individual UNICEF offices on issues affecting children? These groups need not have voting power, but at least youth would have a voice."

She leaned back in her chair. "I wouldn't want to impose such a policy on the various UNICEF offices."

After thirty minutes, I was still getting nowhere, and as a final attempt to interest her in getting youth involved in this organization, I proposed that an advisory committee of young people be created to put together suggestions for her personally. Perhaps this group of young people could meet over the Internet and every month submit ideas to be looked over by her assistants.

She paused and thought about it. Then she said, "I wouldn't want children to have to be involved in such bureaucracy. It's my hope that the involvement of young people in UNICEF will eventually evolve naturally. It's not my role to force it on the organization."

I left the headquarters of UNICEF that day wondering how the involvement of young people in the organization could ever "evolve naturally" if the executive director would not support it.

Young people must have a voice. They need opportunities to participate and find solutions to their own problems. According to the United Nations' own Convention on the Rights of the Child, youth have that right and that responsibility.

CHAPTER **16**

What Is Childhood?

THE NIGHT BEFORE I WAS scheduled to come home from South Asia, a radio talk-show host in Toronto told the public he thought I was "not normal." At thirteen, he claimed, I should be thinking about sex and girls, and not about human rights or child labour. Others have asked me if I feel I have lost my childhood, since I have become so caught up in the fight against child labour.

What is a good and normal childhood in the world today? In my travels I have found two extremes. In many developing countries, children are often asked to work long hours at hazardous jobs with no opportunity to play or to go to school. They are not allowed to develop physically, intellectually, and emotionally as they should. They support entire families. They fight in wars. They are given too much responsibility at too young an age.

On the other hand, in many industrialized countries everything is done for children. They are segregated most of their lives with members of their own age group and are given little opportunity to assume responsibility, to develop a social conscience, or to learn through interaction with adults. Through media they learn to be consumers, to gain their self-image through the electronic toys they own and the labels they wear. They, too, are exploited. They see violence and suffering on the news every day but are told that they are too young to do anything about it. They are conditioned to become passive bystanders. This is the other extreme. Marian Wright Edelman, founder of Defence for Children International, once said, " 'Affluenza' and lack of moral purpose are more dangerous viruses than influenza for millions of America's and the world's children."

We want to help free children from both extremes.

Children are not simply empty vessels to be filled. They are people with ideas, talents, opinions, and dreams. Children believe they can fly, that there is nothing to stop their dreams from coming true. Some may call that wishful thinking, or simply being naïve. Some call young people idealists, as if it were a stage they need to outgrow. But I feel the world could do with more idealists, that there are never too many dreamers.

It was the dreamers of the world who thought that one day the Berlin Wall would fall, that apartheid in South Africa would end, and that a human would walk on the moon. Because we are young, full of ideals, and full of dreams, we are not afraid of taking an idea that to some seems impossible and striving to make it a reality. Because children are dreamers, they are unstoppable. Because they are idealists, they always have faith in a better tomorrow.

People sometimes ask me how I am able, as a teenager, to deal with all of the horrific things I have seen. They do affect me. At times, I find myself frustrated and angry. At other times, my hatred for what I have seen can turn to despair. But I have come to realize that none of these emotions really accomplish anything. We can yell as much as we want, or cry our eyes out, but it won't improve the lives of children.

As difficult as it might be, people have to channel all of these emotions into hope. My anger must move me to action; my sadness, to a determination to help.

For each time that I have felt overwhelmed by all of the suffering and hatred in the world, I can also remember a time when I felt hope. It is because of children such as Munnilal, who never gave up the hope he would again see his mother, that I never give up hope that change will come about.

Travelling has given me a better perspective on life. I feel closer to true spiritual values when I talk with the poor and underprivileged people I meet. And I have come to realize that money, power, and fancy titles mean little in this world, that true power lies in the hands of those who can help improve the lives of others. The world around me has taken on an entirely different light, a clearer one.

Before I left for South Asia, my bedroom was rather simple, with some sports posters on the walls and a few books on a shelf. But now the room is filled with the mementoes from my travels. Some are souvenirs of places I have been, others are reminders of people I will always want to remember.

On my bed-side table is a green stone Buddha I bought on my first trip to India. The statue reminds me of Alam — always calm, always trying to help those around him. Because the Buddha is laughing, it brings back memories of all the fun times we had during that trip.

On my desk there is a carved wooden statue of a young girl balancing a pot on her head. When I purchased the statue from an elderly lady in Haiti, she told me in French that half of her country's economy is balanced on the heads of women like herself.

There is a bow and several arrows hanging over my bed to remind me of my trip to Kenya. I was staying at a wildlife sanctuary, and when I arrived the guards asked me what weapons I had to defend myself. "A pocket knife," I said, smiling. Once they stopped laughing, I asked them if they would teach me how to use a bow and arrow. They spent several hours doing just that.

I have a growing line of Coke bottles, starting with my first, from the bus station in Dhaka. The writing on them ranges from Bengali to German, Arabic to Italian, and many languages in between.

One of my most treasured gifts is a soap carving of a fleur-de-lys, which was made by a child in Bosnia during the war. He gave it to me in Sarajevo after I was sworn in as Child Ambassador of the First Children's Embassy. When I look at the carving, it reminds me how, even in times of great sorrow and destruction, the human spirit survives.

These are merely the tangible things. They brighten up my room. But it is the memories of people I have met that are most important to me.

Sometimes people say to me, "It must be thrilling to meet famous people." It is true, I have met many well-known people in my recent travels with Free the Children – Pope John Paul II, Shimon Perez, Jane Goodall, Queen Elizabeth, U.S. Vice President Al Gore, the Dali Lama, and others. It was exciting, I have to admit. But it is not the memories of meeting these people that I cherish most. Nor are they the ones who have been my greatest inspiration.

It is the children I've met who are my real heroes. It is their courage and hope for a better world that ring clearest in my mind. When I am discouraged, it is the memories of these young people that I return to for faith in what I am doing.

To be inspired takes a belief in oneself. A belief, as Mother Teresa would say, that a single person can make a difference. People have to have faith in themselves and faith that they can change the world. Because it *is* true – we *can* change the world, one person at a time. Imagine if all the students in a school came together on one issue they believed in. Imagine the power they would have. If people across a community, across a country, across the continents, united to tell the world that no child should have to live in poverty, in abuse and neglect, the power they would have would be incredible. Others would have to stand up and listen, and learn there is a better way for all people to live.

Adults need to believe in the potential of children. They need to believe in the young people they encounter every day. Free the Children has grown because the children involved are lucky enough to have parents and friends who believe strongly in the abilities of young people. A child with adult support and one without can mean the difference between an international movement such as FTC or an idea that never goes beyond a child's mind.

As I look back on all the decisions I have made over the years, I can honestly say that I do not have a single regret. Because I have been fortunate to attend the very innovative Mary Ward High School in Toronto, where all eight hundred students follow independent programs of study, I have been able to travel the world and to complete my studies at the same time.

Right now, I'm happy doing my juggling act between Free the Children, school, family, and being a teenager. When I travel, as I often do with other FTC members, we always take time out for a little fun, even on the most heavily booked trips.

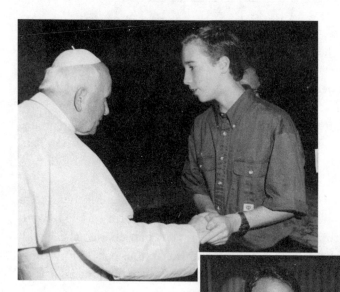

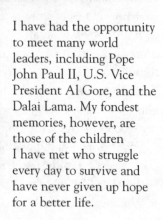

I have had the opportunity to meet many world leaders, including Pope John Paul II, U.S. Vice President Al Gore, and the Dalai Lama. My fondest memories, however, are those of the children I have met who struggle every day to survive and have never given up hope for a better life.

To this day, one of my greatest friends is my older brother, Marc. He, too, is actively involved with Free the Children, and now acts as a mentor for many other children the way he did for me. This photo was taken at a wildlife sanctuary in Kenya, where Marc worked as a volunteer for several months.

In some ways I think I am the luckiest kid in the world. I have supportive parents and great friends. They have allowed me to gaze at the sky and set no limit. I have come to realize just how fortunate I am to have a place to sleep and food on the table. I have been able to learn, to grow, and, most importantly, to help others through my actions.

Free the Children and I have been recognized for our work. Yet the true reward for me is simply in meeting the children and helping to make their stories known.

There is one award, however, that has special significance for me. Perhaps it is because it was the same one that was presented to Iqbal Masih a few months before he was killed. And because it was presented to me on the same stage in Boston where Iqbal had received it.

As I sat listening to my introduction at the Reebok Human Rights Awards, I realized I was sitting in the very chair in which Iqbal had sat two years earlier, preparing to speak to many of the same people and, in a very real sense, deliver an identical message. Iqbal's mission had continued. We had proven that a bullet can't stop a dream.

Without notes, speaking from the heart, I felt that a torch had been passed to me. I knew Iqbal was watching over us.

In the past year, I have had the opportunity to travel and to meet children in many countries, including several in South Asia, Haiti, Brazil, the Philippines, Canada, and the United States.

I have seen children living in the streets in some of the world's largest cities – sleeping on concrete, in gutters, with rats, in the cold. I met children as young as five years old sold as domestic servants, children in factories pouring molten metal with no protective gear, children working as bonded labourers in carpet factories twelve to sixteen hours a day. I stood with children working in sugar-cane fields in Brazil, wielding huge machetes as they cut cane that ends up on our tables in our sugar bowls and on our cereal each day. I saw children in Haiti on the street half dazed from sniffing glue to dull their misery and pain. I even walked the streets of Patpong in Bangkok, Thailand, with an undercover agent who in my presence was promised an eight-year-old boy for his sexual pleasure. Children...all children.

But it is not only in Third World countries that children are suffering. One in four children live in poverty in the United States, fearing for their lives in drug-ridden neighbourhoods. Even in Canada, thousands of children, robbed of their culture and their dignity, sniff glue and gasoline to ward off the cold and boredom.

These children have no voice, no vote, and no economic power. Many of them are subjected to the most inhumane forms of exploitation. I am here today to speak for those children.

In 1990, leaders from around the world gathered together and drew up the United Nations' Convention on the Rights of the Child, which lists the rights of children to an education, to be protected from abuse and exploitation, to be treated with dignity and worth. Yet this child abuse continues. This convention is the most ratified convention in the world – having been adopted by 191 countries – yet this child abuse continues.

Do all children, even the poorest of the poor, even street children, have the right to go to school? Are all children created equal? If child labour is not acceptable for white, middle-class North American kids, then why is it acceptable for a girl in Thailand or a boy in Brazil?

Freeing children is never a question of money. Freeing children is a question of political will. We simply do not believe that world leaders can create a nuclear bomb and send a man to the moon but cannot feed and protect the world's children. We simply do not believe it.

Street kids have something to teach us all. Street kids take care of one another. These children don't have very much in terms of material possessions, but they do have their friends. If a child in India is crippled or has no legs, other street kids will carry him around from place to place. When I gave a street girl in Thailand an orange to eat, she immediately broke it into several pieces and shared it with her friends.

When I was in Brazil, I spent the day with a group of street children between the ages of eight and fourteen. They welcomed me into their world and talked to me about their lives. They even showed me where they slept at night, in a bus shelter covered with cardboard boxes. They were very careful not to let anyone see us go to their secret hide-out for fear that the police would find out and beat or even shoot them. Then they asked me to play soccer with them. I looked around, but didn't see any ball. Street children are poor; they have no soccer ball with which to play. Suddenly, one of them picked up an old plastic bottle on the ground. He kicked the bottle around and we began to play. We had lots of fun until one of the children accidentally fell on the bottle and squashed it and the game was ended.

The day went by and it was getting dark, it was time for me to go. One of the street boys, José, and I had become good friends, and he wanted to give me something to take back to Canada to remember him. But he had nothing. He had no home, no food, no possessions. So he gave me the best thing he owned. He took off his soccer shirt, which was well worn with a few small holes in it, and he asked me to take it as a gift. It did not matter to him that he would be cold that night. It did not matter to him that he had no other shirt to wear. He took off his shirt, because it was all that he had to give. Of course, I refused. But he insisted, and he placed it on my shoulder. So I took my shirt off – a cheap, plain T-shirt – and gave it to him. Although his was dirty, I got the nicer shirt.

I framed that soccer shirt and put it on my wall, and I plan on keeping it for the rest of my life to remember what giving, what being generous, is all about. You see, if there were more Josés, if there were more people who had the heart of a street child and were willing to share, there would be no poverty or suffering of children in this world.

Being recognized here today is a great honour. But the real heroes are the boys and girls who work in darkness, alone and forgotten. The real heroes are the children who have only their hands, their hearts, and their dreams.

And by your actions you can set these children free!

Epilogue

IN MARCH 1998, I WAS PART OF a twelve-day trip through India. This time we weren't two drifters, never quite knowing what adventure the next day would bring. Instead, we were nine members of Free the Children, ages twelve to seventeen, from across Canada and the United States, accompanied by four chaperones, including my brother, Marc, who is now a university student. Marc has become a strong advocate for FTC and volunteers much of his free time helping to coordinate our international groups.

On the day before our flight from Toronto, we went through the contents of our luggage and chatted excitedly. My sense of anticipation, and the many preparations, were a vivid reminder of the days leading up to that first trip of mine to Asia. A parent of one of the FTC members travelling with us had packed a two-week supply of bottled water. Another had prepared a medical kit that rivalled my mother's!

We were headed to Asia to take part in the Indian segment of the Global March Against Child Labour. This march, which had started in the Philippines in January, was to pass through eighty-two countries by the time it arrived in Geneva, Switzerland, in June 1998, to coincide with the International Labour Organization's conference on child labour.

The march was organized through SACCS in India. A key organizer of the march was none other than my former travelling companion, Alam Rahman. Within a month of Alam and I saying goodbye to each other in Bombay, he had taken up an offer from Kailash Satyarthi of a job at SACCS. He soon found himself in charge of coordinating this worldwide march, a massive effort to draw attention to the struggle for the rights of children.

This time in Calcutta, instead of marching with a few hundred protesters, I was marching with many thousands. It was incredible to be walking side by side with young people who had travelled from across the world to raise their voices against child labour. With our fists high in the air, we chanted our protest loud and long.

Upon our arrival in Calcutta the day before, I was reunited with Swapan Mukherjee. Since our first meeting, Free the Children has grown enormously, and has expanded far beyond Canada. Swapan is now chairperson of FTC in India. He was the one who had organized the segment of the Global March in Calcutta, and it was his invitation that brought us all to India.

After Swapan released me from his bear-hug, my eyes fell on his son, Suprio.

"You've grown!" I exclaimed.

He gave me a strange stare, followed by a long laugh. "So have you!"

"Are you up to a game of carom? Maybe some badminton in the hallway?"

We all laughed together. We had been thousands of kilometres apart, but our friendship had only grown stronger.

Swapan filled me in on the activities of FTC India. They were helping children who had been trafficked as camel jockeys and beggars to Persian Gulf countries. With the camera equipment we had sent them they were gathering evidence so these children could be reunited with their families.

While in Calcutta, we went to visit the mission house of the Sisters of Charity. It had been less than six months since the death of Mother Teresa. She had touched my life deeply, and, as I knelt beside her tomb and prayed, I knew that she continued to watch over Free the Children, remaining a powerful influence in our work.

On her memorial was a small plastic tub with a few wild flowers hanging limply from it. Perhaps it had been left there by a child or one of the street people of Calcutta. In this simple gesture I could see just how much love there was for her memory.

We went to visit Mother Teresa's orphanage and delivered some of the school and health kits we had brought with us from North America. It was our own simple gesture, a small thank-you to Mother Teresa and all the Sisters of Charity for being such an inspiration.

In Delhi, I returned to Mukti Ashram. Here the members of our group heard firsthand the stories of children who had been bonded labourers in the carpet industry. The stories they told were again of appalling abuse. But, like the children I had heard two years before, these children were now free. Their smiles and the songs and dances they performed for us during our visit were proof that with freedom there can come the joy of being children once again. I noticed that the centre was overcrowded. I was pleased that FTC had decided to raise funds to help build another rehabilitation centre for freed child labour in Alwar, India.

"Nagashir," I heard someone say. When I turned around, my eyes fell on a familiar face in the distance. I could hardly believe it. I immediately ran up to him. "Craig," I said, pointing to myself.

Nagashir remembered me right away. I was thinking of our first encounter, of the press conference, and our trip to the gates of the prime minister of India's residence, where we were almost arrested! I smiled broadly, and he did the same.

Within seconds, another familiar face came into view – Mohan. It was an incredible reunion. The stories of these two boys had had a tremendous impact on my life. Not only that, but they had forced the head of the Canadian government into confronting the issue of child labour.

I hugged them, barely able to contain my excitement. We sat on the grass and, through a translator, caught up on what had happened since my first visit to India. "And what are you doing now?" I asked each of them.

Nagashir works full-time travelling through the rural areas near his village, visiting families and telling his story. He does it to warn others

I returned to India with a group of Free the Children members from the United States and Canada. Fourteen-year-old Melissa Joffe befriended one of the street children who begged at a restaurant near our hotel. Every time Melissa walked by, the boy would hold up his toothbrush, from the health kit she had given him, and grin with pride.

of the false promises of the middlemen who frequent the villages and try to entice parents into letting their young children work in carpet factories. Nagashir has discovered that his calling is to do all he can to save other children from the abuse and exploitation that he himself had been forced to endure.

Mohan is attending a boarding school not far from Delhi. He hopes to complete high school and go on to college. Such an accomplishment would be unheard of for anyone from his village. He still has his mind set on being a police officer. In fact, he seems more determined than ever. "One day," he told me, his voice rising in excitement, "when I am the chief of police, I will make sure the factory owners are prosecuted. There will be an end to corruption in the courts."

Mohan and Nagashir were in Delhi to participate in the Global March. They would speak at a rally and tell their stories once again. They would continue to be an inspiration to all who heard them.

Later during our visit to Mukti Ashram, as the other FTC members met with children at the centre, I went in search of someone who might be able to tell me of the whereabouts of Munnilal, the friend I had made after the raid on the carpet factory near Varanasi. I waited outside an office as a human-rights worker went through the hundreds of files of children who had come to the centre over the past two years. He came out of the office with a file in his hand and a smile on his face.

Munnilal had indeed come to the centre, he told me. "When he finished his program here, he returned to his village. According to this file, the last time a worker visited him in his village he was living with his family and still going to school."

I was overjoyed. The human-rights worker, as a favour, promised that he would check on Munnilal from time to time to see how he was doing, and that he would send me any news he received about him. He also promised to get a message to Munnilal, that the boy from Canada who had travelled home with him on the day he was freed from the carpet factory was thrilled to hear that he was still in school. "Please let him know that I have never forgotten him. Wish him the best of luck, and tell him I will forever count him as a friend."

During our time in Madras, I tried to locate the young girl who, during my first visit to the city, we had discovered separating syringes. I went to the area where I had first seen her, in the darkened room, squatting before the pile of needles, but I was unable to find her or anyone who knew her whereabouts.

We took a bus to the village outside the city to visit Sister Rita Thyveettil from the SOCSEAD organization. With the help of funds from FTC, she has initiated a project in two villages to help families earn alternative income with milk-producing animals and sewing machines so children can be removed from the gem-cutting industry. It was wonderful to see that our donation helped provide the opportunity for schooling and improved health care.

Soon FTC members were speaking with children in the village to learn more about their lives. And before much longer, many of us were playing games together. That night, some of the local people entertained us, with skits about social issues in their villages, with songs and traditional dances.

At one point all the guests were brought in front of the audience. A child of ten or eleven taught us one of the dances, much to the amusement of the two hundred villagers present.

At the end of the evening, we were asked to share some songs from our own culture. We quickly improvised a routine – a medley of "O Canada," "Happy Birthday to You," and "Lean on Me"! A couple of us even performed an impromptu dance, and were quickly joined by dozens of people from the audience. The villagers found my attempt to teach the wild dance moves to several of the women uproariously funny.

That night we ate dinner at the home of one of the villagers. It was a simple meal served on a banana leaf, but the combination of spices made it the best meal I had on the entire trip. It brought back the wonderful memories of my first encounters with Asian food.

It was during our bus ride back to Madras, with our return to North America not far away, that we all had time to reflect on what this trip to a developing country meant to the group. We recalled the first night we had arrived. We had all gone into the markets of Delhi, so those who had not been to Asia before could experience its energy, and also see its hardship and poverty. They were simply overwhelmed by it all – the surging bodies, the people begging for money, the smell of sewage.... Walking home, passing under a low bridge, we came across entire families of homeless people, seeking a bit of concrete as shelter for the night. We literally had to step over bodies as we found our way through the darkness.

The poverty was worse than anything they had ever imagined. Back in the hotel room, a deep gloom settled over the group, and those who had not been to Asia before broke down crying.

After that first night, they were able to move on, to realize that their emotions must take another direction. Instead of despair, they felt a call to action.

This is the same call to action that moves human-rights workers from the developing world, adults and children alike, to risk their lives.

This is the same call to action I continue to hear, that propels me forward with the intensity I felt that morning in 1995, when I first read about Iqbal.

And this is the same call to action that must motivate people everywhere. We must not turn our eyes away from the millions of children working in abusive and hazardous conditions. As citizens of the world, we are all responsible for one another.

"We must be the change we want to see," Gandhi said.

That change starts within each one of us. And ends only when all children are free to be children.

APPENDIX

Get Informed...
Get Involved

I HOPE THAT THIS BOOK WILL be seen as more than just the story of a trip. I hope it will awaken in many people, especially young people, the urge to do something to end exploitative child labour.

A booklet written by Kathleen Ruff, which supplements the information on the causes of child labour in this book, is available through our Free the Children office. In any human-rights struggle, the first step is to become informed. Information is power. Being upset about child labour is not enough. The challenge to each one of us is to find out what are the underlying causes. The next step is to get involved and be part of the solution. What follows are some statistics to illustrate the extent of the problem, and examples of actions taken by the young people of Free the Children. Perhaps they will inspire you with ideas of how you can help.

Creating Awareness Through an International Network of Children

It was the Ontario Federation of Labour's pledge of $150,000 to help address the problem of child labour in developing countries that put

Free the Children on the front page of the *Toronto Star*. It was the press attention from the meeting with the Canadian prime minister in Islamabad that propelled the organization to national prominence. And it was the appearance on "60 Minutes," in prime-time on U.S. television, that launched us internationally. That program, and a call-in show on CNN called "Question and Answer," were picked up by TV stations around the world. What started as a group of kids over pizza and pop dreaming of changing the world has grown to an ever-expanding network of young people in over twenty countries.

To really be effective, we need a world-wide network of children helping children. Not only to improve the lives of poor and exploited children, but to create awareness of the problem and give all young people a voice and the opportunity to participate in the search for solutions.

Through the Internet, children are now communicating with people from around the world, as far away as Hong Kong, Saudi Arabia, Peru, and Japan. And through their speeches, art displays, poetry, theatrical and musical performances, distribution of literature, and letters to the press, children have made exploitative child labour an issue on an international level. The world's youth must join forces in one strong voice if we are to convince our countries' leaders to make the rights of children a priority.

The Wealth Gap

Poverty is the biggest killer of children. It is the strongest driving force of exploitative child labour. We must challenge government leaders and the citizens of the world to make the elimination of poverty their number-one priority.

- More than 1.3 billion people (one quarter of the world's population) live in absolute poverty, struggling to survive on less than a dollar per day. Seventy per cent of them are women and children.
- Thirty-five thousand children die every day as a result of poverty.
- The wealthiest 20 per cent of the world's population has sixty times as much wealth as the poorest 20 per cent, and the gap is growing every day.

At a meeting of the UN General Assembly nearly thirty years ago, rich countries promised to give 0.7 per cent of their gross national product (GNP) as development aid to the poorest countries. With the exception of a couple of the Scandinavian countries, it is a promise that they've failed to keep. The country that gives the lowest proportion of its GNP in aid is the United States. It is the richest country in the world, but it gives only 0.1 per cent of GNP in development aid. Denmark ranks at the top of the list, giving 1 per cent, a rate ten times higher than that of the United States.

Canadian prime minister Jean Chrétien has admitted that "the gap between rich countries and poor, strong nations and weak, is far too wide." Yet Canada has been cutting back development aid. It was projected to sink to 0.24 per cent of GNP in 1998/99, the lowest level since 1991.

It is estimated at present that only about 10 per cent of development aid from industrialized countries goes towards basic human needs such as primary education, health care, nutrition, and clean water. That is because many industrialized countries require that a large portion of their aid be used to increase exports from the recipient country.

People say, "We can't end world poverty, it just can't be done." But the 1997 UN Human Development Report carries a clear, well-documented message that world poverty can be ended – if we make it our goal. It states that the world has the material and natural resources, the know-how, and the people to make a poverty-free world a reality in less than one generation.

Learning How To Share

Friendship Schools
Most people agree that good primary education is one of the best ways to eliminate exploitative child labour. Nearly one quarter of the world's children between the ages of six to eleven never go to school. Most of these children live in developing countries, and two thirds of them are girls. Schools in many developing countries are overcrowded, teachers are poorly paid, and they lack basic supplies.

It would only cost an extra $6 billion a year to put every child in the world in school by the year 2000. Political leaders say it just is not possible to find this enormous sum of money. Our societies cannot afford it. Yet somehow it is no problem for our societies to afford $800 billion each year for military spending; $400 billion for tourism; $400 billion for cigarettes; $250 billion for advertising; $160 billion for beer; $85 billion for wine; $40 billion for golf.

One of the most distressing realities for me was when I met a young girl who was working as a prostitute in order to buy school books and a mandatory uniform in order to attend school. In response to this need, Free the Children has initiated a program called "Friendship Schools" to link children and schools in industrialized countries with poor schools in the developing world. We are challenging schools in North America, Europe, and industrialized countries around the world to help improve opportunities for the education of the world's children. Schools can become Friendship Schools by collecting school and health kits, by paying for a teacher's salary, or by raising money to help open a rural school in a developing country. As part of the program, children can exchange letters, art, and photos with one another so they will learn more about the country's culture, traditions, and way of life.

One girl from Ghana, who had attended school for a short period and was forced to quit, wrote to our office in despair. She said she loved going to school, but her family couldn't afford to pay for her school supplies. She wrote, "My school requirements are: pens, exercise books, a dictionary, toothbrush, toothpaste, soap, and a school bag. Please save me." The letter was signed *Doris*.

When I spoke to 2,500 young people at a youth convention in Michigan and told them about Doris's problem, they responded by putting together more than a thousand school and health kits. Most of the students sewed cloth bags themselves and chose the school supplies to send. For many of them, it was a very special experience in sharing.

Other children have held fundraisers to pay for a teacher's salary. One group of children raised enough money from their page on the Internet to build a school in Pakistan.

Rehabilitation/Education Centre
Children are often forced to work in dangerous and abusive jobs because they are poor and have no other alternative. One of the first decisions that Free the Children made after my return from South Asia

was to help the South Asian Coalition on Child Servitude (SACCS) build a second rehabilitation and education centre for children freed from labour in the carpet and glass-blowing factories of India. It was decided that half of the cost of the centre would come from the money I raised from my speech at the Ontario Federation of Labour, and the other half from the fundraising activities of children. The new live-in centre has been built on a large treed piece of land in Alwar, India. It serves as a transition centre for up to a hundred freed bonded child at a time, with dormitories, vocational training areas, offices, meeting/ school rooms, and a live-in area for the staff. As well as vocational training in four areas, the freed children learn basic reading, writing, and math, and receive professional counselling to help them recover from their abuse.

Income for Families
Free the Children has also been involved in projects that create alternative sources of income for families and children so that they can be removed from hazardous labour and sent to school. One such project operates in two villages in the Tamil Nadu region of Southern India. In these villages, many children are working in the gem-cutting and polishing industry. The precise work involved can cause severe eye-strain and other health problems due to the poor quality of the air and the long hours of labour in cramped conditions.

Money is being directed to supply the families of these children with milking animals such as cows or goats. The milk provides food for the family, and any excess can be sold as a source of income. Each family to receive a milking animal must mate the animal and give the first calf to another family in the community to spread the benefits of the program.

Providing women with sewing machines is another aspect of the program. A meal a day, and regular medical check-ups, are also included. This project helps to empower women in the community and gives children the opportunity to leave work and to go to school. We are now looking to initiate a similar program in South America.

Young people throughout Canada, the United States, Hong Kong, Germany, Italy, Australia, and other countries around the world have contributed to making these projects a success. The five- to nine-year-old members of the Homework Club in Hudson-on-Hastings, New

York, organized a bake sale and collected $137. At St. Joan of Arc School in Michigan, a group of ten-year-olds sold their own toys at a garage sale and established a fundraiser called "Chores for Children," in which they did odd jobs in the community to raise money to pay the salary of a teacher in India. At an international school in Hong Kong, students organized a "dress down day," with the donations going towards the cost of daily meals for children in the FTC rehabilitation centre in India. One eight-year-old boy from Canada wrote to Free the Children, saying, "I am not rich, but I have more than these children do. I want to help to Free them." He collected pop bottles at the trailer camp where he lives and sold them to raise $31.27. Isaac Nigiel of San Diego, California, donated $518, all the money he received at his bar mitzvah.

Challenging Governments and Business

Children and young people are looking for ways to become involved and to help. Many are organizing petition and letter-writing campaigns to urge government leaders to make the welfare of children a priority in their decision making. They are questioning how their own countries' policies, and those of international bodies like the World Bank and the International Monetary Fund, are affecting the poor of developing countries.

- According to the 1997 United Nations Development Report, the inequality of international trading rules causes developing countries to lose up to $60 billion per year on agricultural and textile markets.

Through selective buying, young children are challenging the labour practices of multinational corporations. On October 25, 1997, a local newspaper in San Luis Obispo County, California, reported: "In a crusade highlighting the alleged human rights abuses of Nike, a high school club is asking the sporting goods goliath to 'Just don't do it.' The Free the Children club at Paso Robles High School organized a boycott this week, collecting from their classmates 14 pairs of new and used Nike shoes and numerous shirts and sweatshirts. Club president Maria Campoverde, a junior, said the goods were to be shipped back Friday to Nike headquarters in Beaverton, Oregon, to Chief Executive Officer Phil Knight. A letter enclosed asked Knight to change his company's employment practices in Southeast Asia regarding children and young adults."

We realize that removing children from factories is not enough. These children need alternatives – school, daycare, and skills training. Their families need a source of income. Companies should be prepared to put money back into countries where they are getting cheap labour. Companies must be challenged to pay their adult workers a liveable wage so that children do not have to work to supplement their parents' income.

A Labelling System

I was deeply moved by the stories of Munnilal, Mohan, and those of other children who had been rescued from the carpet factories in India. Our research in that country led us to the discovery of Rugmark, a label attached to hand-knotted or hand-woven carpets to indicate they are made without child labour. Rugmark is a solution initiated by people in South Asia and not by the Western world. In its contracts with carpet dealers, the Rugmark Foundation states that it will immediately revoke the right of any dealer to use the label if it is found that exploitative child labour has been used in the production of their carpets. Support for Rugmark is strong among UNICEF, the International Labour Organization, and several other international organizations.

The young people from Free the Children contacted Toronto rug importers and retailers and organized a seminar to promote the idea of Rugmark. We explained that a portion of the proceeds from the sale of each carpet goes back to South Asia to help open schools for children freed from the raids on carpet factories.

A group of eleven- to fourteen-year-olds from German Mills Public School in Thornhill, Ontario, asked their teacher if they could study the Rugmark concept in class. They then helped to organize a launch at Toronto's City Hall to announce the arrival of Rugmark in Canada. The city's mayor, human-rights activists, many students, as well as Kerry Kennedy-Cuomo, the daughter of Robert Kennedy, spoke at the launch. In her speech Ms. Kennedy-Cuomo said, "When you walk on a Rugmark carpet, you know that you are not walking on the dreams of children." The event proved to be a tremendous success, with carpet dealers showing more interest in the Rugmark program.

During my visit to Brazil, I became acquainted with a similar labelling system being used in that country for products made without child labour. The Canadian government has since funded a learning circle where interested organizations can examine labelling systems as one of various approaches to help end abusive child labour. Through newsletters and the Internet, Free the Children is now working to encourage the expansion of Rugmark into other countries.

Youth of Today, Leaders of Today

One of the most important truths I learned on my trip to Asia is that we in the industrialized world are a large part of the problem for children living in poverty who are forced into exploitative child labour. I will always remember the wise words of the UNICEF representative in Bangladesh who suggested that instead of putting all of our efforts into raising money for a project in that poverty-stricken country we should take that money and use it to educate people, especially young people, back home. We must understand that the extreme poverty around the world is partly due to the government policies, greed, and wastefulness of so many of us in the industrialized world. We must create a new generation willing to help and to share with the impoverished people of the world.

In our work with Free the Children we soon realized the need not only to free children from abuse and exploitation, but also to free children from the idea that they are powerless and have nothing to contribute to changing the world. This is why we organize youth leadership sessions where young people can develop public-speaking, leadership, and research skills to draw attention to children's issues on a local and international level. One such program is called "Young Heroes," where young people from twelve to fourteen years of age meet for eight Saturdays to develop leadership skills and gain confidence in their own abilities by participating in community projects helping others. Another program is a leadership/human-rights summer camp for young people from ten to sixteen years old. We see no reason why today's youth should not also be today's leaders.

I am certainly not the only young person from Free the Children travelling and speaking on children's rights. When Melissa Joffe, a leader of an FTC group in her school in Thornhill, was twelve she addressed United States Department of Labour Hearings in Washington, D.C. At the age of eleven, Laura Hannant, leader of an FTC group in Ottawa, travelled with me to Sweden, where she spoke to student groups. She was also the keynote speaker at an international conference on the rights of the child at St. Francis Xavier University in Chicago. Tanya Roberts Davis, age fourteen, was one of two FTC representatives at the alternative meetings on children's rights at a recent G-8 economic conference in Denver, Colorado. Adam Carter, fifteen, from Falls Church, Virginia, has made presentations to many school groups, and to a Congressional Committee on Child Labour in Washington. Dianna English, fourteen, volunteers at the Children's Law Center in Willimantic, Connecticut, and has addressed a number of teachers' groups on children's issues.

The list goes on and on. Kimberly Santos and Paul Marin in Australia, Isabel Fernandez in Chile, Davide Massaro and Francesco Tremul in Italy, Joo Peng and his classmates in Singapore. I could name dozens more FTC young people who have committed themselves to speaking out for the rights of children.

In some cases, the action taken by youth has been directly as a result of violation of human rights in their own country. The branch of Free the Children in Calcutta, India, organized a rally to protest the kidnapping of handicapped children in West Bengal, children forced to work as beggars and drug runners to Persian Gulf countries. The Indian government is now promising to take action to put a stop to this practice. Daniel Strand, fourteen, and the young people of FTC Brazil helped to convince their government to invest more than one million dollars in projects to alleviate child labour in Salvador de Bahia. These young people are now playing an active role in the implementation of these projects.

Looking at Our Own Backyards

We do not have to look to developing countries to see children suffering. One in five Canadian children lives in poverty. Canada's National

Anti-Poverty Organization has found that 40 per cent of people who use food banks are under the age of eighteen, and 25 per cent of the homeless are children. In the United States, the statistics on childhood poverty are even more alarming. Fifteen million children in the United States – more than one in every four children under the age of twelve – live with hunger. In both countries, whenever there are cutbacks in government budgets, children are usually among the first to be affected.

Free the Children has broadened its mission to encourage youth to get involved in their own communities. Young people organize food and clothing drives, and volunteer at "out of the cold" projects for the homeless. They set up fundraising events for abused women and children. They challenge our own governments to live up to the promises they made in the UN Convention on the Rights of the Child. Young people must become aware of the suffering in their own country at the same time as they fight for the rights of children in the developing world.

United Nations Convention on the Rights of the Child

The most important and comprehensive international agreement to protect the rights of children – the United Nations Convention on the Rights of the Child – came into force on September 2, 1990.

As of February 1998, every country in the world had ratified this convention, except two: the United States and Somalia. This makes the convention the most widely ratified human-rights treaty in history.

The convention obliges countries to give top priority to protecting the basic human rights of children. In particular, the convention says that each country shall protect children from all forms of physical or mental violence, injury or abuse. They shall make primary education compulsory and available free to all children. Children must be protected from economic exploitation and from performing any work that is likely to interfere with their education or be harmful to their health or physical, mental, spiritual, moral, or social development.

Since world leaders made this "solemn commitment" to improve the lives of children, what has happened? Not much. Why are children still being abused and exploited and going to bed hungry? As UNICEF points out, "In a $28 trillion global economy, the problem is surely not a lack of resources."

Change Is Coming About

It is true that child labour is so complex and ingrained in the social structure of some countries that this abuse cannot be ended overnight. It will take years of hard work on the part of many individuals and many organizations. However, around the world, there are signs that change is coming about.

Recently, government leaders from South Asian countries met and promised to eliminate the most exploitative forms of child labour by the year 2000, and all child labour by 2010. In June of 1998, leaders from government, business, and labour unions met in Geneva to ratify a new International Labour Organization convention which would immediately ban the most intolerable forms of child labour.

Pakistan has announced that the amount it spends on primary education will rise from less than 1 per cent of its national budget to 3 per cent. It has promised to build over a thousand literacy centres.

Brazil has introduced a product-labelling system, with over two hundred products carrying certificates verifying that they are "child-labour free."

Companies such as Reebok, The Gap, and Levi Strauss are now allowing independent monitoring in their factories.

And now all major companies which produce soccer balls will be forced to ensure that their products are produced without child exploitation. Schools have been set up for children dismissed from these factories.

A Final Word

Every struggle to end injustice seems at first overwhelming and impossible. People who campaigned to end the slave trade across the Atlantic met enormous opposition and were told they could never succeed. Women who called for the right to vote were laughed at. When Rosa Parks refused to sit at the back of an Alabama bus in the southern United States, she started a fight for racial equality that most people said she could never win.

But these people, though few in number, and frequently the targets of cynicism and sometimes violence, refused to give up their dream of justice. The world is a better place because of them.

Advances in human rights have always been won by people who are bold enough to believe they can make a difference. They refuse to give up when the rest of the world tells them: It's not possible; You're being unrealistic; It's far more complicated than you think; These things can't be changed; There will always be injustice; Give up.

As Margaret Mead said, "Never doubt that a small group of thoughtful, committed citizens can change the world. Indeed, it is the only thing that ever has."

Free the Children has become an international children's organization, with charitable status in Canada, the United States, Mexico, and Italy. An adult board of directors handles legal and financial matters, including accounting, auditing of books, and ensuring the safety of children when they travel.

Young people are the heart and soul of Free the Children. Adults never represent the organization at meetings. Adults never speak for children; children speak for children. Children decide what actions will be taken by the organization. Children represent children at all government hearings, human-rights meetings, conferences, and conventions.

To contact Free the Children:

Free the Children International
16 Thornbank Rd.
Thornhill, Ontario
L4J 2A2
Canada
Phone: (905) 881-0863   Fax (905) 881-1849

Free the Children USA
12 East 48th Street
New York, NY 10017
USA
E-mail: freechild@clo.com
Website: http://www.freethechildren.org